D1175175

The rise and fall
of the Victorian Sunday

DEDICATION: To my Mother and the memory of my Father.

John Wigley

THE RISE AND FALL OF THE VICTORIAN SUNDAY

Manchester
University Press

© John Wigley 1980

Published by
Manchester University Press
Oxford Road
Manchester M13 9PL

British Library cataloguing-in-publication data

Wigley, John
    The rise and fall of the Victorian Sunday.
    1. Sunday – History
    2. Sunday legislation – Great Britain – History
    I. Title
    263'.4'0941   BV130

    ISBN 0–7190–0794–1

Computerised Phototypesetting
by G.C. Typeset Ltd., Bolton, Greater Manchester

Printed in Great Britain by
UNWIN BROTHERS LTD
The Gresham Press
Old Woking, Surrey

contents

acknowledgements

The work upon which this book is based was made possible by a grant from the Social Science Research Council.

I am particularly grateful to Mr H. Legerton and his colleagues at the headquarters of the Lord's Day Observance Society, who made available to me their invaluable records, although I suspect that they may disagree with some of my conclusions.

I am indebted to the staff of the British Library for their patience and resourcefulness in producing a great deal of obscure material and to that of the Public Record Office for their unfailing courtesy and efficiency.

I have also benefited from the service given by the staff of the House of Lords Record Office, the Institute of Historical Research, the British Rail Record Offices at York and Paddington and those of the Leeds, Liverpool, Manchester, Sheffield, Birmingham, Sydenham and Dover public libraries.

To Dr J. C. G. Binfield of Sheffield University I owe particular thanks, for without his painstaking advice the book would be far more imperfect than it is.

I am grateful to John Murray for permission to make quotations from Osbert Lancaster's *All Done from Memory* and to Hodder & Stoughton for permission to include an extract from F. W. Dillistone's *C. H. Dodd: Interpreter of the New Testament*.

I have not included a separate list of sources or a bibliography because the vast majority of such material is encompassed within the footnotes.

J.W.

abbreviations

B.L. Add. Mss.	British Library, Additional Manuscripts.
P. BRR.	Paddington, British Rail Records.
S.C. of H.C.	Select Committee of the House of Commons.
S.C. of H.L.	Select Committee of the House of Lords.
A.S.T.U.	Anti-Sunday Travelling Union.
C.O.S.R.A.	Cab and Omnibus Men's Sunday Rest Association.
I.S.A.	Imperial Sunday Alliance.
L.D.O.S.	Lord's Day Observance Society (Society for Promoting the Due Observance of the Lord's Day).
M.S.R.A.	Metropolitan Sunday Rest Association.
N.L.D.R.A.	National Lord's Day Rest Association.
W.M.L.D.R.A.	Working Men's Lord's Day Rest Association.
N.S.L.	National Sunday League.
C.A.S.S.I.L.S.	Central Association for Stopping the Sale of Intoxicating Liquors on Sundays.

Remember the sabbath day, to keep it holy. Six days shalt thou labour, and do all thy work: But the seventh day is the sabbath of the LORD thy God: in it thou shalt not do any work, thou, nor thy son, nor thy daughter, thy manservant, nor thy maidservant, nor thy cattle nor thy stranger that is within thy gates. For in six days the LORD made heaven and earth, the sea, and all that in them is, and rested the seventh day: wherefore the LORD blessed the sabbath day, and hallowed it.

[Exodus 20:8–11]

If thou turn away thy foot from the sabbath, from doing thy pleasure on my holy day; and call the sabbath a delight, the holy of the LORD, honourable; and shalt honour him, not doing thine own ways, nor finding thine own pleasure, nor speaking thine own words: Then shalt thou delight thyself in the LORD; and I will cause thee to ride upon the high places of the earth . . .

[Isaiah 58:13–14]

introduction

The English Sunday has a reputation for boredom and languor. We have all heard the phrases 'like a month of Sundays' and 'like a wet Sunday afternoon'. The 'Victorian Sunday' has a reputation for boredom and languor in the extreme.

There is some evidence to justify that grim reputation. Ruskin did not draw on Sundays until he was middle-aged and for the fifty-two years that he lived with his parents screens were placed in front of all his pictures on Sundays. Compton Mackenzie and H. G. Wells have written how respectable Victorian children were forbidden to play with toys on Sundays and pressed into a regime of dark suits, stiff collars and church attendance. Somerset Maugham recorded the traumatic effect which this had upon his own childhood. As for the politicians; F. E. Smith's father was told to leave home for skating on a Sunday; and the young Bonar Law only dared to read Walter Scott on Sunday by lying under a bed in a darkened room, but that was in Glasgow.[1]

In 1825 William Cobbett lamented that the old English Sundays of meat dinners, best broadcloth coats and courting were being swept away. He described the inhabitants of the countryside, whilst Ruskin and his like belonged to the middle classes who had overwhelmed rural England and its values with their commercial and urban society. In 1884 that society's philosopher, Herbert Spencer, told how a dispute about opening a reading room on Sundays could split a mechanics' institute.[2]

Francis Place, the Radical leader, and Lord Brougham, the militant Whig, claimed that the most decisive changes of attitudes and manners took place between 1780 and 1830. So did Charles Dickens, who in the early 1830's heard debates on Sunday observance as a parliamentary reporter. They moved him to write that although Sunday in the large towns was often a day of dissipation, religious fanatics were trying to make it a day of gloom and despondency. As an alternative to both he described a really idyllic English Sunday complete with meat dinners, best clothes, family outings and good feelings.[3]

In fact the Victorian Sunday had no single form. Each social group had different values and manners and each modified them over the course of the century. In its opening years the upper classes made Sunday a day of card and music parties and their children amused themselves by releasing rats in Eton College chapel. But fear of the French forced the upper classes into church, and by the end of the century the Eton boys promenaded on Sunday mornings in top hat and tails (a practice which spread throughout the public schools of England) and spent part of the day doing scripture exercises in the form of their 'Sunday Questions'.[4]

Some members of the lower classes began the century with drunken riots but towards its close contented themselves with hurling patriotic abuse at Mr Gladstone's house. The sober members of the same class began it by having their dinners cooked in bakers' ovens and took their families to the suburbs on Sundays, much as Dickens had recommended; closed it with bicycle trips to the countryside and high teas at home.[5]

The respectable middle classes, deeply divided within themselves, had even more diverse Sunday manners and behaviour, and it was on this class that contemporary attention fastened. In *Little Dorrit* Charles Dickens condemned Mrs Clennam, whose strict Sunday habits scarred her son's childhood, repulsed him in manhood and eventually brought about her own downfall, using the story to attack religious harshness and inhumanity. It is this class too which has attracted the attention of historians. However, most of those who have concerned themselves with the Victorian Sunday have approached it under the influence of their own religious or ideological preconceptions, and liberal-minded people such as G. M. Young have seldom given it a more than passing and usually impressionistic glance. Until recently G. M. Trevelyan's remark that the significance of the English Sunday had not been properly examined remained true. It is the aim of this book to correct that situation.[6]

The most important influence on the Victorian Sunday was English Sabbatarianism. It appeared to consist of a perverse reluctance to enjoy oneself on Sundays and a determination to stop other people enjoying themselves too. Yet Sabbatarianism was more than a Victorian aberration. It was an integral part of English life and history. It developed in England rather than in Scotland (whose experience, and that of Wales, is dealt with in two appendices) but has survived longer north of the border. Similarly, Sabbatarianism has been uncommon in Europe, but British emigrants have carried it to the colonies, where it has sometimes flourished more vigorously than in its native land.

The origin of Sabbatarianism lay in the Fourth Commandment. It had caused the leaders of the early Church considerable unease. They wished to obey the word of God, but the commandment seemed to refer to Saturday, whereas they kept Sunday, and to require that the day be kept holy by abstention from labour, whereas they emphasised the performance of religious duties.

Both St Augustine of Hippo and St Thomas Aquinas had produced theological interpretations of the commandment, but their ideas had had little practical effect. In 1500 Englishmen were obliged to hear Mass on Sundays, but inns and shops were open during the rest of the morning, and the people were free to take part in traditional sports during the afternoon. This was the festal Sunday of custom, a day with religious and social functions, a holy day and a holiday.

After the Reformation many devout Englishmen, particularly those members of the Established Church commonly called Puritans, began to interpret the Fourth Commandment in such a way as to identify Sunday with the Old Testament Sabbath, and to demand the prohibition of most forms of Sunday labour and all forms of Sunday amusement. These Sabbatarians did not succeed in all their aims, but they convinced many Englishmen that Sunday amusements were contrary to the will of God, and their successors passed the 1677 Sunday Observance Act, thus creating the English tradition of Sunday observance.

When the Evangelical Revival began in the eighteenth century Sabbatarian theology and attitudes were an integral part of that militant movement's precepts. In 1780 Anglican Evangelicals secured an Act which made it illegal to charge for admission to places of entertainment on Sundays. Between 1780 and 1827 the Evangelicals tried to give Sunday a Sabbatical character, and because they were able to build upon the Sunday observance tradition they had a degree of success.

The interaction between the Sunday observance tradition, this didactic Evangelical Sabbatarian movement, and the habits of the people produced the stricter Victorian Sunday as recalled by Mackenzie, Wells and Maughan.[7]

The Sabbatarians' role was important, but important in ways in which they themselves little considered. They believed to be sin what many Englishmen still regarded as acceptable features of everyday life. The Sabbatarians sought to convince them otherwise and to mould a seventh part of their existence. The Sabbatarians' beliefs may seem strange to us, but unless their assumptions and ideas are examined their actions remain a mystery. The battles they fought raised fundamental issues of religious and social authority, of the proper relation between divine and civil law and of the Churches' place in political society. The results of their battles were often paradoxical, because, as we shall see, this was an area of real religious and social difficulty.

Notes

[1] Kenneth Clark, *The Gothic Revival* (Penguin ed., 1964), 179; Compton Mackenzie, *Sinister Street* (Penguin ed., 1969), 61; H. G. Wells, *The New Machievelli* (Penguin ed., 1970), 19, 21, 41, 44; W. Somerset Maugham, *Of Human Bondage* (1966 ed.), 37–47; Earl Birkenhead, *Frederick Edwin, Earl Of Birkenhead* (1933), I, 19; Lord Blake, *The Unknown Prime Minister* (1955), 23.

[2] William Cobbett, *Rural Rides* (Penguin ed., 1967), passim ; Herbert Spencer, *The Man versus the State* (Penguin ed., 1969), 237.

[3] PP., 1834, VIII, *Rept. S.C. of H. of C. into Drunkenness*, 116–17; 3H, vol. 22, col. 472 (5 May 1834); Timothy Sparks (Charles Dickens), *Sunday Under Three Heads* (1836).

[4] Lytton Strachey, *Eminent Victorians* (1967 ed.), 177; Siegfried Sassoon, *The Old Century* (1968 ed.), 216; Robert Graves, *Goodbye to all That* (1967 ed.), 43–4; L. E. Jones, *A Victorian Boyhood* (1955), 305–6.

[5] G. Tuckwell and S. Gwynn, *Life of Dilke*, I (1917), 249.

[6] Charles Dickens, *Little Dorrit* (Penguin ed., 1967), 852; G. M. Young, *Portrait of an Age* (1957 ed.), 50; G. M. Trevelyan, *History of England* (1956 ed.), 453.

[7] Henceforth I use use term 'Evangelical' to mean Anglican Evangelical.

PART ONE

chapter one

EMERGENCE
1500–1827

I   *Origins*

Several scholars have attempted to elucidate the origin and development of Sabbatarianism between 1500 and 1800. W. B. Whitaker, a Methodist, wrote that after the doctrinal confusion of the early Reformation there emerged a distinctly Protestant view of Sunday which by the 1580's was supported by the Sabbatarians. They attempted to bring benefit to the whole community by prohibiting Sunday trade and labour, thus protecting the working classes; and to outlaw Sunday games and amusements, thus eliminating an alternative to religious worship and giving the populace a calm, quiet day.[1]

M. M. Knappen, the American historian who sought to rehabilitate sixteenth century English Puritanism, regarded Sabbatarianism as an example 'of English originality . . . the first and perhaps the only important English contribution to the development of reformed theology in the first century of its history.'[2]

Patrick Collinson, arguing from within the English empiricist tradition, challenged Knappen's view by showing that the English Puritans were aware that Continental reformed theology was moving in a Sabbatarian direction. But he did not demonstrate that a fully Sabbatarian theology emerged on the Continent or that the decisive English theorists were much influenced by Continental ideas. He recognised that special reasons lay behind the Sabbatarian practices which so quickly took root in England.[3]

The most important attempt to analyse those 'special reasons' has been made in accordance with the generally Marxist view put forward by Christopher Hill. He appears to believe that the early Reformers were Sabbatarians who prompted governments to abolish saints' days, to concentrate worship and preaching on Sundays and to produce a biblical argument for keeping Sundays free from labour. They contributed to the emergence of an industrial system by removing a cause of irregular and reduced production and by establishing a convenient and regular weekly rest day. Small manufacturers and merchants then used it to defend themselves from industrial competition and teach a new social morality, acting according to rational economic motives but justifying and defending themselves with appeals to biblical precedents.[4]

Unfortunately, none of these interpretations is quite adequate. Only Knappen is fully aware of the complex evolution of Sabbatarian ideas. Only Collinson attempts to give an adequate definition of Sabbatarianism. Whitaker fails to distinguish between the religious and social factors involved, assuming that religious practices naturally had a beneficial social effect. Hill's approach confuses Sabbatarian and non-Sabbatarian theologians, mistakes their motive, overestimates their influence and fails to identify closely the social groups and economic needs to which he argues Sabbatarianism appealed.

In point of fact, they all neglect to examine the evolution of Christian practices and to study the biblical text. The Fourth Commandment caused the Jews to keep the Sabbath upon the seventh day of the week. Rabbinical interpretations and rulings taught devout Jews to avoid all works in the sense of physical actions external to themselves (except those incurred in saving life which was in immediate danger) but to dress in their best clothes, and to eat and drink in order to call the Sabbath a delight. Little by little the early Christians began to modify these various customs. Acts 20: 7–11 (And upon the first day of the week when the disciples came together to break bread . . .') has been interpreted to mean that they met after the Sabbath had ended at sunset and continued their devotions until the following morning. The Apostle Paul recommended that alms be collected on the first day (I Corinthians 16: 2) and it can be argued that his missions to the gentiles (Colossians 2: 16, 'Let no man therefore judge you . . .') involved some relaxation of the

Sabbath law for them.

Revelation I: 10 ('I was in the spirit on the Lord's day . . .') is said to indicate that the first day had acquired not only a Christian function and nomenclature, but a spiritual character as well.[5]

Both days were observed for many decades because Jewish converts clung to their customs and law and because gentile Christians, scattered throughout the Mediterranean world, lacked authoritative guidance. However, during the second and third centuries the gentiles of Rome and Alexandria began to abandon the Sabbath (*dies Sabbatum*) lest they be mistaken for Jews, suffer from anti-Semitism and be accused of practising an illegal religion. Conversely, they began to hold the Lord's day (*dies Domenica*) in greater regard, and their influence helped to create and to intensify diversity among the various Christian communities.[6]

Close identification between the Lord's day and the Resurrection was impossible whilst Easter day was determined entirely according to the Jewish lunar calendar, which allowed it to fall on any day of the week; but the growth of the Church as a corporate body and Constantine's proclamation in 313 making Christianity the official religion of the Roman Empire led to the consolidation and regularisation of many Christian practices, particularly when the Bishops of Rome began to extend their authority.[7]

In 314 the Council of Arles required all Christians to observe Easter on the same day, in 321 Constantine decreed that 'the day of the sun' (*dies Solis*, the Mithraic holy day) was to be used throughout the Empire as the day for weekly Christian worship (henceforth popularly called Sunday) and in 325 the Council of Nicea (which promulgated the Nicean Creed) required all Christians to observe Easter day on a Sunday, although without specifying which.[8]

Henceforward Saturday was slowly separated from Sunday. Constantine had decreed that no work in the sense of regular occupational labour, except in agriculture, should be allowed on Sunday. In 304 the Council of Laodicea enjoined that 'Christians shall not . . . be idle on Saturday . . . but the Lord's day they shall especially honour'. They should work on Saturday and leave Sunday free for worship. In 379 and 386 Theodosius forbade the performance of civic business and holding of public spectacles on Sunday and attempted to enforce his wishes throughout the Empire.[9]

Despite these pronouncements both Saturday and Sunday were kept by Christian men as days of worship rather than days of religious rest. Augustine of Hippo (354–430) held services on both days; the monastics of the Near East kept both days as feasts. Jerome (340–420) who produced a definite Latin translation of the Bible, later called the Vulgate, interpreted the Fourth Commandment as applying to manual toil, called servile labour, but thought that even that might be performed on Sunday afternoons. Indeed, during the fifth century Rome itself appointed Vespers (sung when the evening star appears in the sky on Saturday) as the liturgical beginning of Sunday, a situation which still obtains in the Roman Catholic and Eastern Orthodox Churches.[10]

In the British Isles the small but flourishing Celtic Church kept a Sabbath from sunset on Friday until sunset on Saturday, interpreting the prohibition on work in the Jewish manner. This Church regarded Sunday as a day of essentially minor religious significance and sanctity upon which the liturgy might be celebrated and labour might be performed. It calculated the date of Easter in its own way.[11]

Meanwhile the Roman Church struggled to eliminate such major variations. In 538 and 585 the Councils of Orleans and Macon required Christians to abstain from agricultural labour on Sundays. In 604 Gregory I spoke out against the observance of Saturday and for that of Sunday. Roman ecclesiastics slowly persuaded the Celtic Church in Ireland to observe Sunday and (as Bede records) fought to have its adherents in England take up the Roman method of calculating the date of Easter. The Synod of Whitby (620) settled the latter question, but in some parts of Scotland Saturday itself was kept during the eleventh century, and in parts of England Sunday was kept from Saturday evening until Monday morning during the tenth.[12]

Augustine of Hippo had offered the Church a theological interpretation of the Fourth Commandment. According to him mere physical rest was of no spiritual value, for it created an opportunity for the dissipation which was less desirable than labour. Complete physical rest was spiritually inappropriate, for God upheld his Creation on the Sabbath and Christ healed upon the day. The commandment was a figurative injunction to abstain from sin and devote oneself to the things of the spirit.[13]

Even Augustine had given little practical advice about how to regulate Sunday behaviour, and his views were replaced in the Western Church by a new movement which demanded the observance of Sunday as a Sabbath, applying to it those parts of the Old Testament Sabbath code forbidding all work, all buying and selling and most travelling. This movement appeared at the end of the seventh century, was evinced in 789 when Charlemagne forbade all Sunday labour and was powerfully reinforced in 886 when the so-called 'Epistle of Christ', which was said to have fallen from heaven on to the altar of St Peter's in Rome, called for the Sabbatical observance of the Lord's day.[14]

During the remainder of the ninth century and during the whole of the tenth the new movement spread throughout Western Christendon, soon reaching England. In 906 King Edward the Elder laid down that no one be executed on Sunday if possible. In 925 King Athelstan forbade Sunday trading. In 1020 Canute proclaimed that no trading or assembling was to take place on Sundays, and the Laws of the Northumbrian Priests, issued a few years later, at York, prohibited 'all buying and selling on Sunday, and all assembling of the people, and all travel'.[15]

It proved difficult to enforce such provisions, and abstention from even servile labour on Sundays was not made part of the general law of the Roman Catholic Church until 1234, when Gregory IX issued his *Decretals*. The Roman Church was not given a fully coherent interpretation of the Fourth Commandment until the thirteenth century, when Thomas Aquinas, an Italian Dominican made professor of theology at Paris in 1256, expounded one in his *Summa Theologica*, left unfinished in 1273. He was ignorant of the historical evolution of Sunday observance and so (like most subsequent writers on the subject) used his theological principles to reconcile the biblical text with contemporary Sunday behaviour, and vice versa.[16]

He assumed that the commandment had originally appointed

Saturday as a weekly holy day and so tried to explain how
Christians could obey the Law of God yet keep Sunday, then to
elucidate in what manner the day was to be kept. The
commandment reflected the moral law, which was permanent
and applied to everyone, and the ceremonial law, which was
temporary and applied only to the Jews. The former required
that all men gave some time to the things of God, and the
commandment obviously provided for such time. The latter
governed the particular fixing of that time and its religious
nature. It was codified for the Jews elsewhere in the Old
Testament, whereas Christians were to be guided primarily by
the contents of the New.[17]

J. K. Carter, a scholar who has made a detailed study of
Aquinas' views on this matter, suggests that his application of
these points exhibits certain internal inconsistencies. Be that as
it may, Aquinas concluded that the first day was recognised by
the Apostles and since their time was more properly called the
Lord's day. It was a religious, not a secular, feast and so should
be kept by being strictly devoted to worship, edification and
good works; in order that the soul of the believer might repose in
the heart of God.[18]

Some Continental theologians based a complex scheme of
obligations and prohibitions on Aquinas' work, turning from the
prohibition of labour to the prohibition of alternatives to man's
religious duties. In England, Sunday behaviour was largely
regulated by a pervasive but undefined popular feeling which
kept the day free from regular labour and frowned on secular
activities during morning Mass, but countenanced morning
shopping and outdoor recreation in the afternoon.

In 1388 an Act of Richard II forbade labourers to play tennis
or football on Sundays, but encouraged them to practise archery
instead. In 1448 an Act of the saintly Henry VI prohibited the
showing for sale of goods and merchandise at fairs and markets
on the principal feast days, Good Friday and Sundays; but the
measure did not apply to necessary foodstuffs, and exempted the
four Sundays in harvest. During the remainder of the century
ecclesiastics and preachers placed increasing pressure upon the
people's Sunday behaviour, calling for the closing of all such
shops, booths, stalls, inns and alehouses as had the temerity to

remain open during Mass; and inveighing against recreations which distracted the people from their religious duties and defiled the holy day.[19]

Wycliffe was influenced by this trend, but stood first and foremost in the tradition of St Augustine. Wycliffe referred neither to the seventh nor to the first day but regarded Sunday as the eighth. He taught that the Fourth Commandment should be obeyed not outwardly and formally, but inwardly and spiritually. On Sundays men should abstain from labour and should shun fairs, markets, drunkenness, gluttony and plays, but they should concentrate upon worshipping God in thought, word and deed.[20]

The early leaders of the Reformation in England and on the Continent, Frith and Tyndale, Luther and Calvin, regarded Catholic Sunday theology and its sometime prohibitory emphasis as an aspect of the superstition in which Catholics held all the numerous saints' and holy days. They hoped to wean the people from the belief that Sunday had a holy character in itself by preaching, teaching and writing that labour be allowed on Sundays in cases of necessity. In their commentaries on the Fourth Commandment they arged that its full moral and ceremonial force applied only to Jews. Christians were required simply to set aside a convenient day for bodily rest and to take a devout and joyful part in the duties of religion.[21]

II   The English Reformation

Archbishop Cranmer equipped the English Church with a theology of Lord's day observance which was a subtle compromise between Roman Catholic and early Reformed opinion. The *Bishop's Book* of 1537 and the *King's Book* of 1543 taught that the command to rest from bodily labour on the seventh day was part of the ceremonial law applying to Jews, whereas Christians were only obliged by the moral law to observe a spiritual rest. The Sabbath had been succeeded by Sunday in memory of the Resurrection, so 'Men must have special care that they be not over-scrupulous or rather superstitious in abstaining from bodily labour'.[22]

Normally, men should give themselves to God's service in

worship, in prayer, in religious instruction and by visiting the sick. They should not waste their time in idleness and dissipation, for the service of their Prince and even working in the fields was preferable to that, as Augustine had implied. This teaching was repeated under Edward VI in the Injunctions of 1547 and in Cranmer's *First Book of Homilies*, published the same year.[23]

Henry and Edward opposed both Sabbatarianism and an excess of saints' and holy days. An Henrician ordinance of 1536 reduced the number of such days and transferred the feasts held to commemorate the dedication of churches to the first Sunday in October, directing that they be conducted peacefully and in an orderly manner. An Edwardian Act of 1551 enjoyed men to labour on the remaining saints' and holy days and on Sundays in time of harvest and in cases of necessity. Edward himself often conducted government business on Sundays in order to show his Protestant freedom from Catholic superstitution.[24]

However, Mary, a devout Roman Catholic, repealed the Act of 1551 in 1553 and in 1554 the Visitation Articles of Bonner, Bishop of London, asked if people had hunted, hawked, baited bears and watched plays, or laboured and opened shops, on Sundays, 'contrary to the laudable custom of the Catholic Church'.[25]

The Elizabethan Injunctions of 1559 repeated the substance of those of 1547 and the thirty-fifth of the Thirty-nine Articles (which were approved by Convocation in 1562 and included in the Prayer Book in 1563), Of Homilies, judged the *Second Book of Homilies* to contain 'a godly and wholesome Doctrine'. The eighth Homily, Of the Place and Time of Prayer, was based on Cranmer's earlier work and rejected Jewish authority for that of the law of nature, but taught that Sunday was the Christian Sabbath, so included a list of religious duties and attacked idleness and dissipation without making any allowance for public or harvest work.[24]

III   *The Elizabethan settlement*

The early Elizabethan Church did not have a unified outlook on Sunday observance, apart from insisting upon attendance at the service of the Church of England, as laid down by the Act of Uniformity of 1551. Neither the Injunctions nor the eighth Homily were included in the Prayer Book, and so the Church's teaching was obscure. The Prayer Book did enshrine an ancient custom in the rubric which provided that 'the Collect appointed for every Sunday . . . shall be said at the Evening service next before'; but on the major issue the Church was in no position to make an impact upon the people.

Almost every bishop had his own opinion about Sunday. Aylmer, Bishop of London, followed Calvin's practice of playing bowls on Sunday afternoons. Cooper of Winchester approved of Sunday bowls too. When Archbishops Parker and Grindal issued Visitation Articles in 1569 and 1576 they were mainly concerned with the hours of service, showing little interest in the remainder of Sunday.[27]

Elizabeth herself made a distinction between disorderly and orderly Sunday sports. In 1569 she licensed archery, leaping, running, wrestling, throwing the hammer and pitching the bar. In 1574 she licensed similar traditional sports, provided that they were not indulged in during service time and were not otherwise illegal, but forbade bear and bull baiting.[28]

Given the methods by which the Reformation had been carried through and the Elizabethan settlement imposed, theological diversity and official caution were only to expected, but it was not long before the ferment which these events had unleashed took the matter of the Fourth Commandment out of the hands of the bishops and the queen.

Within the Roman Church, the Council of Trent published an urbane Latin exposition of the Fourth Commandment in its Catechism of 1567. This taught that the commandment merely appertained to the moral but belonged to the ceremonial law, and that Sunday was not the Sabbath but the Lord's day. It should be dedicated to religion, and distracting activities should be avoided, but the Catechism did not specify which, and so the Roman Church avoided the prohibition of all Sunday amusement, in later years being bitterly censured by English Sabbatarians.[29]

In Protestant England devout laymen and clergy had begun to seek the truth for themselves. As far as the Fourth

Commandment was concerned the materials were at hand. In 1538 Henry had ordered English Bibles to be placed in all churches, the Prayer Book of 1549 had taught catechumens to 'keep holy the Sabbath day', that of 1552 had included the whole of the Fourth Commandment in its Catechism and included all the commandments in its Communion Service, and that of 1559 authorised them to be read in place of sermons if necessary. In 1560 Elizabeth ordered the Ten Commandments to be painted on boards and hung adjacent to the Communion table.

As these men searched the Scriptures they concluded that Sunday was in some sense a Sabbath and should be kept holy by the avoidance of virtually all labour and recreation. In 1577 Thomas White, the founder of Zion College, preached this view in a Paul's Cross sermon; in 1578 John Stockwoode, Master of Tonbridge School, preached from the Cross against Sunday plays; and in 1579 John Northbrooke, a controversial minister, wrote against Sunday pastimes. During 1582 the Dedham Classis discussed 'the right use of the Sabbath'.[30]

Before long some of the most acute minds of the age turned to the Fourth Commandment: on the one hand divines like Launcelot Andrewes, university scholars who wished to give the English Church a fully consistent and logical theology; on the other, devout pastors like Richard Greenham and Nicholas Bownde, who wished to give Church, as they thought, a far more biblical character.[31]

During the 1580's Andrewes delivered a series of lectures at Cambridge, suggesting that the Fourth Commandment was part of the moral, not the ceremonial, law and applied to Christians, the day which it governed having been changed in the Apostles' time. In 1592 Greenham published similar ideas in his *Treatise of the Sabbath*, but this was overshadowed in 1595 when Bownde, his step-son, published his own *The True Doctrine of the Sabbath*.

Bownde believed the Fourth Commandment to be an integral part of the moral law, fully binding upon Christians, the example of the Resurrection having applied it to Sunday. He wrote that it required Sunday to be devoted entirely to religion, that all 'works', except those of the most urgent necessity, and all recreations were prohibited:

It is . . . certain that we are . . . commanded to rest . . . from . . .
all . . . things which might hinder us from the sanctifying of the
Sabbath . . . We must not think it sufficient that we do no work on
the Sabbath, and . . . be occupied about all manner of delights,
but we must cease from the one as from the other . . . Therefore
upon this day all sorts of men must give over utterly all shooting,
hunting, hawking, tennis, fencing, bowling, or such like, and they
must have no more dealing with them than the artificer with his
trade or husbandman with his plough . . .[32]

IV   *Controversy, 1580–1642*

Elizabeth had already responded to the new atmosphere, in
1580 forbidding Sunday plays in the city of London, causing the
players to move to Southwark, where in 1583 they were reproved
by Philip Stubbes. When Parliament had met in 1584 the first
Bill of the session sought to promote the stricter observance of
the Sabbath day, and it passed both Houses before the Queen
vetoed it. The publication of Bownde's book in 1595 caused an
immediate controversy, giving courage to the devout laymen and
clergy, now called Puritans.[33]

Bownde's followers wished to abolish the remaining saints'
and holy days and to prohibit virtually all work and recreation
on Sundays, quoting 'Six days shalt thou labour . . . but the
seventh is the sabbath . . .'. They made a particular point of
calling upon the godly civil power to enforce their policies.
Elizabeth held to a less draconian concept of religion and
society. She considered that saints' days and holy days and
Sundays should fulfil both civil and religious functions; they
were days upon which men might worship God and relax: holy
days and holidays. The people should attend chuch and then
might amuse themselves harmlessly, subject only to the
requirements of good order.

In 1597 William Hooker, another divine who hoped to provide
the English Church with an acceptable religious character,
attempted to resolve the situation by suggesting in *The Laws of
Ecclesiastical Polity* that the precise regulation of holy days and
Sundays was the responsibility of each national Church. But
controversy broke out afresh, and in 1599 and 1600 Archbishop

Whitgift and Chief Justice Popham suppressed Bownde's book; noting no doubt with interest that it was dedicated to the Earl of Essex, who led an ill-planned rebellion in 1601. In the same year another Bill for the better observance of the Sabbath passed both Houses, only to fail to gain the royal assent.[34]

The controversy deepened under James I. In 1603 the Puritans presented the Millenary Petition, which mentioned the need to keep the Sabbath holy. At the Hampton Court Conference in 1604 they asked for royal action to prevent the profanation of the Lord's day. James replied by trying to define the civil and ecclesiastical law on the matter.

He issued the substance of Elizabeth's Licence of 1574 as a Declaration, allowing traditional Sunday sports outside service time provided they were peaceful. He ensured that the Canons of 1603 followed the Injunctions of 1547 and 1559 in placing Sunday on a level with holy days, Canon XIII being entitled 'Due Celebration of Sundays and Holy Days'. It exhorted the people to spend all such days in the duties of religion and charity, without mentioning either amusement or work. In 1604 the Act of 1551 was restored to the statute book, albeit without the provision allowing Sunday harvest work.

The king's position was thus quite clear, but in 1606 Bownde's book was published in a new edition, and in that and the following year a Bill was introduced into the Commons to prohibit Sunday morris dances, hunting, coursing, hawking, church ales, dancing, rush-bearing, May games, Whitsun ales, and wakes.

Bownde's ideas were now spreading rapidly among devout people everywhere. Bishop Bayley of Bangor and his brother-in-God Davenant of Salisbury inconvenienced King James by refusing to travel on Sundays. In 1611 the Authorised Version translated the Fourth Commandment and its attendant texts in the form which had been followed by all English Bibles since Tyndale's, rendering Sabbath with a lower-case 's' as an adjective rather than with a capital 'S' as a proper noun, implying that it was merely a 'rest' day without any other theological or chronological implications. Despite this subtlety the wide distribution given to the Authorised Version worsened what was rapidly becoming a rancorous controversy, and in 1614

another Bill was introduced into the Commons, on the first day
of the new session, but, like its predecessors in 1606 and 1607,
failed to become law.

Magistrates in Lancashire now began to forbid Sunday sports
on the ground that they were disorderly. James saw the situation
for himself in 1618 when he was returning from Scotland (in
which he had spent the first thirty-seven years of his life at a time
when that country was not yet Sabbatarian) and issued his
Declaration of Sports, commonly called the *Book of Sports*, as a
definitive statement of the law and of his own policies. Bear and
bullbaiting, interludes and plays and bowling (this latter for the
'meaner sort') were forbidden on Sundays. Archery, leaping,
vaulting, May games, Whitsun ales, morris dancing and rush-
bearing were all allowed provided they took place after the
afternoon or evening service had ended. James favoured these
Sunday activities in order that the people might have some
recreation from their labours, learn to respect the moderate
policy of the English Church and have an alternative to talking
sedition in ale houses and conventicles.[35]

The *Book* was received with outrage in the country, because
Bownde's ideas had become as much a part of the prevailing
outlook within the Church as had a militant
Calvinism—although Calvin had been no Sabbatarian, as we
noted. George Abbot, the Archbishop of Canterbury, opposed
the *Book* and persuaded James that it should not be read in
churches. The obstreperous Sir Edward Coke, whom James had
dismissed in 1616 from his position as Chief Justice, claimed in
his *Institutes* that Sunday trade was illegal at common law,
quoting an edict of King Athelstan, and in 1621 supported a Bill
for punishing of abuses on the Sabbath day, notably dancing and
May games. A lawyer from Lincoln's Inn who pointed out that
the Sabbath was Saturday was expelled from the Commons.
James forbade M.P.'s to legislate against any Sunday recreations
allowed by the *Book*, and the Bill was abandoned; but Coke, who
used any and every issue which arose during the session to
attack the king, was deprived of his seat on the Privy Council at
the end of the year. In 1624 James vetoed a similar Bill and
quietly repealed the 1388 Act.[36]

In 1625 Parliament passed a Bill which declared illegal

Sunday bear and bull baiting, and travelling out of one's parish
to take part in legal Sunday games. In 1627 both Houses
endorsed a Bill which prohibited Sunday travel by carriers and
drovers, etc., and Sunday killing and selling by butchers. In
order to allay the growing storm Charles I, who had succeeded
his father during 1625, gave these Bills the royal assent; but the
matter was not to be settled so easily.

Several devout magistrates in Somerset had begun to prohibit
the feasts and wakes which had been authorised by Henry VIII
in 1536; so in 1633, when the Arminian Laud had succeeded
Abbot as Archbishop, Charles revised his father's *Book of Sports*
with an additional clause asserting the legality of Sunday wakes.
This caused a prolonged storm of protest. Like the previous *Book*
it was ordered to be read in churches, but by this time even more
churchgoers regarded its provisions as contrary to the very word
of God. They protested so vehemently and challenged the royal
policies so effectively that Laud and his supporters felt the need
to defend the government by producing their own interpretation
of the Fourth Commandment.

The theological attack on the Sabbatarians had begun in 1607
when Thomas Rogers, chaplain to Archbishop Bancroft,
published a diatribe against them; in 1622 John Prideaux,
Bishop of Worcester, had preached against Sabbatarianism, but
the attack did not flourish until it was promoted by Laud. In
1635 Francis White, Bishop of Ely, followed his lead, and in 1636
Gilbert Ironside, Bishop of Bristol, Robert Saunderson, Bishop
of Lincoln, and Peter Heylin, chaplain to King Charles (to
whom his book was dedicated), did so too, claiming to defend
the Church as defined by the formularies of the previous
century.[37]

The Laudians studied the Old Testament texts referring to the
Sabbath, but concentrated their attention on the New
Testament. They catalogued Christ's behaviour on the Sabbath
and examined his replies to Pharasaical criticism. Christ taught
in the Synagogue (Mark 6:1–6), allowed the Disciples to pluck
ears of corn (Matthew 12:1–8, Mark 2:23–8, Luke 6:1–5);
healed the man with the withered hand (Matthew 12:9–13,
Mark 3:1–4, Luke 6:6–10), the man with the unclean spirit
(Luke 4:33–6), the infirm woman (Luke 13:11–15), the man

with dropsy (Luke 14:1–5), the crippled man (John 5:1–19) and the blind man (John 9:13–16).

Christ defended his use of the Sabbath by pointing out that according to the Pharisees' interpretation of the Fourth Commandment King David had broken the law, that the Temple priests did so when performing ritual acts; and that doubtless the Pharisees themselves protected and watered their animals on the Sabbath. He claimed that it was 'lawful to do well on the sabbath', that God required 'mercy and not sacrifice' and that 'The sabbath was made for man and not man for the sabbath'. He argued that 'the son of man is Lord even of the sabbath day' and that 'my Father worketh hitherto and I work'—an allusion to a rabbinical controversy about whether an all-powerful God needed a day's rest and whether He would so withdraw His support from Creation (points which had influenced Augustine).

The Laudians were unfamiliar with this issue. They accepted that the commandment as it stood prohibited labour and recreation, but reasoned that it had been promulgated by Moses and belonged primarily to the ceremonial rather than to the moral law, applying to Jews with its original force but not to Christians, having been relaxed by Christ.

They elaborated a theology of the commandment according to which the Apostles and the early Church had been led by Christ's example and resurrection to abandon the sombre Jewish Sabbath, Saturday, whose abstemious character commemorated God's rest on the seventh day of Creation; and to instutute the joyful Christian Lord's day, Sunday, whose festal nature commemorated the Resurrection which had inaugurated the first day of the Christian dispensation.

In practice Sunday was not 'the Sabbath' or 'a Sabbath' from which all labour and recreation was forbidden but the Lord's day, meet for worship and for good works of all kinds even if they involved labour and recreation. In cases of dispute the Apostles' successors – the bishops – had the authority to adjudicate and to call upon the civil power to arbitrate.

The Laudians were accused of abrogating the fourth of the Ten Commandments, of thereby challenging the authority of the other nine, and of making the king and his government their accomplices. They were opposed even more strongly by Bownde's followers, led by the ever more militant Puritans, who defined their own views and went beyond Bownde himself to produce the full Sabbatarian position.

The Puritans wrote that God had rested on the seventh day of Creation and blessed and sanctified it (Genesis 2:2–3), that it was kept as a holy Sabbath in the wilderness (Exodus 16:25–6) and codified in the Ten Commandments (Exodus 20:8–11) as a sign and commemoration of Creation. This day of holy rest – a Sabbath – then marked an everlasting convenant between God and His chosen followers (Exodus 31:13–17). The Jews kept this Sabbath on Saturdays, but by and through the Resurrection God moved both the day and the holy character to the first day of the week, Sunday, as a sign of the New Covenant. He caused it to be called the Lord's day in New Testament times in token of the fact that it 'belonged' to Him and was to be used for Christian devotions, being the Christian Sabbath.

The Puritans believed that the essence of the commandment lay in keeping the Sabbath 'holy' and strove to do so in several ways. First, by preparing themselves on the previous day (Exodus 16:22–3). Secondly, by avoiding work such as harvesting (Exodus 34:21) and gathering fuel (Numbers 15:32–6). Thirdly, by prohibiting buying and selling (Nehemiah 13:15–22; Jeremiah 17:19–27) and in some cases by refusing to cook (Exodus 35:3). Fourthly, by refusing to travel except to church (Exodus 16:29). Lastly, they took Isaiah's phrase 'turn away from doing thy pleasure on my holy day' to mean that an absolutely integral part of keeping the Sabbath 'holy' lay in proscribing all forms of worldly enjoyment.

Similarly, the Puritans, like the Jews and some medieval theologians, took 'work' to indicate not merely servile labour but almost all physical acts. Thus after searching the New Testament they concluded only that Christ had allowed 'works' of necessity and mercy towards humans and animals. He had in no wise relaxed the proscription of 'pleasure' and worldly enjoyment.

The Sabbatarians held strongly to several further convictions. First, that because the day was holy and had been blessed and sanctified it had an inherently sacred nature. Secondly, that its nature was desecrated and profaned when men engaged in worldly labour or pleasure or neglected the positive religious duties of worship. Thirdly, that God would punish Sabbath-breaking. Fourthly, that Sabbatarians should restrain their countrymen as Nehemiah had done; and fifthly, that the English were God's chosen people, whose national success depended on pleasing Him by keeping the Sabbath. They might use the examples of the Palace Guard (II Kings 11:5–9) and of Nehemiah to mount military and police activity on the day.

Two sharply opposed camps had emerged. The Sabbatarians were led by educated Puritan members of the Established Church who appeared to be supported by many magistrates, country gentlemen and members of the House of Commons and to derive their greatest strength from the most economically advanced areas and classes of England. They claimed that the Bible taught simply and authoritatively that men should do their labour and take their recreation on the ordinary days of the week, but never on the Lord's day, which was the Sabbath and reserved for religion. They themselves devoted the day wholly to religion and sought to compel the people at large to give up Sunday labour and recreation in order to obey the commandment itself and increase their chances of receiving instruction.

The Laudians were supported by the king and court (where the Privy Council met for business and to swear in new members, and masques were preformed on Sundays), by large parts of the aristocracy, traditionalist members of the gentry and by the common people, who valued their age-old Sunday recreations. They claimed to defend the reformed faith and law of the English Church, which had been bequeathed to them by its founders but was now being overwhelmed by Puritanism. They themselves kept a sober Sunday and compelled the people to keep only a moderate one.

This division had profound political implications. It obviously touched the national conflict at several points, especially as a clash between rival systems of authority: the Bible and its Calvinistic expositors opposed the Arminians and their apparently over-subtle interpretations, and the Commons and provincial magistrates opposed the Stuarts and their court.

V   *Apogee, 1642–60*

Between 1642 and 1660 the Sabbatarians sought to codify their ideas and to make an alliance with the civil power. They achieved the former in the Assembly of Divines, which drew up Westminster Confession of 1644, this part of which was principally formulated by Englishmen. The Confession itself, and the Larger and Shorter Catechisms which are associated with it, contained and explained the following imperative exposition of the Fourth Commandment.[38]

> As it is in the law of nature, that, in general, a due proportion of time be set apart for the worship of God: so in His word, by a positive, moral, and perpetual commandment, binding all men in all ages, He hath particularly appointed one day in seven for a sabbath, to be kept holy unto Him: which from the beginning of the world to the resurrection of Christ, was the last day of the week, and, from the resurrection of Christ, was changed into the first day of the week, which in scripture is called the Lord's Day, and is to be continued to the end of the world, as the Christian Sabbath.
>
> The Sabbath is then kept holy unto the Lord, when men, after a due preparing of their hearts, and ordering of their common affairs beforehand, do not only observe an holy rest all the day from their own works, words, and thoughts about their worldly employments and recreations; but also are taken up the whole time in the public and private exercises of His worship, and in the duties of necessity and mercy.

A parliamentary ordinance of 1644 applied Sabbatarian principles to retail trading in general, declared illegal any Sunday 'games, sports or pastimes whatsoever' and called in for burning all copies of the *Book of Sports*. In 1645 the Act which replaced the Prayer Book with the new *Directory of Public Worship* echoed the phraseology of the Confession, and an Act of 1647 abolished the remaining saints' and holy days, Christmas and Easter, substituting the second Tuesday in every month as a holiday for apprentices. In 1657 two Acts forbade between them milling, cloth-making, tallow-melting, baking, brewing, soap-boiling and distilling—trades in which natural contingencies, market pressures and technical considerations made it difficult to avoid Sunday work.[39] By that date also profanation of the

Lord's day had been made a reason for ejecting ungodly ministers and schoolmasters and for disenfranchising electors.[40]

But the period between 1642 and 1660 was too short to establish a fully Sabbatarian system. Parliament met on Sundays in time of emergency, and Cromwell was no Sabbatarian. In addition, radicals and sectaries in politics and religion were challenging many Sabbatarian ideas. Even before the Civil War disputes about the commandment's meaning had raised disconcerting issues of principle. If the Fourth Commandment no longer applied in its full and original force, did the other nine? If it applied to all men, was a servant right to disobey his master's order to work on the Sabbath? Who should judge in such cases? Now extremists claimed that the Sabbath should be kept from sunset on Friday till sunset on Saturday, mystics believed that Sabbath-keeping destroyed true spiritual religion, the Quakers taught that there should be no distinction of days and the Diggers began to cultivate St George's Hill on a Sunday. No less a person than Milton thought that the only true guide and authority in such matters was the individual's own conscience.[41]

VI   *Diffusion and the Evangelicals, 1660–1827*

Following the Restoration in 1660 the active alliance between Sabbatarianism and the civil power was broken and the legislation which it had produced lapsed, but the English religious outlook had been decisively changed even before the Civil War had begun. Many men in all classes of society had been convinced that it was against the will of God to engage in sports and recreations on Sundays. They were thus able to repudiate the events of the war years as the product of extreme times whilst preserving the substance of their convictions. Parliament persuaded Charles II to include in his Worcester House Declaration of October 1660 a promise 'to take care that the Lord's day be applied to holy exercises, without unnecessary divertisements', and in 1662 the Commons asked him to write to the Archbishop of Canterbury about the necessity for Lord's day observance.

Members of the House of Commons soon pressed for

legislation. In order to forestall their demands a Bill was drawn up in the Lords, sent down to the Commons and given the royal assent as the 1677 Sunday Observance Act. It did not, therefore, concern Sunday recreation but was designed to deal with Sunday labour and trade and with the law itself.

The preamble to the Act acknowledged the divine origin and spiritual importance of Lord's day observance and reminded the people of their religious duties. The Act itself was a codification of the Act of 1627, the Ordinance of 1644 and the Acts of 1657. It prohibited on Sundays all worldly labour, except for 'works' of necessity and charity, and all retail trade, except for the sale of milk and the provision of meat in inns, cookshops and victualling houses. It severely restricted Sunday travel and declared Sunday a *dies non juridicus*, rendering illegal Sunday arrest for civil offences.[42]

Breaches of the Act cound be reported and prosecution initiated by any citizen – the common informer – and any person over fourteen found guilty was liable to a fine of five shillings. The interpretation and implementation of the Act caused enormous trouble, for by the end of the seventeenth century Sabbatarianism had begun to lose its grip on the community. In the countryside and small towns magistrates drove the people to church and prohibited Sunday trade and recreation, but in the large towns they concentrated on the hours of service, leaving custom and opinion to regulate the remainder of the day.

The middle classes maintained the age-old custom of having the best meal of the week at mid-day on Sundays and largely retained the Puritan suspicion of Sunday recreation. This combination of a festal tradition with the most marked characteristic of Sabbatarianism created the sober English Sunday, which was remarked upon by so many foreign visitors.

For instance, in the next century Samuel Johnson disliked Sundays in Lichfield, where he accompanied his father to church, attended family Bible reading, and was shut in his room to read *The Whole Duty of Man*, although only on Sunday was a fire lighted in a chamber other than the kitchen. In his manhood in London Johnson always attended church and usually dined off a meat pie, but insisted that Sunday should not be kept with 'rigid severity and gloom, but with a gravity and simplicity of behaviour'. He thus sometimes gave a Sunday dinner party and enjoyed a Sunday walk, without, however, neglecting to read the Bible when at home or works of devotion which he took with him when away.[43]

On their accession William and Mary issued a Declaration for the Better Observance of the Sabbath Day and the bishops pointed out to the German George I what effect promotion of Sunday sports had had upon the early Stuarts. Some pious members of the Established Church had taken heart from William and Mary, and between 1689 and 1738 Societies for the Reformation of Manners gained more convictions for Sunday trading than for any other single offence.

For several decades the matter did not generally concern the bishops, but it was a live issue for some of the lesser clergy and their followers. In 1728 William Law, a non-juror who had refused to accept the supremacy of the Hanoverians, implied in his *A Serious Call to a Devout and Holy Life* that a Sunday devoted to religion was a mark of devoutness but that Sabbatarianism could become a form of hypocrisy. In the 1730's John Wesley thought that diversions which did not directly promote religion were unsuitable for Sundays. In the 1750's John Newton perfectly combined spiritual and civil powers as captain of a slave ship and enforced an exemplary Sabbath. In 1757 a group of High Churchmen, followers of Wesley and Whitefield, and Dissenters called upon the magistrates to suppress desecration in London.[44]

Because this earnest religious spirit was shared by some members of the Established Church it gained some support from M.P.'s, and the 1757 Militia Act exempted Sunday as a day for drilling. In 1780 the Evangelicals roused Bishop Porteus of Chester to the dangers of Sunday assemblies and meetings, and he gained government support for a Bill which became law as the Sunday Observance Act of 1780. It imposed £200 fines upon the organisers of Sunday amusement, debate or other entertainment for which admission was charged.

During the 1780's Sabbatarianism enjoyed a considerable revival, and developed many of its nineteenth century features. In 1784 Porteus explained that the House of Hanover had respected the Sabbath day and so could rely upon the loyalty of the Sabbatarians. During the French wars Sabbatarians recoiled with horror when the French regicides introduced the Decadal Calendar, which abolished Sunday, stressing their own patriotism and the connection between anti-Sabbatarianism and Jacobinism. Wesleyans emphasised their Sabbatarianism and their loyalty. Dr Joseph Priestley, a Unitarian anti-Sabbatarian who wanted political reform, had his house burned down by a patriotic mob.[45]

Some Sabbatarians gave a social justification for their ideas. The working population was warned that only by religiously abstaining from Sunday amusements did it establish a right to a day's rest. Men who decried William Paley's anti-Sabbatarian theology adopted his argument that Sunday rest was economically desirable. In an over-populated country 'the addition of the seventh day's labour to that of the other six would reduce the price. The labourer himself would gain nothing.'[46]

These views were exceptional, for the movement's basis was incontrovertibly religious and Evangelical. Hannah More drew up a Sunday code. William Grimshaw prohibited Sunday football, disguised himself as an old woman in order to track down and stop the games which replaced it, and fetched his parishioners to church with a riding crop. During 1784, the last year of his life, when he knew that death was not far off, Dr Johnson begged his friends to devote Sundays to religion, and persuaded a reluctant Joshua Reynolds to promise never to neglect to read the Bible and (as if in anticipation of Ruskin) never to paint on Sundays. Wilberforce, who in 1786 had spent Easter Sunday sunbathing, improved his own Sunday behaviour and then turned to that of English society at large.[47]

He tried to recreate an alliance between Sabbatarianism and the civil power. In 1787 he persuaded George III to issue a Proclamation for the Encouragement of Piety and Virtue, founded a society to carry it into effect, helped to prosecute Sunday shopkeepers under the 1677 Act, conspired to produce a Bill to prohibit Sunday newspapers and backed the Society for the Suppression of Vice when it prosecuted Sunday traders on its own account.[48]

The parliamentary class reacted against this spiritual extremism. In 1794 the London Bakers Act clarified the cookshop clauses of the 1677 Act, allowing bakers in the metropolitan area to work on Sundays from 9.00 a.m. to 1.00 p.m., when they might sell bread and bake meat, puddings and pies (the poor man's Sunday dinner). During 1795 the House of Commons rejected outright a Bill intended to tighten up the Sunday trading clauses of the 1677 Act, members arguing that some Sunday trade was necessary to meet the needs of the poor, whose circumstances obliged them to shop on Sundays.[49]

In 1799 Wilberforce and Lord Belgrave promoted a Bill to suppress Sunday newspapers and Pitt indulged his friend Wilberforce by supporting it, until he was told that most of them supported his government. Pitt realised that it was impossible to subordinate the essential processes of politics to the wishes of enthusiasts. In the midst of the French wars the 1803 Militia Act allowed Sunday drilling, but provided that persons with religious scruples might be excused if they served on another day in lieu. After Pitt's death in 1806 Greville's Militia Bill proposed to use Sunday as a normal training day, arousing the Sabbatarians' fears.

The Sabbatarians' hopes were raised in 1809 when Spencer Perceval became Prime Minister. He often searched the Book of Revelation to produce parallels between Napoleon and Anti-Christ. He allowed Wilberforce to persuade him to assemble Parliament on Tuesdays rather than on Mondays in order to save M.P.'s from the sin of travelling on the preceding Sunday. After he was shot dead in the lobby of the House of Commons in 1812 the Rev. Daniel Wilson paid a Sunday afternoon visit to his imprisoned assassin in an unsuccessful attempt to persuade him to repent. Wilson's mother was the daughter of one of Whitefield's trustees and his father a prosperous silk mercer with premises in Cheapside. The young Daniel worked in his uncle's silk warehouse before being converted by the Rev. John Newton, the former slave-ship captain, and was later to produce the definitive Evangelical interpretation of the Fourth Commandment, so inspiring a major assault upon the English Sunday.[50]

Sabbatarianism now entered a phase of intensification. In 1809 Evangelicals in London, where the threat to the Sabbath was greatest because of the presence of a cosmopolitan upper class and a vast urban population which was difficult to control, had set up a society to suppress Sunday trading, and a second one was established in 1810. Their tracts and pamphlets and the ever-increasing number emanating from individual Sabbatarians resulted in the movement becoming more militant in its demands and more precise in its practices. In 1821, for example, Frank Newman, John Henry's brother, caused a family row by refusing to copy a letter for his father on a Sunday, and the future cardinal, at this time a youthful Evangelical, was called upon to adjudicate.[51]

Such action overtook the earlier Evangelical leaders. Neither Elliot nor Venn was Sabbatarian, and Thornton wrote and posted letters on Sundays. In 1797 Wilberforce had stressed the moderate nature of Lord's day observance in his *A Practical View* and in 1821 defended Sunday letter writing: 'often good people have been led by the terms of the Fourth Commandment to lay more stress on the strictness of the Sunday than on its spirituality'.[52]

Nor did the intensified movement impress Parliament. In 1820 Lord Belgrave failed in his second attempt to outlaw Sunday newspapers. In fact, Parliament was in the course of modifying the 1677 Act to meet the needs of London's highly urbanised society. The process had begun as early as 1698, when the Billingsgate Act allowed the Sunday sale of mackerel and the River Thames Act allowed forty watermen to ply for hire. In 1710 the Hackney Coaches Act had allowed Hackney coaches and chairs to ply and in 1762 the Fish Act had allowed fish carts to travel freely on Sundays.

In 1821 a Bread Act extended the provisions of the 1794 Act to the whole of England, with the proviso that work might continue until 1.30 p.m., and deliveries might be made on Sundays and that dough might be prepared for baking on Mondays. The 1822 London Bread Act applied these provisions to the metropolitan area with double fines; and in 1836 yet another Bread Act extended them to the whole country.

Meanwhile, in 1827 the River Thames Act allowed boats to freely ply for hire on Sundays, and in 1831 the Hackney Carriage Act allowed Hackney carriages to stand and ply on the same terms as on weekdays. The only moves towards restriction were made in 1765, when the Westminster Tolls Act imposed tolls on

Sunday traffic, and in 1831 when the Game Act declared illegal the Sunday killing and taking of game.

By the 1820's, however, the Sabbatarians had emerged as a determined group, with a strong sense of mission. They had overwhelmed most non-Sabbatarian theologies, notably those which argued that Christ, the Apostles or the early Church had relaxed the Fourth Commandment, technically called the Dominical school, and sought to enforce their own views.

Although Sabbatarianism was relevant to the social conditions of the period from the 1520's to the 1820's, it was really the product of a particular religious culture. By 1500 most Englishmen already rested from their labours on Sundays, and so were able to indulge in shopping and recreation, against the latter of which the Sabbatarians directed most of their energy. Sabbatarianism took root and grew in England because the Bible was available to devout men who understood it in a limited way. They took 'holy' to mean 'other-worldly' and 'pleasure' to mean not 'will' but 'enjoyment'; and so moulded the understanding and behaviour of many other Englishmen.

By and large, Sabbatarians were newcomers to national political life, men of property who valued authority and wanted to draw the bonds of social discipline tighter than the country's traditional rulers thought necessary or wise. By 1800 they looked for political allies not to the landed class but to M.P.'s with mercantile and professional backgrounds like Wilberforce, Pitt and Spencer Perceval. Their own movement was falling into the hands of a new generation of leaders like Wilson who gave it a strident tone and uncompromising outlook. That tone and outlook were bringing about the changes in attitude and manners noticed by Place, Brougham and Dickens, and were soon to produce the Victorian Sunday.

Notes

[1] W. B. Whitaker, *Sunday in Tudor and Stuart Times* (1933); *The Eighteenth Century English Sunday* (1940).

[2] M. M. Knappen, *Tudor Puritanism* (Chicago, 1969), 442.

[3] Patrick Collinson, '*The Beginnings of English Sabbatarianism*', in *Studies in English Church History*, I (1961), 207–21.

[4] Christopher Hill, *Society and Puritanism* (1966 ed.), 145–218.

[5] J. Danielou and H. Marou, *The Christian Centuries* (1964), 13; J. G. Davies, *The Early Christian Church* (1965), 62.

[6] L. Harding, *The Celtic Church in Britain* (1972), 48, 75.

[7] Danielou and Marou, *op. cit.*, 42, 74, 75; Davies, *op. cit.*, 154.

[8] L. Harding, *op. cit.*, 76.

[9] *Ibid.*, 93.

[10] Indeed, to the present day Roman Catholics attend Confession on Saturday night as a preparation for Sunday Mass, and keep a Saturday vigil before Easter Sunday, Pentecost and the Embertides; whereas for the Orthodox all Saturday nights are vigils. Sunday afternoon services were uncommon until spread by the Reformation and even among Protestant Churches Sunday evening services were uncommon before the mid-nineteenth century, when the acceptance of gas lighting coincided with a desire to take religion to 'the people'. Even today, Roman Catholic churches rarely hold services on Sunday evening, the Orthodox do not regard it as part of the liturgical or religious day, and members of the Abyssinian, Armenian and Nestorian Churches preserve an even older custom by observing both Saturday and Sunday.

[11] Harding, *op. cit.*, *passim*.

[12] Bede, *A History of the English Church and People* (Penguin ed., 1965), 102–8.

[13] John Burnaby (trans.), *Augustine: Later Works* (Lib. Christ. Classics, S.C.M., vol. VIII), 1955, 216–17.

[14] R. Cox, *The Literature of the Sabbath Question I* (Edinburgh, 1865), 366–9.

[15] Margaret Deanesly, *Sidelights on the Anglo-Saxon Church* (1962), 119, 122, 182–3.

[16] F. C. Copleston, *Aquinas* (Penguin ed., 1965), 9–10.

[17] J. K. Carter, 'Sunday Observance in Scotland, 1500–1606', unpublished. Ph.D. thesis, Edinburgh University (1957), 10–30; T. Aquinas, *The Summa Theologica of St. Thomas Aquinas* (trans. Fathers of the English Dominican Province, revised by the Rev. D. J. Sullivan), 1955, II, 253, 256, 260, 301, 314.

[18] J. K. Carter, *op. cit.*.

[19] P. F. Skottowe, *The Law relating to Sunday* (1936), 65; G. R. Owst, *Preaching in Medieval England* (Cambridge, 1926), 100, 193.

[20] H. E. Winn (ed.), *Wyclif: Select English Writings* (Oxford, 1929), 180–2; Thomas Arnold (ed.), *Select English Works of Wyclif* (Oxford, 1871), II, 55–7; R. Vaughan (ed.), *Tracts and Treatises of Wycliffe* (Wycliffe Soc., 1845), XVIII, 4–6; S.P.C.K. (pub.), *Writings of the Reverend and Learned John Wickliff* (1831), 69–71.

[21] J. K. S. Reid (trans.), *Calvin: Theological Treatises* (Lib. Christ. Classics, S.C.M., vol. xxii), 1962, 111–13; *Institutes of the Christian Religion* (*ibid.*), 394–400; W. Tyndale. *Tyndale's Answer, &.* (Parker Soc., Cambridge, 1850), 67, 98; C. Hill, *op. cit.*, 210–11; K. Wace and C. A. Bucheim, *Luther's Primary Works* (1906), 47–51; T. G. Tappert (ed.), *Luther: Selected Writings 1517–1520* (Philadelphia, 1967), 136–70.

[22] E. Cardwell, *Documentary Annals of the Reformed Church of England* (Oxford, 1844), I, 15–16.

[23] D. Wilkins, *Concilia*, III (1727), 823, 841.

[24] E. Lloyd, *Formularies of Faith* (1825), 142–8, 306–11.

[25] E. Cardwell, *op. cit.*, 155–9.

26 *Ibid.*, 220–1.

27 *Ibid.*, 236–7, 247, 409.

28 *Ibid.*, 311–12, 345–6.

29 R. Cox, *The Literature of the Sabbath Question I, op. cit.*, 371–82.

30 Thomas White, *A Sermon* (1578); John Stockwood, *A Sermon* (1559); John Northbrooke, *A Treatise* (1579); R. G. Usher (ed.), *The Presbyterian Movement in the Reign of Queen Elizabeth* (R. Hist. Soc., Camden Soc. Third Series, vol. VIII), 1905, 27–35, 75–6.

31 Launcelot Andrewes, *Catechistical Doctrine* (Oxford, 1854), 152–69; G. B. Elton, *England under the Tudors* (1965), 422.

32 R. Cox, *op. cit.*, 141–51.

33 J. E. Neale, *Elizabeth I and her Parliaments* II (1957), 60.

34 William Hooker, *The Laws of Ecclesiastical Polity*, V (1597), paras. 69–72; P. McGrath, *Papists and Puritans under Elizabeth I* (1967), 337, n. 3; J. E. Neale, *op. cit.*, II, 394.

35 James Tait, 'The Declaration of Sports for Lancashire', *Eng. Hist. Rev.* (1917), 561.

36 J. P. Kenyon, *The Stuart Constitution* (1968), 131.

37 Thomas Rogers, *The Catholic Doctrine of the Church of England* (Parker Soc. ed., Cambridge, 1854), *passim*; John Prideaux, *The Doctrine of the Sabbath* (1622); Francis White, *A Treatise of the Sabbath Day* (1635); Gilbert Ironside, *Seven Questions of the Sabbath* (1636); Robert Sanderson, *A Sovereign Antidote Against Sabbatarian Errors* (1636); Peter Heylin, *The History of the Sabbath* (1636).

38 J. K. Carter, *op. cit.*, 41.

39 C. H. Firth and R. S. Rait, *Acts and Ordinances of the Interregnum 1642–1660* (1911), I, 421–2, 598–9; II, 1762–70, 1194.

40 *Ibid.*, I, 81; II, 977, 1048.

41 C. Hill, *Oliver Cromwell, &c.* (Penguin ed., 1972), 190, *Society and Puritanism, op. cit.*, 210–13.

42 P. F. Skottowe, *op. cit.*

43 Christopher Hibbert, *The Personal Life of Doctor Johnson* (1971), 9, 11.

44 L. Radzinowciz, *A History of the English Criminal Law* (1956), II, 3, 8; III, 145–6, 186–7; William Law, *A Serious Call, &c.* (1965 ed.), 64; John Telford, *The Letters of John Wesley* (1931), I, 78; James Pope Hennessy, *The Sins of the Fathers* (1970 ed.), 274–5.

45 Beilby Porteus, *A Sermon on the Sabbath* (1784); J. L. and Barbara Hammond, *The Town Labourer* (1966 ed.), 301; J. Hughes *An Essay on the Christian Sabbath* (1804); Joseph Priestley, *Letters to a Young Man* (1792).

46 William Paley, *Moral Philosophy* (1785), Bk. V, ch. 7; William Bolland, *The Christian Sabbath* (Cambridge, 1809), 60, 68.

47 Christopher Hibbert, *op. cit.*, 311.

48 L. Radzinowciz, *op. cit.*, III, 145–6, 186–7.

49 W. B. Whitaker, *Eighteenth Century English Sunday, op. cit.*, 151–68.

50 J. L. and B. Hammond, *op. cit.*, 229; Josiah Bateman, *Daniel Wilson* (1860), I, 138.

51 G. Faber, *Oxford Apostles* (Penguin ed., 1954), 22.

52 R. I. and S. Wilberforce, *The Correspondence of William Wilberforce* (1840), II, 451–2.

chapter two
Resurgence
1827–37

I   *Daniel Wilson*

During the autumn of 1827 Daniel Wilson preached three
sermons on Lord's day observance. After leaving the silk
warehouse he had graduated from St Edmund Hall, Oxford,
briefly returned as a tutor, held a curacy in Surrey and
ministered to the cream of Evangelical society at St John's
Chapel, Bedford Row. He was at present rector of St Mary's,
Islington, and soon to be made Bishop of Calcutta. In 1828 Dr
Whately, soon to be made Archbishop of Dublin, published a
Dominical Sunday theology. In 1830 C. J. Blomfield, Bishop of
London, issued *A Letter on the Present Neglect of the Lord's Day*,
calling upon the inhabitants of London and Westminster to
improve their Sunday behaviour.[1]

Later in 1830 Josiah Conder, the scholarly but militant
Congregational editor of the *Eclectic Review*, attacked Whately's
theology and demanded legislation to secure the better
observance of the Lord's day. Wilson considered unsatisfactory
the distinction which Conder made between 'religious' and
'political' legislation, so preached seven more sermons on the
subject and published them in 1831, hoping, in the words of his
biographer, to establish Sabbatarianism upon a base
'incontrovertible and immoveable', and to gain legislation in
accordance with its principles.[2]

Wilson's first three sermons had inspired his parishioners to
found a Lord's Day Society during 1827, and in the same year
the parishioners of St Margaret's, Westminster, founded a
Sabbath Observance Society. During 1830 Apsley Pellatt, a
Congregational glass manufacturer from Southwark, supported

a Sunday Trading Suppression Society, and other metropolitan Nonconformists formed a Sabbath Protection Society, both of which hoped to persuade shopkeepers to close their shops on Sundays.[3]

Wilson wrote from within the Fundamentalist outlook developed by the earlier Sabbatarians, and long since accepted by all English Protestants, regarding the Bible as a divinely inspired historical record. He devoted almost half his efforts to dealing with biblical chronology and concluded that Christ had not relaxed the Fourth Commandment but swept away a host of Pharasaical accretions and restored it to its original purity.

Wilson shared the Puritan understanding of 'work', of 'holy' and of 'pleasure'. He warned that 'Works of necessity and charity must not be multiplied without just cause' and told his readers to spend Sundays absorbed in the worship of God, shunning all amusement and recreation.[4]

He placed the Christian Sabbath at the heart of revealed religion: 'The glory of God is peculiarly concerned in the due observance of the Sabbath. It is the day which he is pleased to call his own, and with which he has connected most of the practical blessings of salvation.' If English men and the English nation desecrated and profaned the Sabbath, God would punish them with war, rebellion, fire, flood and commercial distress.[5]

The prosperous householders for whom he wrote should suppress such desecration as came within their authority: 'The head of every family has a charge of souls, as it were, committed to him; he is a priest in his own house.' Magistrates and legislators should similarly use their authority to suppress national profanation.[6]

Wilson's book was published in January 1831. On the 25th he and his brother Joseph gathered a band of friends into the latter's house near Clapham Common (a noted Evangelical area, popularly renowned as the home of the 'Clapham Sect'). They set up a committee, appointed Joseph its hon. secretary and resolved to found a society. On 8 February they hit on the name of 'The Society for Promoting the Due Observance of the Lord's Day' (more commonly called the Lord's Day Observance Society and hereafter referred to as the L.D.O.S.), and adopted Daniel's draft of a Primary Address, intending to act upon his interpretation of the Fourth Commandment.[7]

During March the L.D.O.S. took an office in Exeter Hall, the Evangelicals' headquarters, and during May a sub-committee used Conder's book to check on the Sunday observance laws (inviting him to their society's A.G.M. the next year as a gesture of appreciation). In July the full committee decided to try and pass a Bill to strengthen the law, and in February 1832 the sub-committee produced a draft. After a prolonged search amongst Evangelical M.P.'s the L.D.O.S. persuaded Sir Andrew Agnew, a right-wing Scottish Whig, to act as its parliamentary spokesman. Early in July the House of Commons accepted his proposal to set up a select committee on 'The Laws and Practices Relating to the Lord's Day', and he packed it with Evangelical M.P.'s.[8]

The committee heard evidence, much of it orchestrated by the L.D.O.S., that Sunday morning markets flourished in the poor districts of London, that pigeon shooting and gambling were commonplace, that cattle were driven to market and that streets were often full of drunkards as divine service began. It feared that such violations would provoke the wrath of God and recommended that something should be done immediately.[9]

II   *Sir Andrew Agnew*

Sir Andrew Agnew was born in 1793 in Ireland. He had been baptised into the Irish Church and had spent his childhood in that country before enjoying the fashionable life of Edinburgh, Oxford, London and Cheltenham in the company of his negro manservant. He despised religious enthusiasm but was impressed by the Rev. Gerard Noel's preaching, read devotional works by Edward Bickersteth and Thomas Chalmers and was deeply influenced by that well known evangelical work *The Dairyman's Daughter*. Whilst recouping his overstrained finances by living austerely on his large Scottish estate he heard a powerful sermon by the Rev. Thomas McCrie (his biographer's father) and adopted a convinced Sabbatarian position. Agnew's doctrinal views were vague: he held to a strongly anti-Catholic Protestantism and supported the Established Churches of the United Kingdom, although he transferred his sympathy to the

Free Kirk of Scotland between its foundation in 1843 and his own death in 1849.

In 1830 he had entered Parliament for Wigtonshire as a principled and unopposed Independent. He hoped to support Peel and was very suspicious of Wellington, the Prime Minister, but refused to vote in the division which encompassed his downfall and thought the Whig Reform Bill which shortly followed to be too extreme. But by deciding at last to support it he achieved fame as one of the three timorous and irresolute men who ensured its successful second reading. He then went on to oppose the Whigs' Irish Education Bill, to oppose Wood's Bill to admit Nonconformists to Oxford and Cambridge and, by attacking Russell's Irish Church reforms, helped bring down Grey's government. Henceforth he supported Peel and in 1837 stood as a Tory for the constituency of Wigton Burghs.[10]

Sir Andrew Agnew was not a 'House of Commons man'. He exuded an air of good nature, had an even temper and possessed a reserve of moral courage; but he had a weak voice, a cold and subdued manner when speaking and was essentially a man of one issue. He had only reluctantly taken up that issue and lamented his own unsuitability for the task, but felt constrained to press forward; even when taunted by M.P.'s such as Hume and O'Connell, men whose advanced and Catholic views, and Radical and Irish followers, he cordially detested.[11]

During January 1833 the L.D.O.S. tidied up its draft Bill, and George Rochefort Clarke, a committee member and solicitor, and Sir Andrew Agnew, used it as the basis for the Bill which Agnew was to introduce in April.[12] The provisions of his Bill included stringent fines for shopkeepers found guilty of opening on a Sunday; the speedy transfer of fairs and markets from Monday to Tuesday to avoid Sunday business; the prohibition of all Sunday travel except that to divine service, and all Sunday hiring of cabs except by clergymen and doctors; and restrictions on the Sunday departure of ships. Licensed premises were to be closed except to travellers, and fines were to be imposed for drunkenness and for gambling, hunting, shooting, baiting, cock and dog fighting, or attending wakes, fairs, newsrooms and public debates. All 'pastimes' which took the form of 'public indecorum' were to be forbidden.[13]

Agnew introduced the Bill in that form in 1833, 1834 and 1836, but it was defeated on each occasion. In 1837 he amended it slightly and it passed its second reading but lapsed with the dissolution caused by the death of William IV; and he himself was defeated in the consequent election. He complicated matters in 1833 and 1834 by introducing a Scottish Bill, and in 1834, 1836 and 1837 by introducing a Fairs and Markets Bill, which sought to transfer Saturday and Monday markets to other weekdays, to reduce Sunday travelling. His only success was a Bill to transfer elections (to corporations, livery companies and the like) from Sundays to the Saturday preceding or the Monday following, which reached the statute book as the Elections on Sundays Act of 1833.

His position was further complicated by Bills introduced by other M.P.'s. In 1833 William Peter, Whig member for Bodmin, introduced a Bill inspired by pressure from his constituents and drawing its details from the pious upper classes' Sunday observance tradition. This Sunday trading Bill sought to restrict the opening of shops, especially during the hours of divine service. In 1833 and 1835 P. H. Fleetwood, Tory M.P. for Preston, and in 1835 J. S. Poulter, Whig member for Shaftesbury, introduced similar Bills. They received greater support in the House than did Agnew's and might have passed had they not been filibustered by the Radicals and Irish.

Besides this Agnew found it extremely difficult to find a seconder for his Bill. Lord Ashley promised to act in this capacity if no one else would, but Agnew did not call upon him, and he spoke on the Bill on only one occasion. The M.P.'s who did support Agnew amazed the Commons by treating each occasion as an opportunity to give a personal testimony and to call down the wrath of God.[14]

Their arguments highlighted the last century's preoccupation with the limits of personal and public freedom: on what grounds, in any, was personal and social behaviour to be restricted and what was to be State's role in the process?

Quite simply, Sabbatarian laymen wished to put Wilson's ideas into practice, claiming the authority of God to use the power of the State to enforce them. The high Tory Evangelical, Sir Robert Inglis, M.P. for Oxford University, thought it was the 'bounden duty of every Christian Country to provide for the religious observance of the Lord's day'. J. P. Plumptre, moderate Tory M.P. East Kent, thought that M.P.'s ought to go 'as far as temporal authority could go to enforce the injunctions of the sacred scriptures . . . one of the most important and binding duties which Parliament had to enforce was the observance of the Lord's day'.[15]

These men believed that the State had rightly established the Anglican Church and that it should enforce that Church's current teaching. Irish Catholic M.P.'s quickly objected to the State's adopting and enforcing a mistaken religion. Philosophic Radicals objected to its adopting and enforcing any particular religious truth at all. *The Times* commented, 'Outward observance of religion, if compulsory, makes men hypocrites but will never make them practical Christians; and if restraints or prohibitions be applied to things which . . . are indifferent . . . , there is no calculating the alienation of the heart which they may engender to one and all [its] principles, as well as [to] the authorities under . . . which encroachments have been directed against individual liberty.'[15]

Agnew himself adopted the ideas of his acquaintance Lord Ashley (who became Lord Shaftesbury in 1851), to whom he had advised Parson Bull to entrust Sadler's Factory Bill, and claimed that his own Bill would forbid one man to employ other men for pleasure or for profit on Sundays, thus protecting the poor from Sunday labour and enabling them to attend church. Here he was opposed by M.P.'s who held to *laissez-faire* ideas, believing that the State should play no part in relations between masters and men, and that legislative interference would disrupt the nation's economic life. Some Radicals pointed out that stringent control of Sunday shopping and suchlike would not affect the well-to-do but would make life burdensome for the poor.[17]

However, protection from Sunday labour was not the principle behind the Bill, for its specifically exempted the labour of domestic servants. Whilst Agnew was explaining that legislative interference with the domestic affairs of the rich could set an unfortunate precedent for interference with those of the poor, he declared that the Fourth Commandment gave masters complete religious and civil authority over their servants.[18]

The principles behind the Bill were Sabbatarian ones. Its real aim was neither to protect the labourer nor to give him an opportunity to worship; neither to save the conscientious religious man from the unfair competition of those shopkeepers who opened on Sunday, nor to compel the easy-going not to offend the scrupulous. The Bill did not deal with either personal or social morality but with sin. It sought to impose the religious duty of obeying God by abstinence from desecrations and profanations which included some forms of labour and as many forms of amusement and recreation as could be included in its provisions. Its very title – 'A Bill to Promote the Better Observance of the Lord's Day' – indicated what its preamble explained, that its aim was to have the State base its own law on God's as far as was practically possible; thus having the effect of treating sin as crime.[19]

The Commons only listened at all because of Agnew's persistence – 'he meant to go on, little by little, till at last he had brought the House round to some conclusive measure' – and because of pressure from outside the House. In 1833 and 1834 members referred to the strength of feeling in their constituencies and in the country, and Sir Oswald Mosley, Whig member for North Staffordshire, begged the House to settle the matter quickly before the pressure became unbearable, pointing out that only anti-slavery petitions had borne a greater number of signatures than those for the Bill.[20]

In fact Agnew himself did not speak at any length until 1836 but then declared roundly:

'It had been asked why persist in a course which had been so often repudiated by Parliament? . . . surprise had been expressed that such a question should have been reserved for a Reformed Parliament, which it was supposed would be less inclined to religious questions than the former House of Commons. He . . . supported the Reform Bill, from the conviction that it would, by enfranchising the middle classes, bring to bear on the Commons . . . a great accession of moral power. Such a question as that of providing for a due observance of the Sabbath, stood no chance in an unreformed House . . . , but would have been put down by some hundreds of gentlemen . . . having no constituents . . . Every Member of the House [now] had constituents, and in every constituency were some men of moral weight. By the influence of such men he was supported; and he trusted he should be enabled to stand up year after year in the same cause.[21]

Clearly, political calculations would be made as M.P.'s, parties and governments reacted to what was for most men a new and strange issue. In 1833 Lord Althorp, the Whig Chancellor of the Exchequer and Leader of the House of Commons, spoke strongly against Agnew, causing the Tory Inglis to complain that the government used the whole weight of its influence against the Bill. But although it was defeated forty-eight Whigs and Liberals had voted for it in the company of twenty-five Tories. In 1834 Sir Robert Peel, the leading Tory in the Commons, hardly knew what attitude to take when speaking on Agnew's Fairs and Markets Bill.[22]

Agnew did not introduce his Bill whilst Sir Robert Peel was briefly head of a Tory administration in the spring of 1835, although, at the first reading of Poulter's Bill, Goulburn, the Chancellor of the Exchequer, spoke for Poulter and took twelve members of the Ministry into the 'aye' lobby with him. But as soon as his government had fallen Peel made a devastating attack on the Bill's details and called for its defeat on principle.[23]

In 1836 at the first reading of Agnew's own Bill ten members of Peel's late administration and nine members of the Whig Ministry voted for it, but at the second only two of the Tories supported and three of the Whigs opposed it. In the following year similar tactics caused J. H. Roebuck to complain that members wished to gain credit for supporting the Bill and to throw the odium of defeating it on to Radicals like himself.[24]

On 7 June 1837 Thomas Spring Rice, Whig Chancellor of the Exchequer, spoke against Agnew at the second reading but took only one other Minister into the lobby with him. Goulburn voted for Agnew alongside six other Tory ex-Ministers. The Bill passed by 112 to 66, with seventy-six Tories on the majority side and only seven on the minority, a notable reversal of the 1833 position.

Agnew wrote jubilantly, 'We had a famous [first reading] debate . . . many old opponents voted with me (the pressure from without) . . . Our triumph [at the second reading] delights our

friends ... Mr. Spring Rice took a very foolish part, not having
an idea that I was to beat him ... The conservatives supported
me with very few exceptions—not that I have moved an inch
towards them—they have come to me.'[25]

The Evangelical weekly *The Record*, a staunchly Sabbatarian
publication, thought that the Bill was carried because the
members of the Carlton Club voted for it in a body. The Tory
party's electoral agent, F. R. Bonham, had certainly voted for it
at both readings. It is possible that the Tories supported Agnew
for purely tactical reasons. Spring Rice's declaration gave them
an opportunity to discomfort the Whigs. The end of the session
was near at hand, so they could vote for the Bill knowing that it
had no chance of becoming law. In any case, William IV was
critically ill and his death (which occurred on 20 June) would
necessitate a dissolution, a general election and a new
Parliament.[26]

There were also longer-term factors at work. Many high Tory
M.P.'s and Tory newspapers had regarded Agnew's Bills with
distaste, the product of Scots or Dissenters. But Agnew's support
from within the Established Church had influenced many M.P.'s
and caused even anti—Evangelicals like Williams Wynn to
moderate their opposition. Backwoodsmen like the eccentric
Colonel Sibthorpe were often able to overcome their suspicion
that Sabbatarianism was alien to 'old England' and assimilated
it to the Sunday observance tradition. Sabbatarian ultras like
Inglis, who had begun his political career as Lord Eldon's
private secretary, had an established place in the party and
Goulburn was a close friend of Peel's.[27]

The Whigs were in a quite different position. Although Agnew
began as a right-wing Whig, neither he nor the Scottish Whigs
who supported him had much in common with the aristocratic
Whig leaders, who were untouched or repelled by
Sabbatarianism. Lord Melbourne, the Whig Prime Minister in
1837, took a peverse pleasure in travelling on a Sunday, 'being
adverse to the Sabbatarian heresy which prevails in the country'.
Agnew was no doubt happy to withdraw his support from such a
man. Nonconformist M.P.'s who followed the Whigs—John
Wilks who had founded the Protestant Society in 1811; Edward
Baines I, owner of the *Leeds Mercury*; Joseph Pease, the Quaker

railway owner; Mark Philips, a Unitarian and one of Manchester's first M.P.'s; and Richard Potter, member for Wigan—were suspicious of or opposed to Agnew's Bills. The Radicals and Irish were strongly against him.[28]

III   *The Lord's Day Observance Society*

Whilst Sir Andrew Agnew was so occupying the House of Commons, the L.D.O.S. committee had begun to organise its own society. It had placed advertisements in newspapers in order to attract members, developed close contacts with *The Record* in order to spread its message, and its own members had written tracts designed to convince the doubtful. Each M.P. had been sent material supporting Agnew's Bill, and the committee had concentrated on collecting signatures to petitions in its favour.

Only three of the original eighteen who met in Joseph Wilson's house were clergymen. Daniel Wilson needs no further description. The Rev. Henry Blunt, incumbent of Trinity Church, Sloane Street, was a pillar of the Evangelical cause, a noted pastor and preacher. The Rev. S. C. Wilks was on familiar terms with the Evangelical 'establishment', having studied at St Edmund Hall while Wilson was tutor and since 1816 edited the *Christian Observer*.

The fifteen laymen included one member of the landed class, Sir George Grey, and one M.P., Henry Maxwell. Grey's mother had been deeply influenced by Wilberforce and he himself married the eldest daughter of Henry Ryder, Bishop of Lichfield (the first Evangelical to reach the Episcopal bench, albeit under the patronage of his elder brother the first Earl of Harrowby), later enjoying a long Ministerial career as a Whig. Maxwell was of a different stamp, having made his name by fighting against Catholic emancipation as Grand Secretary to the Orange Lodge of Ireland, a militant back-bench Tory.

In subsequent years clergymen joined and left the committee in response to particular crises. Grey had no further contact with it and although Maxwell remained a member he gave it very little support. It was therefore dominated by members of the metropolitan professional class. In 1834 three of the fifteen lay

committee members were solicitors, three were barristers, one
was a banker, one a magistrate and one a 'merchant'. This
pattern persisted through the mid-century until the 1880's saw
an influx of military men.

The L.D.O.S.'s membership, with an annual subscription of
10*s* 6*d*, was mainly middle class, with a small number of bishops
and M.P.'s and a handful of the gentry and aristocracy. The
L.D.O.S.'s committee was entirely, and its membership almost
entirely, Anglican. The society had very few links with other
denominations except the Wesleyan Methodists, whose Annual
Conference resolved to support Agnew in 1833. But even these
contacts were infrequent, and the L.D.O.S. found that Jabez
Bunting was not an easy colleague. Postal contact with Joseph
Sturge, the radical Birmingham Quaker, who shared his
denomination's theological anti-Sabbatarianism, but was
attracted by Agnew's claim to provide Sunday rest for the poor,
was wholly exceptional.[29]

The bishops who lent their names to the L.D.O.S. were safe
men, members of the upper class with a bent for religion which
was traditionally infused with a mild Sabbatarianism. Sumner
of Winchester was a moderate Evangelical and a protégé of
George IV, Grey of Hereford was elevated by his brother the
Prime Minister, and Davys received Peterborough as a reward
for having tutored Queen Victoria.

Some of the Evangelical M.P.'s to whom it looked before
finding Agnew were a little extreme in the expression of their
faith. Sir Thomas Baring, the financier, restricted his charity to
the pious poor. William Evans supported his father's policy of
commanding his employees and tenants to send their children to
the church and Sunday school hard by the cotton mill from
which his family derived its prosperity. Sir Robert Inglis, whose
fortune was founded in the Indies, had won Oxford by
challenging Peel to defend his policy of Catholic emancipation.
Spencer Perceval, the late Prime Minister's son, stood up in the
Commons with Bible in hand and lectured the House on the
need for national days of fasting and humiliation.

Other M.P.'s with whom it had contact in the early
1830's—Sir Oswald Mosley, who owned much of Manchester;
Andrew Johnstone, whose Scottish accent was too marked to be

understood by many M.P.'s; and Able Smith, a wealthy banker—were less extravagantly devout.

The aristocrats who supported the L.D.O.S. were untypical of their class. Lord Henley wanted to ban the bishops from the House of Lords. Lord Winchilsea had challenged the Duke of Wellington to a duel over his administration's support for Catholic emancipation and in 1850 was to urge the government to declare war on the Papal States as a punishment for restoring the Roman Catholic hierarchy in England. The society's other aristocratic supporters, the Dowager Duchess of Beaufort, the Marquess of Cholmondely and the Earl of Chichester, were all notoriously religious.

Agnew stood at the edge of a complex system of family and business relationships. It included the Noels (Earls of Gainsborough), the brewing dynasties of Hanbury and Buxton, the banking houses of Barclay, Bevan and Hoare, the Kinnairds and (through the latters' financial interest in Coutts & Co.) the Earls of Harrowby, who in turn were later related by marriage to W. H. Smith, the wealthy stationer.

The Hon. and Rev. Gerard Noel had given evidence to Agnew's select committee, and the equally Hon. and Rev. Baptist Noel had attended the L.D.O.S.'s A.G.M. in 1833. The society had approached Sir Thomas Fowell Buxton, M.P., Granville Ryder, M.P. (a grandson of the first Earl of Harrowby), and Lord Sandon (who in 1842 became the second Earl). They and their relatives and descendants were to be intimately associated with the evolutiuon of the Victorian Sunday.

In party political terms the various M.P.'s reflected the vote on the second reading of Agnew's Bill in 1833. Evans and Smith were Liberals and Johnstone, Mosley and Buxton were Whigs; whilst the Harrowby family were but moderately Tory, although Baring, Perceval and Inglis were immoderately so. However, few were prepared to speak up for Sabbatarianism in the House in more than a perfunctory way, and so Inglis's emergence as the Sabbatarians' champion indicated that its support in the future was to come more and more from the Tories, as Agnew found in 1837.

Socially speaking, this group represented not the landed

interest as such but that strand in English society seen earlier in Pitt and Spencer Perceval senior, the supremely successful merchants and professional men whose wealth had given them a stake in the country and whose loyalty had won them a place in political life, thus demonstrating that process of assimilation so often noted by contemporaries and historians.

IV   *Nonconformists and propaganda*

Most leading Nonconformist ministers had remained aloof from Agnew's campaign because its Evangelical progenitors and their parliamentary spokesman opposed them on so many denominational issues (as Agnew had voted against the admission of Nonconformists to the ancient universities) and because they were turning to the 'Voluntary Principle' according to which the State should not interfere in religious matters. In 1837 the L.D.O.S. committee recorded its belief that the majority for Agnew's Bill 'would have been greater . . . but at this time the dissenting denominations put forward with unusual prominence, as a fundamental principle, that it was wrong to legislate in regard to religion'.[30]

Most Nonconformists were Sabbatarians in theology and in practice and desired to see the Fourth Commandment obeyed, and so searched for arguments which minimised the State's religious role. Conder had written that the State should not compel men to fulfil positive religious duties, but legislate to give all men the opportunity to do so. To compel men to refrain from desecration in order to provide rest was neither an imposition upon the conscience nor an infringement of liberty, because they were neither forced to do something forbidden by their own religion nor to act for religious reasons.[31]

Conder recorded that his tract was 'very coldly and suspiciously received by the Dissenters', and his arguments certainly did not convince Nonconformist M.P.'s. They generally followed the Radicals, who believed that Agnew's Bill was contrary to *laissez-faire* principles and would disrupt economic and social life.[32]

The Sabbatarians therefore followed Daniel Wilson's recommendation to make every effort to spread their views.

Sabbatarians feared the wrath which God would pour forth upon Sabbath-breakers. They regarded the English as the Sabbath-keeping chosen people and contrasted themselves favourably with the Scots and the Jews. They regarded the French as either Sabbath-breaking Catholics or atheists, and warnings about the dread 'Parisian Sunday' were amongst the most used of Sabbatarian cries.

They appealed first to the upper and parliamentary classes, telling how poor men attributed to Sabbath-breaking their first step into a life of crime which led to the gallows. Josiah Conder explained how Sunday schools saved the community the expense of providing schools itself and saved the government the trouble of policing the lower orders. The Society for Promoting Christian Knowledge thought that Sabbath-breaking implied contempt for the civil government. In a tract entitled *An Appeal to the Rich* the L.D.O.S. warned that once the poor had broken God's law they might logically reject all human authority.[33]

Much of the Sabbatarians' literature was devoted to explaining away objections to their ideas. In his widely-distributed *A Letter To The Friends Of The Sabbath Cause* Agnew denied that he sought to enforce 'a peculiar religious observance by force of law or to "make men religious by Act of Parliament"'. Conder denied that Sabbatarian measures would place heavier burdens on the poor than on the rich by maintaining that if all shops and suchlike were closed on Sundays then all classes would be equally unable to use them. When replying to the argument that the rich could use their superior domestic resources to circumvent such measures he admitted that it was impossible to restrain the rich as well as the poor in their violations of the Sabbath day without 'sacrificing privileges which are amongst the most valuable in our constitution'.[34]

The Sabbatarians' distinction between 'private' and 'public' behaviour enabled them to avoid a fundamental challenge to the rights of property. They defended the right of the private property owner to use his servants, his horses and his grounds without any interference; but claimed the right to regulate that which was corporately or nationally owned, such as railways and the Post Office.[35]

Nor was economic theory forgotton. In his *Letter* Agnew explained how Sunday employment would increase the supply of labour and produce unemployment and lower wages during the week. James Bridges, a close friend, explained that the 'philosophically certain and practically proved' laws of Paley and Malthus showed that Sunday work would result in economic disaster. In any case, God held in reserve the threat of a divinely inspired commercial panic.[36]

V   *The provinces and the voters*

The L.D.O.S. committee had quickly appreciated the value of rousing the country to obtain support for Agnew's Bill. Joseph Wilson corresponded with a multitude of Evangelical clergymen, and received especially strong support from the Rev. William Leake in Derbyshire and the Rev. Herbert Smith in Hampshire. At Easter 1833 three members of the committee spent a week touring the country to establish local societies, and the committee itself employed the Rev. William Rogers as a part-time travelling secretary.

The society's Annual Reports claimed that England was quickly covered by 'Auxiliaries', but the Minute Books indicate that most such bodies had no permanent organisation, and were usually the product of the local Evangelical clergy. Both the clergy and the auxiliaries were widespread, but they were concentrated in the south, where they received some support from members of the professions and the gentry. The petitions which they raised (in 1833 1,061 bore 261,706 signatures, and in 1834 1,076 bore 204,413) had impressed the Commons but were probably untypical of the feelings and opinions of most Englishmen.

The three strongest auxiliaries, those at Bath, Derby and York, drew their strength from opposing Sunday railway-building and the provision of Sunday train services. It was no coincidence that Derby and York were railway centres and Bath on the Great Western line from London to Bristol.

The Derby auxiliary was supported by one Tory M.P., Sir George Crewe, and by W. L. Newton, a director of the Midland Counties Railway. Sabbatarian meetings held at Bath and York in the late 1830's were invariably replete with lawyers, surgeons and solicitors. Most supporters belonged to that class of self-employed men who dominated the L.D.O.S. in its earlier years, and the predominance of military men at Bath anticipated the society's later support.

Sir Andrew Agnew was convinced of the value of local societies as instruments for exerting pressure upon their own M.P.'s and upon the Commons in general. But although the Derby society was active and the *Derby Mercury* regularly produced a quarter column of 'Sabbath Intelligence' and recorded the votes of local M.P.'s on the issue, no apparent result was produced. Sir George Crewe continued to support the L.D.O.S., whilst Edward Strutt, radical scion of the Unitarian cotton-spinning family, consistently voted against Agnew and supported opening the British Museum on Sundays. He kept his seat until removed for bribery in 1847.[37]

However, the situation was very different at Bath, the scene in 1837 of a notable election contest. The fight was between two Liberals—J. A. Roebuck, by now a leading anti-Sabbatarian, and Major General C. Palmer—and two strong Tories—Lord Powerscourt and W. H. L. Bruges. Bath had a particularly strong L.D.O.S. auxiliary, and about eight weeks before the election the Tory *Bath Chronicle* opened an article on 'Mr Roebuck and the Sabbath Question' with the words:

> We have a question to ask of the Dissenters of Bath, a large proportion of whom are the supporters of Mr. Roebuck. Are they prepared to vote at a future election for a man who has declared 'that it is not part of Christianity to observe the Sabbath?' We hope—indeed we do believe—that they will not. There is in Bath a Dissenting Chapel, five of whose deacons, and the son of whose minister, voted for Mr. Roebuck. Are they prepared to vote again for him . . . ? This is a matter which calls for most serious consideration of all those among Mr. Roebuck's constituents . . . , and they will have much to answer for to public opinion if they do not take the opportunity of a future election to disclaim, by their actions, all participation in Mr. Roebuck's creed on this point.[38]

As the election approached the *Chronicle* returned to the attack on Dissenting consistency, accusing Dissenters and Radicals of wishing to assail the Established Church and destroy the

Sabbath day as preliminaries to revolution. The London L.D.O.S. joined in with advertisements and pamphlets, all redolent with Old Testament allusions, which recalled French revolutionary infidelity and appealed to tradesmen and mechanics to make the Sabbath issue a test question.[39]

Roebuck tried to explain his attitude to the Nonconformists and defended his views at several meetings but eventually concluded that 'his ... sentiments ... have deprived him of many votes'. Many Tories exploited the Sabbath issue at the nomination, and Roebuck (after having been in second place with 1,042 votes in 1835) came bottom of the poll with 900 votes. Roebuck's wife believed that it was her husband's anti-Sabbatarian views which cost him the seat, but other causes were at work. Roebuck lost the support of local Whigs and right-wing Liberals, the Radical group was so badly split as to refuse to take part in the election, registration had been neglected and the Liberals (in contrast to the Tories) insisted upon a pure campaign.[40]

The situation at the end of 1837 was a complicated one. Wilson had codified Sabbatarian ideas and Agnew had made a considerable impact in Parliament. The L.D.O.S. had taken on the role of both prophet and pressure group, had certainly revived the Sabbatarians, had roused the religious public and had had a significant effect in certain areas and constituencies.

However, Agnew was now without a seat in the Commons and did not wish to re-enter the House. His activities had stirred up a veritable cacophony of Radical opposition, and had so stimulated the pious Sunday observance tradition that several Bills had attempted to solve the problem of Sunday morning shopping. In addition, the organised Sabbatarians themselves came from a rather narrowly based section of society and were clearly finding it necessary to adapt many of their ideas to other religious and social groups.

Thus the evolution of the Victorian Sunday seemed likely to be as convoluted as the emergence of the English Sunday had ever been—but, for some years at least, with two distinctive features. First, that the Sunday observance tradition was well established in those classes and parts of the land which upheld the attitudes of conventional piety. Secondly, that the L.D.O.S. was prepared to mould those attitudes in accordance with its own precise Sabbatarian position and thereby to fight to impose its own precepts upon other classes and upon other areas.

Notes

[1] R. Whately, *Essays on Some of the Difficulties in the Writings of St. Paul* (1828), 163–8; C. J. Blomfield, *A Letter on the Present Neglect of the Lord's Day* (1830).

[2] Josiah Conder, *The Law of the Sabbath Religious and Political* (1830); D. Wilson, *The Divine and Perpetual Obligation of the Lord's Day* (1831); Josiah Bateman, *op. cit.*, I, 212.

[3] PP., 1834, VIII, *S.C. of H.C. Suppression of Drunkenness*, 179.

[4] Daniel Wilson, *The Lord's Day* (1956 ed.), 150.

[5] *Ibid.*, 1.

[6] *Ibid.*, 157.

[7] L.D.O.S., *Minute Book I*, 25 January, 8 February 1831. Thomas McCrie, *Sir Andrew Agnew* (Edingburgh, 1849) 120, states that Joseph was Daniel's brother; but Josiah Bateman, *Daniel Wilson, op. cit.*, I, 20, maintains that Joseph was his cousin, the eldest son of the uncle to whom he had been apprenticed.

[8] Thomas McCrie, *Agnew, op. cit.*, 118–19; PP., 1831–32, *Rept. S.C. of the H.C. Observance of the Sabbath Day.*

[9] *Ibid., passim.*

[10] Thomas McCrie, *Agnew, op. cit., passim.*

[11] James Grant, *Random Recollections of the House of Commons, &c.* (1836) 339–40.

[12] PP., 1833, III, 561, *A Bill to Promote the Better Observance of the Lord's Day.*

[13] *Ibid.*

[14] T. McCrie, *Agneew, op. cit.*, 147; 3H, vol. 15, col. 951 (19 February 1833); vol. 17, col. 1335 (16 May 1833); vol. 22, col. 54 (11 March 1834).

[15] 3H, vol. 17, col. 1333 (16 May 1833): vol. 38, col. 1227 (7 June 1837).

[16] *The Times*, 3 April 1833.

[17] C. Driver, *Tory Radical. The Life of Richard Oastler* (1946), 212; J. L. and B. Hammond, *Lord Shaftesbury* (1923), 20; 3H, vol. 17, col. 1325 (16 May 1833).

[18] 3H, vol. 33, cols. 1070–72 (18 May 1836).

[19] PP., 1833, III, 561, *A Bill to Promote, op. cit.*

[20] 3H, vol. 28, col. 507 (3 June 1833).

[21] 3H, vol. 33, col. 8 (21 April 1836).

[22] 3H, vol. 17, col. 1331–2 (16 May 1833); vol. 22, col. 54 (11 March 1834).

[23] 3H, vol. 26, col. 740 (25 March 1835); *ibid.*, col. 1374 (20 May 1835).

[24] 3H, vol. 38, col. 1229 (7 June 1837).

[25] Thomas McCrie, *Agnew, op. cit.*, 298, 305.

[26] *The Record*, 24 June 1844.

[27] A. Blomfield, *A Memoir of Charles James Blomfield* (1861), I, 154–6; 3H, vol. 17, col. 1334 (16 May 1833); vol. 28, col. 503 (3 June 1835); vol. 118, col. 1726 (29 July 1851).

[28] P. Ziegler, *Lord Melbourne* (1976), 216.

[29] L.D.O.S. *Minute Book III*, 12, 26 November 1841.

[30] J. T. Baylee, *The History of the Sabbath, &c.* (1857), 234.

[31] Josiah Conder, *op. cit.*, 53–4.

[32] E. R. Conder, *Josiah Conder: a Memoir* (1857), 26.

[33] Josiah Conder, *op. cit.*, 33; S.P.C.K., *Sabbath Breaker's Monitor* (1831), 4; L.D.O.S., *An Appeal to the Rich* (1831), 3.

[34] Sir Andrew Agnew, *A Letter To The Friends Of The Sabbath Cause* (1835), 4; Josiah Conder, *op. cit.*, 54.

[35] James Bridges, *The Sunday Railways, &c.* (1849), *passim*; 3H, vol. 164, col. 16 (28 June 1861); vol. 171, col. 525 (8 June 1863).

[36] Sir Andrew Agnew, *A Letter, &c, op. cit.*, 5–6; James Bridges, *op. cit.*, 11–12.

[37] Thomas McCrie, *Agnew, op. cit.*, 284–5; *Derby Mercury*, 19 March 1833, 11 February 1835, 22 July 1840.

[38] *Bath Chronicle*, 25 May, 1 and 29 June, 6 July 1837.

[39] L.D.O.S., *Minute Book II*, 30 June and 5 July 1837.

[40] *Bath Chronicle*, 20 July 1837; *Bath and Cheltenham Gazette*, 25 July 1837; R. E. Leader, *Roebuck, &c* (1902), 101; G. D. H. Cole and R. Postgate, *The Common People* (1964 ed.), 307–8.

chapter three
CONSOLIDATION
1837–47

After Agnew's defeat the L.D.O.S. was without a spokesman in Parliament. Relations with Agnew were uneasy. He did not wish to engage again in the rough-and-tumble of political life but was prepared to campaign in the country for another Fairs and Markets Bill. The L.D.O.S. committee was itself divided between those who insisted on another general Bill and those prepared to support a less extensive measure. Indeed, after 1837 the society not only lost support numerically and financially but its committee began to lose its sense of purpose and direction.

This had become apparent by 1841, when a sub-committee was set up to examine the society's future. It reported that the society was unlikely ever to be able to find an M.P. willing to promote a Bill satisfactory to its principles, much less to pass it through Parliament. The full committee therefore decided to place the society on a firmer organisational base. The services of the Rev. William Rogers had already been dispensed with. Joseph Wilson now retired into the background, and the committee took on the Rev. J. T. Baylee as full-time paid secretary, on the recommendation of the Rev. Hugh Stowell, leader of the Evangelicals in Lancashire.

The extension of the railway system and the institution of the penny post provided him with an opportunity to extend the society's influence, but despite his establishment of a *Quarterly Publication* in 1843, it failed to maintain either the impetus or the support which it had enjoyed in the 1830's. The society concentrated on spreading its ideas, suppressing such desecration as it could, and watching that Parliament authorised no new forms of desecration.

In 1838 Plumptre, who had previously supported Agnew, followed the example of Peter, Fleetwood and Poulter and introduced a Sunday trading Bill of his own. By this date the 1677 Act was almost totally ineffective, for the fines were small, neither the police nor the parochial authorities were willing to operate it and prosecutions brought by individual citizens—the common informer—seldom succeeded. Hence these Bills imposed more stringent fines upon retail sales either during the whole of Sunday morning or during the hours of divine service.

The L.D.O.S. had been suspicious of the earlier Bills and supported none of them because their preambles did not acknowledge the divine standard which the society regarded as being embodied in the 1677 Act, which applied to the whole day. The L.D.O.S. considered, furthermore, that they implied approval of trade at other times of the day and would have the practical effect of replacing and superseding the 1677 Act.

In 1838 the society surprised Plumptre by discountenancing his Bill for the same reasons. In 1846 and 1848 when Charles Hindley, a Moravian and Liberal M.P. for Ashton under Lyne, introduced a Bill it opposed him too; in 1847 and 1850 refused to support Bills introduced into the Lords by the Evangelical second Earl of Harrowby; and in 1851 was to oppose one introduced into the Commons by Williams, the Liberal M.P. for Lambeth.

By that date it had discovered two far more spectacular issues. In 1840 and 1846 Joseph Hume, the Radical M.P. (in 1840 for Kilkenny and in 1846 for Montrose), moved to open the British Museum and National Gallery on Sunday afternoons. He hoped to give the poor an alternative to spending their time in beer shops and public houses (which were open on Sundays from 1.00 p.m. to 3.00 p.m., from 5.00 p.m. to 10.00 p.m., and after 1.00 p.m., respectively). Goulburn and Inglis claimed that Hume's proposal would injure the Christian religion and cause more drunkenness. On each occasion the Whig government maintained a cautious neutrality.[1]

The 1830's and 1840's were the great years of English railway development, and the Sabbatarians exerted themselves to the utmost to prevent the institution of Sunday train services. Many railway companies respected their principles. The Liverpool & Manchester restricted its Sunday services and instituted a scheme whereby Sabbatarian shareholders could donate to charity that part of their dividend earned from Sunday traffic.

The North Eastern, influenced by the Quaker Pease family, instituted a similar arrangement. Many companies adopted the practice of ceasing operations during Church time, and most companies ran only a limited Sunday service, for demand was very small. But they refused Sabbatarian demands for total Sunday closure. The London & Birmingham allowed Joseph Sturge to resign his directorship after rejecting his repeated attempts to close the line on Sundays.[2]

As early as 1835 the Bishop of Hereford had tried to amend the Newcastle upon Tyne Railway Bill to forbid Sunday traffic, and Agnew had followed his example with the Great Western, turning to the Glasgow & Ayr Bill in 1837.[3]

The front-benchers took a very cautious attitude. Lord Wharncliffe, Peel's Lord Privy Seal in 1835, was prepared to consider encouraging excursions. Sir Frederick Pollock, Peel's Attorney General in the same year, was unwilling to close railways except at the time of divine service. Lord John Russell thought legislation on the matter best avoided.[4]

In 1838 the Post Office secured an Act allowing the Postmaster General to compel railway companies to run a mail train at any time on any day. Most companies then began to run at least one train each way on Sundays, and usually attached passenger carriages to secure such fares as there might be. The resulting controversy caused Plumptre to try to amend Gladstone's 1842 Railway Bill to prohibit Sunday trains.[5]

II   *The 1844 railway Bill*

Gladstone was about to lead Peel's government into difficulties as he steered his 1844 railway Bill through Parliament. The Bill would compel the companies to provide a third-class train in each direction on each passenger line every weekday. But the Radical M.P. for Wolverhampton, Thornely, persuaded the Commons to amend it to impose such a duty on all 'days on which passengers are to be conveyed'. Gladstone realised that that would oblige many companies to provide third-class trains on Sundays and reasoned that if the amendment became law then the government would be conducting a direct legal attack upon Sunday observance. He concluded that the vote must be reversed in the House of Lords.[6]

Peel, to whom Gladstone revealed his position, did not support his views. He agreed to back him if need be but outlined his objections to the plan. The government had twice forced the Commons to rescind votes in the present session (on the Factory Bill and the Sugar Duties). To call upon the House to acquiesce in an amendment by the Lords would be substantially a third case, especially since the sense of the House was for Thornely and a number of loyal Tory members were probably for him too. Eighteen government men had voted among the forty-one against Thornely; but over twenty Tories (including the Young England group) had supported him. To press on in such circumstances could only lead to difficulty.[7]

But Gladstone did press on, drawing up a long memorandum defining his position, disregarding Peel's advice not to rely on Blomfield, and extending his proposed amendment to include Christmas Day and Good Friday.[8] His plans quickly went awry. Alexander Pringle, Tory M.P. for Selkirkshire, who had supported Agnew's plea for a select committee in 1832 and was now a junior Lord of the Treasury, acting as a teller for Gladstone in the minority of forty-one, had written to the L.D.O.S. asking it to support the government Bill. The society thought he referred to the Bill as amended by Thornely, so sent an agitated deputation to Gladstone. The Derby Sabbatarians wrote to Peel implying that 1,500 £10 householders were about to convict the government of desecrating the Sabbath.[9]

Confusion continued when the Bishop of Lichfield gave notice of the amendment which Blomfield was to introduce. On the following day, 2 August, Blomfield repeated to the House the substance of Gladstone's memorandum. He was criticised by Whig peers who argued that if the rich could travel on Sundays it was right that the poor should be able to do so too. (Engels attacked him on similar grounds in his *The Condition of the Working Class in England*, published later in the year.) Nor were the Tory peers favourable to Blomfield. Lord Dalhousie, Vice-

president to Gladstone at the Board of Trade, feared defeat if a
vote were taken, so hurriedly consulted their party's elder
statesman, the Duke of Wellington, the epitome of high
Toryism. The Duke, who had fought Waterloo on a Sunday,
moved the adjournment with a speech against Blomfield, who
wrote a pained letter of complaint to Gladstone.[10]

Dalhousie informed Gladstone that 'At the outset it was very
chaos as our people disliked the amendment . . . the Cabinet
must settle the matter.' When the debate was resumed three
days later Lord Wharncliffe was put up to explain the
government's position. He produced a neat compromise by
which the railway companies must attach third-class coaches to
at least one of such passenger trains as they might run on
Sundays. A long and troublesome debate followed. He and
Dalhousie resisted Whig attempts to provide the Sunday third-
class coaches with the same minimum conditions as the weekday
third-class trains, because that would create a better third-class
service on Sundays than on weekdays; the third-class coaches
having to travel at the same speed as the rest, whereas it was
thought that the third-class trains would travel at the minimum
speed of 12 m.p.h. They persuaded the House to accept
Blomfield's amendment as a matter of form, agreed that the
Christmas Day and Good Friday provisions should not apply to
Scotland, and then got the House to accept the government's
clause in place of Blomfield's. Their majority for this was thirty-
five to thirty, and Dalhousie commented: 'Half a length in a race
is as good as a distance . . . Our own people dead against us still
in sentiment.'[11]

It remained for Gladstone to square the Commons. He
advised that because of an 'arrangement to which he had come
with the railway companies' the House should not extend to
Sunday third-class coaches the minimum conditions laid down
for weekday third-class trains, for fear of attracting custom away
from the other classes. Thornely, however, moved that the
maximum charge for third-class passengers be the same on
Sundays as on weekdays, and Gladstone accepted the change.
Henceforwards railway companies attached third-class coaches
to Sunday trains until the clauses were repealed by the Cheap
Trains Act of 1883.[12]

In 1845 officials in the Board of Trade showed their contempt for the Sabbatarians by picking a Sunday as the last day for the receipt of railway plans, and Whitehall was jammed with cabs as engineers fought to meet the deadline. In 1846 Blomfield made a final desparing effort to prohibit Sunday passenger traffic.[13]

III   *The provinces and opposition*

Meanwhile the L.D.O.S. had concentrated upon supporting its auxiliaries, for their enthusiasm had waned as soon as Agnew's campaign had ended. That at Derby comforted itself with the reflection that its members 'though by no means numerous were exceedingly respectable'.[14]

Members of the auxiliaries at Bath, Derby and York generally voted Tory in general elections, and in 1847 the hon. secretary of the Bath auxiliary, Melmoth Walters, spoke for Lord Ashley, who was contesting the seat. J. T. Baylee warned its members to be on their guard against the subversive ideas propagated by the 'vile trash of the Sunday press'.[15]

The Bath auxiliary hired a policeman to patrol the Lansdown Revel (which took place on a Sunday), that at York gained the Lord Mayor's pledge to put down Sunday cricket, and at Derby the Mayor told the auxiliary that nothing 'could be politically right which was morally wrong'.[16]

The auxiliaries failed to secure lasting agreements with masters, mill owners and shopkeepers to avoid Sunday business. They failed to convince the working classes that their aim was to protect them from Sunday labour. Railway labourers in Bath paid more attention to the auxiliary's use of the 1677 Act to prosecute them than to protestations that it did so for their own good.[17]

Nor, indeed, did the auxiliaries object to all Sunday labour. That at Bath regarded the Sunday fuelling of lime kilns as 'necessary' work; and the *Derby Mercury* reflected a common Sabbatarian attitude when it noted that 'The limitations to the principle of protection on the Lord's day are the sacredness of domestic arrangements and the legitimate use of private property'.[18]

In 1834 an auxiliary had been founded in Newcastle upon

Tyne and had made an annual attempt to close the Central Exchange Newsroom on Sundays. In 1846 its activities so irritated Charles Larkin, a Roman Catholic, a leading member of the Northern Political Union and a campaigning journalist, that he led a movement against it, accusing Sabbatarians of seeking an alliance with the 'temporal power' in order to wage war on 'all the innocent recreations and enjoyments of the people'.[19]

There was a tradition of working class anti-Sabbatarianism. During the French wars political meetings had been held on Sundays. The most radical newspapers were published on Sundays. A host of pamphleteers had criticised Agnew on behalf of the working classes.[20]

Some social reformers hoped to use Sunday as a day for non-religious education. William Lovett, who had been brought up a Wesleyan, wanted places of recreation open on Sundays to act as a counter to drink. Joseph Livesey, the pioneer of teetotalism, shocked some devout persons by teaching writing in his Sunday school. Robert Owen, who as a boy had written to William Pitt about the need for stricter Sabbath observance, wished to use Sunday recreation as an element in his plans to educate and civilise the masses. By 1832 Owen was giving Sunday lectures in two London theatres as well as at his headquarters on the Grays Inn Lane. By the later 1830's his followers, such as the Coventry Branch of the Recreative Religionists, were flourishing in the provinces and organising Sunday lectures there.[21]

Owen's Sunday lectures had a number of effects. They excited 'the alarms of the religious portion of [his] members and [caused] great numbers to secede' They gave the police an opportunity to arrest working men for 'unlawfully assembling on a Sunday evening'. They gave the Rev. J. W. Kidd a chance to close down the Manchester Hall of Science by bringing a prosecution under the 1780 Act.[22]

A more important effect was to provide intelligent young men from the lower middle classes with an opportunity to engage in mutual improvement and education as they lost their religious faith. George Jacob Holyoake left the Congregationalists and Charles Bradlaugh the Evangelicals for careers in secularism; George Howell (later to be organiser for the Reform League and secretary of the Parliamentary Committee of the T.U.C.) and Thomas Cooper, the Chartist, abandoned Wesleyanism, each one entering radical politics through Sunday meetings in Owen's Halls of Science. The Chartist leaders—Frost, O'Brien, Harney, O'Connor and Jones for example—commonly used Sundays for political lectures and meetings.[23]

When criticising Agnew's Bill the parliamentary Radicals and *The Times* had revived the theology of the Reformation, and some religious opposition to Sabbatarianism had survived from earlier days. The Quakers still referred to Sunday as 'First Day'. Small congregations of Seventh Day Baptists still existed in London and Tewkesbury, and during the 1840's their co-religionists in the United States inspired the foundation of the Seventh Day Adventists. Dr Priestley's Unitarians maintained their anti-Sabbatarian position. For the most part, however, the development of anti-Sabbatarian theology resulted from struggles to escape from the Sabbatarian interpretation of the biblical text.

The first element came from eccentrics who asserted that the Sabbath was a half pagan, half Catholic institution, or that it should be observed from sunset to sunrise. The second element came from liberal churchmen. Dr. Whately, product of an Oriel College fellowship, had denounced Sabbatarian theology and presented a Dominical one, but hesitated to commend Sunday amusement. Dr. Arnold, also a Fellow of Oriel, and between 1828 and 1842 headmaster of Rugby School, impressed similar views upon his pupils. The third element came from Newman and Keble, also Fellows of Oriel, who abandoned Sabbatarianism as they established the Tractarian movement, Newman criticising its Evangelical proponents and Keble allowing the Hursley villagers to play Sunday cricket.[24]

The L.D.O.S. was unaware of that development, for it was still trying to regain the initiative lost in 1837. It had continued to influence Parliament and gained widespread acceptance for its beliefs, but the extension of the railway network and the growth of a many-sided opposition were challenging its attempt to win control of Sunday. The next decade was to prove vital.

Notes

[1] 3H, vol. 55, cols. 721–6 (14 July 1840); vol. 88, col. 717 (14 August 1846).

[2] G. K. Roberts, 'The Development of a Railway Interest, &c.', London University PhD. thesis (1965), ch. V; David Brooke, 'The Opposition to Sunday Rail Services, &c.', *Jnl. of Transport History*, VI, 1963–64, 95–105; *Railway Times*, 10 March 1838; Stephen Hobhouse, *Joseph Sturge, &c.* (1919), 55; Alexandrina Peckover, *Life of Joseph Sturge* (1890), 54–5.

[3] 3H, vol. 28, col. 646 (11 June 1835); col. 150 (26 May 1835); vol. 33, col. 855 (30 March 1836); vol. 38, col. 855 (17 May 1837); vol. 28, col. 646 (11 June 1835); vol. 32, col. 844 (13 March 1836).

[4] 3H, vol. 28, col. 646 (11 June 1835); col. 150 (26 May 1835); vol. 38, col. 898 (19 May 1837).

[5] PP., 1838, XVI, *Railway Communications, passim*; 1 and 2 Vict., c. 98 *An Act to Provide for the Conveyance of Mails by Railways*; 3H, vol. 56, col. 320 (4 February 1841); vol. 52, col. 703 (30 March 1841); vol. 53, col. 1013 (31 May 1842); vol. 64, col. 183 (18 June 1842).

[6] 3H, vol. 72, col. 256 (5 February 1844); vol. 80, col. 1190 (22 July 1844); B.L. Add. Mss., Gladstone Papers, 44275, f. 207 (Gladstone to Peel, 26 July 1844).

[7] *Ibid.*, F. 209 (Peel to Gladstone, 27 July 1844).

[8] *Ibid.*, 44374, f. 162 (29 July 1844).

[9] 3H, vol. 14, col. 50 (3 July 1832); L.D.O.S., *Minute Book III*, 26 and 31 July 1844, *Quarterly Publication*, No. 5, 41–2 (October 1844); B.L. Add. Mss., Peel Papers, 40548, ff. 31–7.

[10] 3H, vol. 75, col. 1648 (1 August 1844); F. Engels, *The Condition of the Working Class in England* (trans. and ed. W. O. Henderson and W. H. Chaloner, Oxford, 1958), 319 and n.; B.L. Add. Mss., Gladstone Papers, 44361, f. 209 (Blomfield to Gladstone, 3 August 1844).

[11] B.L. Add. Mss., Gladstone Papers, 44361, f. 205 (Dalhousie to Gladstone, 2 August 1844), f. 212 (*ibid.*, 5 August 1844); 3H, vol. 75, col. 1843 (5 August 1844).

[12] 3H, vol. 76, col. 1846 (6 August 1844); 7 and 8 Vict., c. 135, *An Act to Attach certain Conditions to the Construction of Future Railways, &c*; PP., 1847, LXIII, *Regulations of Every Railway Company on the Subject of Travelling on Sunday*; PP., 1864, LII, *Return of the Number of Passenger Railways, &c.*; 46 and 47 Vict., c. 34, *An Act to Amend the Law Relating to Railway Passenger Duty, &c.*

[13] H. Parris, *Government and the Railways* (1969), 101; 3H, vol. 87, col. 27 (5 June 1846).

[14] *Derby Mercury*, 5 April 1837.

[15] *Bath Chronicle*, 11 June 1847.

[16] *Derby Mercury*, 8 March 1837.

[17] *Bath Chronicle*, 19 June 1845.

[18] *Derby Mercury*, 1 May 1833.

[19] Charles Larkin, *No Sabbath in Christianity* (Newcastle upon Tyne, 1846), 3.

[20] Anon., *Sunday in London* (1833); Figaro in London (pseud.), *Sycophantic Saints and Sabbath Sinners* (1833).

[21] William Lovett, *The Life and Struggles of William Lovett, &c.* (1876), 57;

Joseph Livesey, *The Life and Teachings of Joseph Livesey, &c.* (n.d.), clix, n.; Robert Owen, *The Life and Teachings of Robert Owen* (1857), I, 16–17; *id.*, *A New View of Society*, (*c.* 1813), 10–12; PP., 1832, VII, *Rept. S.C. of H.C. Observance of the Sabbath Day*, 73, 90; William Smith, *Scepticism and Infidelity* (1840), *passim*.

²² William Lovett, *Life*, *op. cit.*, 43, 77–8; *The Watchman*, 17 June 1840.

²³ G. J. Holyoake, *Sixty Years of an Agitator's Life* (1900), *passim*; H. B. Bradlaugh and J. M. Robertson, *Charles Bradlaugh* (1902), I, 1–20; F. M. Leventhal, *Respectable Radical: George Howell* (1973), 11–20; Thomas Cooper, *The Life of Thomas Cooper, &c.* (1872), *passim*.

²⁴ Rev. M. W. Jones, *The Sign of the Messiah, &c.* (1879), *id.*, *Sabbath Memorial and Sabbath Observer*; Rev. C. M. Davies, *Unorthodox London* (1876), 135–41; Richard Whately, *Essays on Some of the Difficulties, &c.*, *op. cit.*, 167 n.; Geoffrey Faber, *Oxford Apostles* (Penguin ed., 1954), 22, 143; A. Mozley (ed.), *Letters and Correspondence of John Henry Newman* (1891), I, 127; M. J. Svaglic (ed.), *John Henry Newman, Apologia Pro Vitae Sua* (1967), 86, 260, 262; Owen Chadwick, *Victorian Church* (1966), I, 445; Thomas Arnold, *Christian Life and Doctrine, &c.* (1878 ed.), 184–92.

PART TWO

chapter four

1847–57 (I)
THE CRISIS

I   *Post Office, prize essays and railways*

When in 1847 the L.D.O.S. learned that Rowland Hill's plans for the Post Office involved the startling innovation of transmitting mail through London on Sundays the society opened a campaign against the practice and soon extended it to demand the complete cessation of Sunday collection and delivery as well. The newly formed Evangelical Alliance took up the cry and its Scottish members, dissatisfied with the attitude of most English Nonconformists, set up a Sabbath Alliance of their own. In 1848 the Wesleyan Methodists established a Sabbath Committee of their own.

The Post Office campaign drew on support which had previously lain dormant, and late in 1847 John Henderson, a Glasgow merchant, drew up plans for an essay competition in which the working classes would be invited to write on the temporal advantages of Sabbath observance. Lord Ashley extended the plan to England during 1848 and persuaded Prince Albert, who was anxious to show his interest in social questions, to donate £50 for prizes. The Evangelical Alliance, the Religious Tract Society and a group of Leicester Sabbatarians got up competitions on their own account and the prize-winning essays from all five series were published during the late 1840's and the 1850's.[1]

Within a few years the essays transformed the whole Sabbatarian controversy. J. A. Quinton's *Heaven's Antidote to the Curse of Labour* explained how Sunday work would produce unemployment and low pay—'six days' pay for seven days' labour'—forcing the labourers to 'take refuge in the precincts of some union, or be goaded into the commission of crimes'.[2]

The essayists did not ask for legislative action to protect themselves from Sunday labour. 'A Labourer's Daughter' wrote in *The Pearl of Days* (which was commended by the queen) that the Sabbath limited the employers' power, but that 'comparatively little can be done by the civil ruler in promoting the cause of Sabbath observance'.[3]

The essayists believed that total abstention from Sunday amusements was the answer to their problem. If Sunday amusements spread they would destroy the day's sanctity and lessen the embargo on labour, allowing all forms of industrial work to begin and leading other forms of work to spread as people amusing themselves demanded food, drink, transport and so on.

They were determined to demonstrate their political safety. An essay favoured by the Religious Tract Society condemned strikes as the major cause of working class Sabbath-breaking, because they led men to pawn their Sunday clothes. A loyal Leicester essayist denounced Robert Owen, Feargus O'Connor and Tom Paine: 'the dreams of the socialist, the thoughts of the leveller and the sneers of the infidel'.[4]

The L.D.O.S. had had little to do with the essays because it was completely scriptural and religious in its outlook and in 1849 was again taken up with the parliamentary scene. Joseph Locke, the railway engineer, aided by the Baptist railway contractor S. M. Peto, had introduced a Bill to compel Scottish railway companies to attach passenger coaches to Sunday mail trains which ran under the 1838 Act. Amidst a storm of Sabbatarian protest the Tories accused Locke of 'a direct infringement of the rights of private property', and the Whig government, whilst indicating its right to regulate the railways, advised the House to defeat the Bill in deference to the strength of feeling in Scotland. It was lost by 122 to 131.[5]

However, the L.D.O.S. recommended the Post Office campaign by using the newly formed societies to flood Parliament with petitions and persuaded Lord Ashley to move in the Commons for an end to the Sunday collection and delivery of mail. On 30 May 1850, coincidentally the first day in the newly built House, he defeated Lord John Russell's Whig government on the issue. By that time every M.P. had been sent a lavishly bound volume of the Albertian Prize Essays, and although some doubtless discarded them, Joseph Hume sending his to the Library of the British Museum, Ashley referred to them as authentic expressions of working class opinion. He endeavoured to persuade M.P.'s that the working classes wished to benefit from Sabbatarian legislation. What he did do was to make himself one of the most unpopular men in England, and the vote was reversed later in the same year.[6]

II   *The Crystal Palace and pamphlets*

During 1847 and 1850 Thomas Cooper, the Chartist, used his egotistically titled *Cooper's Journal* to oppose Lord Harrowby's Sunday trading Bill, fearing that its real aim was to enable the government to close the secularists' lecture halls on Sundays. He called for a 'fair stand up fight [against] the Sabbatarians. It would cause so much thought among the people that they would be laughed down.' His co-editor, Frank Grant, backed him: 'The deluge of trash vented on this topic widens the breach between Christianity taught in the churches and the common reason of mankind. Let the bigots do their worst, the sooner we hope to see a strong tide set in and sweep away such monuments of religious folly.'[7]

The fight was nearer at hand than either Cooper or Grant had anticipated. When in 1851 the Great Exhibition was kept firmly closed on Sundays the Sabbatarians waxed lyrical about the bounty which God had bestowed upon His people. But early in 1852 when the Crystal Palace was moved to Sydenham the company formed to run it as a business venture proposed to open it on Sunday afternoons. An article in *The Times* roused the Sabbatarians by claiming that Lord Derby, the Tory Prime Minister, had agreed. A deputation led by Archbishop Sumner of Canterbury, his brother of Winchester, Blomfield of London, Lord Shaftesbury and Sir Robert Inglis waited upon the Prime Minister and condemned the plan. Josiah Conder published a second edition of his book with a preface asserting that the Palace's Sunday opening would cause deeper offence to public morality and give greater comfort to Popery than any official act since the time of James II. The government inserted into the company's charter of incorporation a clause derived from the 1780 Act, that no person should be admitted to the building or grounds on Sundays for a money payment, made directly or indirectly, without the sanction of Parliament.[8]

No one issue encouraged the Sabbatarians as did the Crystal Palace. Clergy and laymen all over the country poured forth leaflets, pamphlets and tracts. Their emotion reflected the impact which the Palace had made on the mid-Victorians and produced material which revealed very significant aspects of their own convictions and practices.

The Religious Tract Society told the middle classes that Sabbath observance was a sure way to distinguish between the righteous and the wicked and recounted that many of the latter perished in the very midst of their Sunday amusements. Middle class ambitions were catered for when the Sabbatarians told how young clerks sacked for refusing to work on Sundays were rewarded with God-given wealth. The class's social position was safeguarded when Sabbatarians advised that masters might use their authority to require servants to keep the Sabbath, but warned servants themselves that they 'must not, under a pretence of keeping the Sabbath day holy, refuse to do any necessary work; such as making fires or beds'.[9]

When dealing with the working classes the Sabbatarians adopted a different approach, producing tracts phrased in what they took to be the working class vernacular and picturing rural villages in which contented labourers observed a Sabbath eve, rose early on Sunday, went to church and then ate a frugal but satisfying meal of hot vegetables and bacon which had been largely prepared on the previous day. The working classes were enjoined to accept their poverty joyfully, to respect their employers and masters and to put aside all false ideas and ambitions. When editing working class essays, Edward Bickersteth (who had been given the living of Watton by Able Smith) apoligised for the occasional 'freedom of remark respecting their position in society'. Shaftesbury was more direct: 'your political rights, how trumpery, how mean, how unworthy of consideration are they, when compared to those rights which assert the sanctity of the Lord's day'.[10]

III　　　　　*The Sunday trade riots of 1855*

During 1854 the L.D.O.S. made a temporary alliance with the temperance movement and forced through Parliament a Bill which severely restricted Sunday drinking hours. In 1855 Lord Robert Grosvenor introduced a Sunday trading Bill, and its prospect of success, combined with irritation caused by the Licensing Act, caused the metropolitan working classes to demonstrate against it. Lord Palmerston, Whig Prime Minister, persuaded Grosvenor to withdraw it and the Licensing Act was rapidly repealed.

Witnesses who opposed Sunday trade Bills before select committees in 1847 and 1850 were certainly Chartists. One of Grosvenor's aims was to free respectable shopkeepers from the competition of costermongers who, as Henry Mayhew found, were ignorant of the Six Points but considered themselves thorough Chartists.[11]

For three Sundays in June and July 1855 the working classes flocked to Hyde Park to demonstrate against the Bill, which had become the symbol of their exasperation with a political system that bowed to every interest except their own, and had produced an embryonic class-consciousness. Henry Beal, who described himself as a table-decker when giving evidence to the Royal Commission which reported on the affair, told how there was 'a general feeling of abhorrence against the measure; that it was a measure to crush the poor, while the rich had their privileges unmolested'.[12]

Chartists whose enthusiasm had survived the debacle of 1848 had posted up placards and circulated handbills, and street singers had distributed satirical ballards. Two Sunday papers, the Chartist *Reynolds' Newspaper* and the Radical *Weekly Dispatch*, had stirred up popular feeling. On Sunday 24 June a crowd of some 150,000 people assembled in the Park and barracked the wealthy promenaders of Rotten Row with shouts of 'Go to church' as Chartists handed out leaflets bearing details of a meeting to plan the revival of their movement.[13]

Karl Marx, who was present, wrote an excited article for the *Neue Oder Zeitung* announcing that 'the English revolution' had begun. On 1 July an even larger crowd, composed of the middle and the working classes, gathered in the Park. They included, according to witnesses to the Royal Commission, socialists who spoke out against the aristocracy, well dressed men who dropped hints of the 1848 revolutions, and a group of foreigners who talked of barricades. The assembly had been prohibited by Sir Richard Mayne, the Metropolitan Commissioner of Police, and large forces of police broke up the crowd. On the next Sunday the Park was comparatively quiet and after milling around the more adventurous moved off through Belgravia, breaking windows.[14]

The commission was set up to satisfy the public outcry against the violence used by the police. Sir Richard Mayne argued that he feared a major outbreak, led by three men present in the Park, but refused to name them. However, one was the international revolutionary Ledru Rollin, and another was the Chartist propagandist G. W. M. Reynolds. Bradlaugh was there and brushed with the police, later giving evidence to the commission, but he did not pose a threat to law and order. Thomas Frost, a Chartist and Radical journalist (not to be confused with John Frost, who had led the rising at Newport and did not return from exile until May 1856) saw staves being distributed among the crowd on the third Sunday, but thought that they were intended to teach the police a lesson. In the event the police remained in the background, so the staves were not used. There is no evidence to suggest that anyone planned a rising, for those activists who were present contented themselves with speech-making and the crowd's own behaviour was largely spontaneous; but the government, enmeshed in the Crimean conflict, had received a severe shock.[15]

IV   *British Museum and Sunday bands*

Crisis followed crisis. The Sabbatarian victory over the Crystal Palace had so provoked Sir Joshua Walmsley, the Radical M.P. for Leicester, that in March 1855 and February 1856 he moved in the Commons to open the British Museum on Sunday afternoons in order to provide a compensation for the continued closure of the Palace and to provide the working classes with an edifying, educational and innocent alternative to

Sunday drinking.

Walmsley's proposal so unleashed Sabbatarian fury that Palmerston used his government whips against the motions. But he was no Sabbatarian and had allowed Sir Benjamin Hall, the Commissioner of Works, to arrange for military bands to play in London parks on Sunday afternoons. By May 1856 the Horse Guards band was playing in Kensington Gardens, the band of the Second Life Guards in Regent's Park and a third military band in Victoria Park. It was estimated that on Sunday 4 May 1856 140,000 people, a tenth of the population of London north of the Thames, gathered in the parks to hear the bands.[16]

The Sabbatarians' fury was unleashed once more. They made prominent use of an argument which had come to the fore during the Post Office campaign; that if the government sponsored national desecration it tainted every citizen with guilt, doubly so if each one did not protest. Palmerston was warned by Shaftesbury, his stepson-in-law, but refused to suspend his bands. Shaftesbury then persuaded Sumner to address a letter of remonstrance to Palmerston and, faced with the growing Sabbatarian storm, the latter told the Commons that he had acceded to the Archbishop's wishes and withdrawn them.[17]

It was an embarrasing episode for the government. Dallas, the United States ambassador, thought that Palmerston had approached Sumner on bended knee. Greville, the diarist, believed that Palmerston had deliberately sought Sumner's intervention to extricate himself from the risk of defeat without losing face. When Palmerston reported to the queen she replied that she could not 'sufficiently express her regret at the incomprehensible blindness and mistaken piety of the so-called "Evangelical Saints" '.[18]

V   *Social Sabbatarianism*

These crises highlighted an essential characteristic of Sabbatarianism. When the Sabbatarians declared that a master exercised spiritual functions over his household, that he should interpret the Fourth Commandment on his servant's behalf and that the servant should obey, then they produced an axiom which (to adapt Macpherson's phrase) may be called possessive or spiritual authoritarianism.[19]

The assertion of authority and the desire to enforce obedience lay at the heart of Sabbatarianism. In 1844 an anonymous Sabbatarian had explained, 'It is an unaviodable inference from the plain word of God that the Magistrate, being God's minister [should use] His authority.' In 1852 the Rev. C. C. Collins claimed, 'We wish for no restrictions upon any man's liberty—none, at least, unauthorized by the sanction of God's holy word.' In 1857 Bishop Blomfield counselled, 'We must deal with society as a Christian man deals with his family.'[20]

When appealing for support the Sabbatarians had moderated their language, but there often seemed to be a gulf between Sabbatarian propaganda and reality, as was apparent in their attitude towards the lower orders. Conder had written, 'It is upon the Sunday that the peasant feels himself a freeman: it is on this day, that, in the house of God, he is lifted up to the level of a man.' However, Joseph Arch, the agricultural labourers' leader, recalled how the labourers, his father among them, were made to wait and approach the altar after the squire and his family had done so. The Fascist Sir Oswald Mosley, descendant of the Whig baronet, looking back to the pre-1914 world, thought that 'class values only emerged strikingly in church'.[21]

Yet there was some reality in Sabbatarian propaganda. William Booth, the founder of the Salvation Army, bitterly denounced socially stratified worship. He had lost his job as a pawn broker's assistant for refusing to work on Sundays, but had been taken back when his master recognised his stand for religious principle, much to the joy of his widowed mother. Sabbatarianism's capacity to satisfy the whole middle class, ranging from those who kept servants to those in Booth's precarious position, and to appeal to each in the shared language of Fundamentalism, gave it its strength.[22]

Sabbatarianism encountered problems with those who neither shared these social conditions nor accepted authoritarianism and Fundamentalism, but the prize essays had provided a way out of part of this difficulty by stressing that the purely voluntary abstention from amusements had the most salutary social effects. This approach was codified in 1856 when a Wesleyan minister, William Arthur, published his pamphlet *The People's Day*, and may be called social Sabbatarianism.[23]

The Sabbatarians quickly filled in the details of this new approach. J. T. Baylee decided that amusements were innocent 'only when limited to ordinary days of the week'. A devout Leicester Sabbatarian explained that 'Sunday pleasure ... encompasses every amusement that the mind of man can invent, from the highest intellectual enjoyment to the most trifling diversion that can be participated in'.[24]

Social Sabbatarianism was of enormous importance. It moulded and enlivened the controversy for almost fifty years. It allowed the Sabbatarians to avoid authoritarianism and to champion the working classes. It allowed Nonconformists to assuage their consciences and to defend the civil observance of the Sabbath. It allowed M.P.'s to reconcile their *laissez-faire* principles with their religious values, for no legislation was called for, merely the defence of the *status quo*.

Notes

[1] L.D.O.S., *Quarterly Publication*, No. 32, p. 223 (January 1850).

[2] J. A. Quinton, *Heaven's Antidote to the Curse of Labour, &c.* (1849), 25,26.

[3] A Labourer's Daughter, *The Pearl of Days, &c.* (1848), 76–7.

[4] Edward Bickersteth (ed.), *Prize Essays, &c* (1850), 4–9; Samuel Foxon, *The Leicester Prize Essays* (1857), 22.

[5] Joseph Devey, *Joseph Locke* (1862), 257–69; 3H, vol. 104, cols. 285 and 835 (3 and 23 April 1849).

[6] 3H, vol. III, col. 471 (30 May 1850).

[7] Thomas Cooper, *Cooper's Journal*, vol. 10, No. 1, pp. 146–7 (9 March 1848), vol. 26, No. 1, p. 40 (29 June 1850).

[8] O. Chadwick, *The Victorian Church (op. cit.)*, I, 462–3.

[9] Religious Tract Society, *The Lord's Day* (Tract No. 14); anon, *The Crystal Palace, &c.* (1855), 20; A Clergyman, *A Commentary on the Ten Commandments* (R.T.S. No. 56), 2; anon, *A Sunday Evening's Present to a Female Servant* (n.d., Houlston's Tracts), 3.

[10] Anon, *The Sabbath was made for Man: a Word to Working Men* (1853); S.P.C.K., *The Working Man's Holiday; or, What Sunday Can Be* (Tract No. 1631); John Hall, *The Sons of Toil and the Crystal Palace* (1853); Edward Bickersteth (ed.), *Prize Essays, &c., op. cit.*, p. x n.; Edwin Hodder, *Shaftesbury* (1886), III, 267.

[11] PP., 1847, IX, *Rept. S.C. of H.C. Sunday Trading in the Metropolis*, 108–11; PP., 1850, XIX, *Rept. S.C. of H.L. Sunday Trading in the Metropolis, passim*.

[12] PP., 1856, XXIII, *Rept. Alleged Disturbances*, 146–7.

[13] B. Harrison, 'The Sunday Trading Riots of 1855', *Historical Journal*, VIII, 2 (1965), 219–45.

[14] K. Marx and F. Engels, *On Britain* (Moscow, 1962), 435.

[15] Thomas Frost, *Forty Years' Recollections* (1880), 257.

[16] O. Chadwick, *op. cit.*, I, 466.

[17] J. T. Baylee, *Letters on the Lord's Day* &c (1849), 14.

[18] G. M. Dallas, *Letters from London* (1870), I, 47; L. Strachey and R. Fulford (eds.), *The Greville Memiors* (1938), VIII, 228–9; B. Connell, *Regina v. Palmerston* (1962), 201–3; H. C. Benson and Viscount Esher (eds.), *The Letters of Queen Victoria* (1907), III, 171, 243.

[19] Cf. C. B. Macpherson, *The Political Theory of Possessive Individualism* (Oxford, 1967).

[20] A Roadside Enquirer (pseud.), *The Sabbath Question Illustrated* (1844), 73; C. C. Collins, *The Sabbath* (1852), Sermon II, 18; Cab and Omnibusmen's Sunday Rest Association, *First Annual Report* (1859), 11.

[21] Josiah Conder, *op. cit.*, 35; *Countess of Warwick* (ed.), *Joseph Arch. The Story of his Life* (1898), 28; Sir Oswald Mosley, *My Life* (Nelson ed., 1970), 11–12.

[22] Richard Collier, *The General next to God* (Fontana ed., 1970), 24–5.

[23] William Arthur, *The People's Day* (1856).

[24] J. T. Baylee, *History, op. cit.*, 258; Florence Griffin, *Leicester Prize Essays, op. cit.*, 10.

chapter five

1847–57 (II)
THE COUNTRY

I   *Sunday labour*

The Sabbatarians therefore claimed to have won the battles
of the mid-century, but before the full significance of these years
can be appreciated it is necessary to examine the state of the
country, where their struggle against desecration and
profanation was in full swing, producing paradoxical effects
which roused Dickens's biographer Cruikshank to suggest that
perhaps 'the taboo was set up to save the tribe from being
worked to death'.[1]

During the eighteenth century some commentators had held
purely expedient attitudes towards Sunday. In 1725 the Rev.
Henry Bourne had even condoned Sunday games as a valuable
relaxation for the poor; but in the 1770's Sabbatarianism itself
was attacked because it gave them an opportunity for idleness
and disorder. In 1784 Arthur Young praised Coke of Holkham
for sending his men to church on Sunday mornings and to the
fields in the afternoons. In 1792 Dr Priestley wrote that Sunday
leisure time benefited the poor only if they used it to educate
themselves or to renew their strength for their labours.[2]

These rational attitudes towards Sunday observance were
overwhelmed by a revived Sabbatarianism which stressed the
supernatural element—God Himself rewarded the Sabbath-
keeper with worldly success. At the same time the holidays of the
poor were reduced and their hours of labour increased. The
Bank of England reduced its holidays from forty-seven days in
1761 to four in 1836. Readers of *A Christmas Carol* will recall that
Boxing Day became an ordinary working day. Steam-powered
mills adopted the twelve-hour day and the six-day week and

hand-loom weavers with whom they were in competition were forced to labour on Sundays in order to survive.

In the 1830's Agnew had claimed that Sabbatarianism would protect workers, but had refused to interfere between masters and servants, and Wilson had asked employers to order their workers' Sunday for them. Sabbatarians were, indeed, concerned far more with social authority than with social problems.[3]

Other men had realised that Sabbatarian authoritarianism could be used to counteract contemporary versions of *laissez-faire* ideas as they were held by many of the factory masters. Richard Oastler, an Anglican and a Tory opponent of Edward Baines I, told how a group of operatives, radicals and Dissenters, led him into the factory movement.

> On Sunday morning when we were all preparing to go to church, about half a dozen working men ... called upon me ... I told them that I was going to church, that on any other day I should be glad to see them. They replied, 'Sunday, Sir, is the only day on which we can come; we are in the mills all the rest of the week, from early in the morning till late at night.' This information brought home most forcibly to my mind, that the factory system and the Fourth Commandment could not work together. I thought the matter over, consulted with Mrs. Oastler, and, seeing that it was clearly a work of charity, remained with them ... to co-operate ... in striving to obtain a change in the factory system.[4]

Oastler, Bull and Sadler had each made the threat to the Sabbath a major part of their arguments for legislation. The first part of their case was that excessive labour in the week made children too tired to attend to their lessons in Sunday schools. The second had been given by Sadler in his speech on the second reading of the Bill which became the Factory Act of 1833: Sadler's argument being that the Sabbath rest was an example of interference between the employers and their employees, which compensated the latter for the reduction of other holidays, and. which, as William Paley had implied, caused a reduction in the hours of labour without reducing wages.[5]

That was a clever argument but had been slow to produce results. The 1831 Factory Act established the principle of a

Saturday half-holiday by limiting the Saturday hours to nine (as compared with twelve on other weekdays) but made no reference to Sunday work or to the religious education which had figured in the Acts of 1802 and 1819. Clause XIII of the 1833 Factory Bill did forbid the employment of children and young persons on Sundays 'thereby depriving such Children and Young Persons of the moral and religious Instruction and the Necessary Rest which the institution of the Sabbath is designed to afford' but the clause was struck out in committee. Sadler's argument was taken up in 1835 by the Radical M.P. James Silk Buckingham, who told the Commons that Sabbatarian restrictions on Sunday train services were a departure from *laissez-faire* principles which helped the railway workers, but such views were not propounded in the House again for eleven years.[6]

During the 1840's investigations made by the Factory Inspectors and Commissioners had shown that most Sunday work took place when other overwork was present. The week was long when the day and the year were long. Work often ceased only late on Saturday afternoons and began again early on Monday morning, with only two universal holidays—Christmas Day and Good Friday—the whole year through. Sunday work was caused by technical problems, fluctuations in demand and the employees' weakness; in all of which cases—because the pressures were strongest—an antidote was most urgently needed.[7]

Some masters had had a religious objection to Sunday labour even when they gave no thought to overwork in general. Several pottery firms refused to fire their ovens on Sundays, and some men in the most competitive and oppressed trades deliberately rested their workers. Mr Davies, a lint scraper, of Bermondsey New Road, took his family and six female apprentices to chapel twice every Sunday and often taught them writing and arithmetic on Sunday evenings, but he was quite exceptional.[8]

The Inspectors themselves had held Sunday observance ideas, and their knowledge of these conditions eventually had led to an important development. Mitchell found that among the West Midlands blast furnaces the larger firms tried to lay off as many men as possible on Sundays or to cease intensive work for at least a few hours but refused, on technical grounds, to close down

entirely. Mitchell countered these objections and suggested the
need for 'a regulation which will apply to all the iron-masters
alike [so] none of them will suffer'. Tancred collected similar
evidence and statistics.[9]

The 1846 Factory Bill had not, however, contained a Sunday
labour clause, although the debate upon it was notable because
the anti-Sabbatarian Whig T. B. Macaulay used the analogy of
Sunday rest to explain how the provision of adequate rest and
shorter hours did not, as some factory owners argued, reduce
production, but would, over a long period of time, actually
increase it.[10]

II   *The Sabbatarian contribution*

The results of the religious census taken on Sunday 30 March
1851 suggested that out of 17,927,609 inhabitants of England
and Wales some 7,261,032 attended a place of worship on that
day but that 5,378,283 were unable to do so because of extreme
youth or age and sickness or necessary work. Inaccurate and
imprecise though the figures are, they do indicate that an
enormous amount of work took place on Sundays.

The Sabbatarians now had an opportunity to show how a
religious prohibition on Sunday labour would save both masters
and workers from the consequences of the former's rather limited
economic rationality. An anti-industrial tone became part and
parcel of Sabbatarian attitudes, and they hinted that anti-
Sabbatarian advocates of opening museums and the like on
Sundays, who were often, like Roebuck and Hume, protagonists
of the purest *laissez-faire* and non-interference ideas, wanted to
force the poor to work for seven days a week.

A small minority of the Sabbatarians maintained that their
doctrine and its practices were in the masters' interests. Conder
insisted that the Sabbath gave the workers just enough rest as
was necessary for them to recover their strength for further
exertion. Baylee told the Bath auxiliary that Sabbath rest was of
'decided pecuniary advantage to the employers'. Such comments
were exceptional. They themselves and most other Sabbatarians
concentrated on the benefit they hoped to bring to the poor.[11]

In particular, the Sabbatarians' concern with the national

desecration caused by the Post Office had involved them with Sunday work there. Despite the reversal of Ashley's motion the Post Office authorities had introduced a system by which if the receivers of sixth-sevenths of the Sunday letters in a postal district petitioned for the discontinuance of Sunday delivery, then it would be ended.

In general Sabbatarians claimed that the best way to help the workers was to obey the Fourth Commandment, not to work on Sunday and to avoid all activities which caused others to work, but their claim contained an inherent fault, for they demanded that servants work and used the formula of 'acts of necessity and mercy' to justify some other Sunday work.

In 1855 W. F. Hook, the noted Vicar of Leeds, published a non-Sabbatarian theology and suggested that public amusement might be allowed on Sundays provided it was free, for purchased amusement would lead to labour. C. B. Adderley, a Tory M.P. and a Sabbatarian, published a tract in reply. He criticised Hook's theology, condemned his advocacy of 'Sabbath desecration' and revealed that Sabbatarians were opposed to certain forms of behaviour on Sundays rather than to Sunday labour in itself: 'Paid for amusements are to be resisted because they lead to labour; but this reason is inconclusive—for if the object be fitting, so is the labour needful for it . . . The mere test of payment for labour incurred would put down public worship itself, which requires the services of beadles and other functionaries; and eating, which requires cooks and waiters.'[12]

During the Crimean War W. H. Smith invoked the formula of 'acts of necessity and mercy' to break his firm's embargo on Sunday labour in order to publish the names of the dead and wounded as soon as they were available. When he later visited Canada he spent Sunday reading the Prayer Book in his hotel in order to avoid walking outdoors as if he were sightseeing, but when his Sunday evening bath was late complained of the self-assertive attitudes of Canadian hotel servants.[13]

Significantly enough, the anti-Sabbatarian Lord Brougham had posed a nice problem for the Sabbatarians by his judgement in the case of Philips v. Innes, ruling that an apprentice to a barber could not lawfully be required to attend his master's shop on Sunday for the purpose of shaving the customers, because shaving was not an act of necessity.

Sabbatarianism was an inappropriate way to provide rest, for it applied a simple, essentially pre-industrial, religious prescription to a complex, essentially urban, social problem. Sabbatarians avoided the difficulties which a complete cessation of labour would have produced for themselves by requiring servants to work and applying the formula 'acts of necessity and mercy', but failed to appreciate that society at large similarly needed the work of some railwaymen, shopkeepers and the like, whose work rhythm ran counter to that of the rest of the community. Sabbatarianism thus justified some Sunday work, but regarded the unjustified as sin meet for condemnation, rather than as a problem suitable for social reform.

Social Sabbatarianism was implicitly a substitute for labour regulation. In 1854 and 1855 Edward Baines II, who had inherited the *Leeds Mercury* and used it to spread the purest voluntaryist and *laissez-faire* ideas, wrote and published two social Sabbatarian tracts. *The Value of the Sabbath to the Working Classes* maintained that part of social Sabbatarianism's special value to them lay in its avoidence of legislative interference with their economic and social life.[14]

III   *Sunday leisure*

Oastler's exclamation that 'the factory system and the Fourth Commandment cannot work together' had been made when he realised that the Churches, the factories and the workers were competing to use the free time which still existed on Sundays. The Churches wanted alert worshippers and pupils, the masters time for their labourers to recuperate, and the workers an opportunity for bodily and mental amusement and recreation. To these latter activities the Sabbatarians were most particularly opposed not primarily in order to give an opportunity for worship and religious instruction, or to remove an alternative to them, but because Sunday amusement and recreation were sinful in themselves.

The Sabbatarians had contributed to this competition. The biographer of Sir Titus Salt, the Congregational industrialist and philanthropist, described how in Salt's youth 'The Sabbath was strictly observed . . . Good Friday was not in their calendar, and the many feast days which human authority originated they did not recognise'. In 1850 *The Watchman* pointed out that 'this Protestant country . . . happily lacks and the idle saints' days of the Romish calendar [but has] the one legitimate weekly holyday that Scripture and reason alone prescribe'.[15]

During the 1850's some London shop workers organised in John Lilwall's Early Closing and Saturday Half Holiday Association tried to attract religious support for the half-holiday by arguing that if Saturday afternoon were free for recreation shop workers would be less inclined to amuse themselves on Sundays. Dr John Cumming, minister of the Crown Court Presbyterian Church, Covent Garden, who patronised the movement, taught that the Fourth Commandment implied that labour should be limited to six days a week but thought that any less was the result of employers' generosity exceeding God's justice. In 1855 one anonymous Sabbatarian wrote that 'the command about the Sabbath day . . . commands work on weekdays'. Daniel Wilson had written, 'Man was created for six days' work . . . the six days, if given up to religious acts, would be idleness, superstition and temptation of God.' In 1856 the L.D.O.S. declined to enter into the Saturday half-holiday movement, merely allowing individual members of its committee to investigate the phenomenon and report back if they so desired.[16]

The Evangelical Sabbatarians had begun their battle against Sunday recreation by attacking Sunday newspapers under the inspiration of Wilberforce in 1799 and 1820. Daniel Wilson, the L.D.O.S. and Blomfield abominated them, the latter describing Sunday newrooms 'as . . . a sort of moral dram-shop where doses of the most deliterious poison are imbibed by thousands of persons'. The attack was conducted along several fronts: Sunday newspapers were a direct profanation, they caused and led to labour, and they supported and spread among the lower classes ideas which were not only opposed to Sabbatarianism but to the whole social order which the Sabbatarians supported.[17]

They hoped to use Sunday school to control and to influence the children of the poor. The earliest Sunday schools were established by pious Evangelicals to keep them off the streets on

Sundays. In 1797 the governors of the powerful Stockport Sunday school printed and distributed copies of the Sunday observance laws and tried to persuade the constables and magistrates to enforce them.

Some early factory masters had acted on Porteus's remark that children left unemployed on Sunday 'are apt to be idle, mischievous and vicious'. Horrockses of Preston employed a man to keep children off the streets on Sundays and Arkwright and others anticipated Evans's practice by compelling all hands under twenty to attend school for four hours on Saturdays and Sundays to keep them out of trouble.[18]

All the Sunday school pioneers taught children to read the Bible and many taught them to write as well, but during the 1790's some Sabbatarians objected to writing, arguing that it was not necessary to be able to write to understand the Bible, and writing was thus a secular employment, unfit for the Lord's day. The controversy gathered force in the early years of the new century as Joseph Lancaster popularised his Lancasterian 'system', which taught reading and writing together, often by means of non-biblical readers.

When the Royal Lancasterian Institution (later the British and Foreign Schools Society) was founded in 1808 the Wesleyan Methodist Conference passed a resolution forbidding the teaching of writing in its Sunday schools. During 1808 and 1809 the Rev. Jabez Bunting made his name by attacking writing in Sunday schools in Sheffield and Liverpool, causing bitterness and upheavals which presaged the later effects of his autocratic conduct on the denomination as a whole.

Conference's decision to stamp out Sunday writing, which was reiterated in 1817 and 1827, may be seen as an attempt by the Wesleyans' governing body, which consisted entirely of ministers, to impose its authority on the independent-minded laymen in the provinces, but such an interpretation is an over-simplification.

The issue was basically theological. Many Wesleyan ministers who objected to Sunday writing provided for writing to be taught on weekday evenings instead. Not all Sabbatarians objected to it. Many Wesleyan laymen did not. In 1805 the Methodist New Connexion supported it and the early Primitive Methodists did so, arguing that it was an act of mercy to teach poor children to write on Sundays.

The issue was not only theological. Some Wesleyan ministers shared the contemporary fear and distrust of the poor, objecting on a 'political consideration, that of placing the poor above their condition of life'. Champions of Sunday writing felt that religion should serve a humane as well as a spiritual purpose and often supported proposals for constitutional change. Thus Jabez Bunting was opposed in Sheffield by James Montgomery, a former Moravian who had been imprisoned for sedition, owner-editor of the reformist *Sheffield Iris*.

Wesleyans regarded the New Connexion and the Primitives as tainted with political radicalism, and after the New Connexion had turned against Sunday writing in 1826, and the Primitives had abandoned it during the 1830's, overwhelmed by the resurgence of militant Sabbatarianism, it persisted only in the most radical denominations, the Baptists, Congregationalists and Unitarians. During the 1840's even the latter had almost all replaced it by weekday evening lessons; and, in any case, the spread of denominational day schools rendered the matter less and less acute.[19]

As the Sabbatarian campaign progressed almost all sections of English society had been affected. There were some oddities. In 1828 the lunatics in Bedlam had been chained to their beds on Sundays and the public had been allowed in to view them. In the late 1830's the inmates of workhouses had not been allowed out to attend their own places of worship on Sundays. In the 1840's private water companies had left parts of London without a water supply on Sundays.[20]

In the West End of London the rich and the fashionable used the afternoon for riding and driving in Hyde Park. In its back streets poor men went to the barber for their weekly shave and then bought their families the ingredients of a good dinner before taking them out for walks. In its suburbs was an intellectual Sunday where J. S. Mill, Grote and Austin met to discuss political economy.[21]

The English towns and cities had a more sombre air, sometimes broken by the voices of open-air preachers; whilst in the villages, as chronicled by Trollope, the people gathered round the church gate to greet the squire. Scattered throughout the land were the religious middle class families like those of Edmund Gosse and Samuel Butler whose Sundays approximated to Wilson's ideal.[22]

Pious members of the upper class ate cold meals on Sundays in order to give their servants relief. They took their families to church on foot and during the rest of the day banished newspapers, secular books, drawing, needlework, riding and driving from their households. Less religious members of the same class attended morning service, ate a gargantuan lunch and then toured their gardens, kennels, stables and grounds before relapsing into somnolent preparations for a light supper which enabled servants to attend their service.[23]

During the 1840's some members of the lower classes had still regarded Sunday as a day not for abstention from pleasure but for abstention from work: they clung to the popular tradition of regarding Sunday as a feast. Poor men and women throughout the country washed on Saturday night, laid out their one set of non-working clothes (their proverbial 'Sunday best'), prepared tea or coffee instead of gruel for breakfast, made a point of having a good lunch ('We always have a good dinner at one; it is very wicked to omit that'), looked forward to an afternoon tea, and invariably went out for a walk on fine Sunday evenings.[24]

The Sunday schools were producing new attitudes. Boys and girls who gave dispassionate accounts of heavy drinking and brutal fighting thought that to play marbles on Sundays was very bad. In the county of Durham Methodism had produced 'great external respect for the Lord's day'. In south Staffordshire the police stopped 'all irregular proceedings' on Sundays.[25]

There was another side to the coin. In Sheffield Ebenezer Elliot, the 'Corn Law Rhymer', complained that groups of men and youths wandered about the country lanes arranging and indulging in gambling and dog fighting. Sunday in Wolverhampton so shocked one Factory Inspector, Horne, that he apologised for the need to describe it 'verbally from my note-book'. Men and women lounged around in their working clothes as their own children played in the filthy streets: 'they did not know what to do with their leisure or with themselves ... nothing seen but squalid disorder, indifference and utter waste, in self-disgust, of the very day, of which, in every sense, they should make the most'.[26]

IV   *The problem of leisure*

Thus the problem in the mid-century lay with those who did not know what to do with their leisure or with themselves. The religious census had also revealed that 5,208,294 people had failed to attend a place of worship although they had the opportunity to do so. The Sabbatarians were particularly interested in this group.

Their predecessors had, as we have seen, eliminated many traditional Sunday sports, and they were in the midst of attacking those which remained, many of which were associated with Sunday drinking. Yet before 1839 there were no statutory restrictions on the Sunday opening of public houses, although they followed the age-old custom of closing during divine service. In the early 1800's bulls had been hunted through the East End by drink-crazed mobs and drunken brawls had been common on Holborn Hill on Sundays. In 1833 Francis Place was convinced that a great improvement had taken place. But the Beer Act of 1830 had allowed beerhouses to open from 1.00 p.m. to 3.00 p.m. and from 5.00 p.m. to 10.00 p.m. on Sundays. Many magistrates complained that it encouraged licensed premises to spring up in rural areas, bringing in their train Sunday cricket and the abuse of churchgoers. The Sabbatarians set themselves the task of eliminating Sunday cricket. 'What,' asked Hippolyte Taine some years later, 'is to be done on the day of rest? There is the church or the pot house . . . but no other way of spending a Sunday.'[27]

The Radical answer to the problem of leisure was to give the poor a substitute for the tea gardens and pleasure grounds which had decayed in the previous forty years of urbanisation and for the drinking which had survived it. In 1834 when giving evidence before a select committee on temperance Edwin Chadwick, the Benthamite social reformer, had suggested that the provision of rational Sunday recreations would diminish drunkenness on that day, and similar suggestions were made to committees on Public Walks, Arts and Principles of Design, and National Monuments and Works of Art. Chadwick's suggestion had culminated in the resolutions of Hume and Walmsley, but they had been heavily defeated by the Sabbatarians.[28]

The businessmen's answer had been to provide Sunday trains. During the 1840's company after company had replied to Sabbatarian enthusiasts who interrupted their shareholders' meetings that Sunday trains enabled the working classes to visit the countryside and to refresh themselves innocently and soberly. Much of the railway interest regarded itself as the agent of social progress which the Sabbatarians were trying to obstruct. Thus the L.D.O.S. had warned that Chartists supported Sunday trains and pointed out that Sunday excursions incited the humbler classes. Equally, in 1849 eight known railway directors had voted for and two against the first reading of Locke's Bill whilst two of the railway newspapers, the *Railway Record* and *Herapath's Journal*, strongly supported it.[29]

The battle intensified in 1850 when the Great Western began a series of cheap Sunday excursions out of London. By 1854 it had been joined by the South Western, Brighton, Blackwall and Tilbury & Southend companies. During the 1850's the L.D.O.S. recorded interventions by its supporters in the affairs of almost fifteen railway companies in an attempt to stamp out the innovation. They feared that it would breath new life into the remains of Henry VIII's wakes besides being an entirely new desecration.[30]

V   *Sunday drinking*

The Sabbatarians seemed curiously slow to tackle Sunday drinking itself because their support came from Anglicans who were seldom temperance enthusiasts, whilst the later teetotalers were often militant Nonconformists with whom they were reluctant to co-operate. Indeed, one of Daniel Wilson's few comments on Sunday drinking implied approval of beer, and Blomfield was suspicious of temperance societies. Thus although the L.D.O.S. had hoped to amend the 1830 Beer Act to further restrict Sunday opening, the society supported mealtime opening and 'off' sales on Sunday to meet the needs of the working classes.[31]

Agnew's Bill would have closed licensed premises, except to travellers, and in 1834 Lord Wynford had introduced a Bill to close public houses on Sundays; but the main impetus to restrict Sunday licensing hours came from traditionalists and moderate Tories who hoped to protect the hours of service, to improve public order and to clear the drunken lower classes out of the sight of respectable churchgoers. These feelings had secured the 1839 Metropolitan Police Act, which closed London's public houses from twelve midnight on Saturday until one o'clock on Sunday afternoon. Several northern towns had then procured similar local Acts. In 1845 the National Temperance Society, an Anglican body, had proposed a Sunday closing Bill, but the L.D.O.S. did not interest itself in the matter until 1847. In 1848 Lord Harrowby set up a select committee to investigate the effects of the 1839 Act and himself secured an Act which closed public houses until 12.30 p.m. on Sundays (or until the usual hour at which divine service ended, if later) throughout the rest of England.[32]

In 1853 the temperance movement, now dominated by teetotalism, was strong enough to force the Forbes Mackezie Bill through Parliament. This closed public houses in Scotland on Sundays, except for *bona fide* travellers at inns and hotels. Emboldened by the national Sabbatarian crisis, the L.D.O.S. threw its resources into raising petitions demanding a similar measure for England, closing all public houses and beer shops on Sundays. In 1854 it placed its support behind Colonel Wilson Patten, a Tory who, like Forbes Mackenzie, sat for Protestant Lancashire, and had fallen under the influence of the militant temperance interest which had its roots there.

He secured a select committee on public houses, managed it with great skill and rushed his Bill through both Houses—it passed its first reading in the Commons on 13 July and gained the royal assent on 7 August. It restricted Sunday drinking hours in England to 1.00—2 p.m. and 6.00—10 p.m. That did not satisfy the L.D.O.S., which decided to open another campaign for a total closing Bill 'in accordance with the Command of God'.[33]

However, before the L.D.O.S.'s campaign could begin the Sunday Trading riots had taken place. They unnerved the government, and it allowed the Radicals, who wished to give the poor a free choice between visiting places of rational recreation or public houses on Sundays, to set up a select committee of their own. It emphasised what the Metropolitan Police Commissioners, Sir Richard Mayne and his predecessor, Colonel Charles Rowan, had reported to the committees which had investigated Sunday trade and drinking during the previous ten years, that there was a limit beyond which the people should not be pushed. Thus in 1855 the Radicals won an Act which overturned Wilson Patten's and extended Sunday drinking hours to 1.00—3.00 p.m. and 5.00—11.00 p.m.[34]

In point of fact the campaign never took place, for the alliance between the Sabbatarians and the teetotallers was a transient one. In 1848 Buxton, of Truman Hanbury & Buxton, supported Sunday trade Bills; during the 1850's Robert Hanbury gave his time and money to the L.D.O.S.; and the many select committees of the 1850's illustrated the different outlooks of the two movements.[38]

When giving evidence before the Commons select committee on public houses in 1854 J. T. Baylee told its members that 'I am not a teetotaller and I do not think that it [alcoholic drink] is in itself wrong'. Several of the carefully prepared witnesses whom he produced explained how the working classes might store beer in stone bottles in order to drink it on Sundays if the public houses were closed.[36]

On the other hand Joseph Livesey injured Sabbatarian susceptibilities by holding open-air temperance meetings on Sundays. He could not understand how Parliament could refuse to open the Crystal Palace and British Museum yet refuse to close public houses on Sundays. When Nathianiel Card, founder of the prohibitionist United Kingdom Alliance, and Dr F. R. Lees, one of its formost propagandists, gave evidence before the 1854 committee they appeared to favour opening places of rational educative or health-giving recreation on Sundays.[37]

Notes

[1] R. J. Cruikshank, *Charles Dickens and Early Victorian England* (1949), 101.

[2] Henry Bourne, *Antiquities of the Common People* (1725), ch. XIX; E. Evanson, *The Sabbatical Observance of Sunday* (1788), 22; E. Royston Pike, *Human Documents of Adam Smith's Time* (1974), 121; Joseph Priestley, *Letters, op. cit.*, 48, 49.

[3] D. Wilson, *Lord's Day, op. cit.*, 149.

[4] Samuel Kydd, *The History of the Factory Movement* (n.d.), I, 123–4.

[5] *Ibid.*, 175, 219; 3H, vol. 11, col. 344 (16 March 1832).

[6] PP., 1833, II, *A Bill to Regulate the Labour of Children, &c.*; 3H, vol. 28, col. 150 (26 May 1835).

[7] PP., 1842, XVI, and 1843, XIII, *Children's Employment Comission, passim*; PP., 1843, XII, *Employment of Women and Children in Agriculture, passim*.

[8] PP., 1842, XVI, *op. cit.*, c. 83, c. 90, F. 257.

[9] PP., 1842, XVI, 53–9; PP., 1843, XIII, *op. cit.*, cxxxvi, cxlii, cxliii, 502, App. 131.

[10] 3H, vol. 86, cols. 1036–40 (22 May 1846).

[11] Josiah Conder, *op. cit.*, 37–8.

[12] W. F. Hook, *The Lord's Day* (1855); C. B. Adderley, *Reflections on the Rev. Dr Hook's Sermon* (1856), 13–14.

[13] Viscount Chilston, *W. H. Smith* (1965), 33, 72–3.

[14] Edward Baines, *A Correspondence, &c.* (1854), *The Value of the Sabbath, &c.* (1855), *passim*.

[15] R. Balgarnie, *Sir Titus Salt* (1970 ed.), 10–11; *The Watchman*, 21 May 1850.

[16] John Lilwall, *The Half Holiday Question* (1856), 27; Dr J. Cumming, *Sunday, &c.* (1856), *Labour, Rest and Recreation* (n.d.); anon, *The Ten Commandments* (1859), 22; Daniel Wilson, *Lord's Day, op. cit.*, 172, 187; L.D.O.S., *Minute Book IV*, 6 March 1856.

[17] R. W. and I. Wilberforce, *Wilberforce, op. cit.*, II, 338, 434–5; 3H, vol. I, col. 545 (26 May 1820); A Layman, *Observations upon Sunday Newspapers, &c.* (1820); C. J. Blomfield, *A Letter, op. cit.*, 15–16; J. T. Baylee, *Statistics and Facts, op. cit.*, 5, 17; *Bath Chronicle*, 16 May 1841.

[18] Sidney Pollard, *The Origins of Modern Management* (Penguin ed., 1968), 228.

[19] E. P. Thompson, *The Making of the English Working Class* (Penguin ed., 1968), 389; W. R. Ward, *Religion and Society* (1972), 137–40; W. T. Laqueur, *Religion and Respectability* (1976), 132–45.

[20] G. W. E. Russell, *Collections and Recollections* (1898), 109; PP., 1837, XVII, Pt. I, *Poor Law Amendment Act*, 8,106,122, 123; PP., 1851, *Metropolis Water Bill*, 674.

[21] H. Taine, *Notes on England* (1872 ed.), 68; Henry Mayhew, *London Labour and the London Poor* (1861), I, *passim*; J. S. Mill, *Autobiography* (World's Classics ed., 1969), xii, 71.

[22] A. Trollope, *Barchester Towers* (New American Lib. ed., 1963) 217, 225; Edmund Gosse, *Father and Son* (Penguin ed., 1970), 165, 169; Samuel Butler, *The Way of all Flesh* (Penguin ed., 1966), 123, *id., Erewhon* (Everyman ed., 1965), 50.

[23] T. McCrie, *Agnew, op. cit.*, 334–5; E. C. Mack and W. H. G. Armytage, *Thomas Hughes* (1954), 106; G. W. E. Russell, *One Look Back* (1912), 155–97, *id.*,

A Short History of the Evangelical Movement (1915), 136–7.

[24] PP., 1842, XVI, *Children's Employment in Mines*, I, 83.

[25] *Ibid.*, 67, 74, 87, 148; PP., 1843, XIV, *Children's Employment, Manufacturing Districts*, D. 7.

[26] PP., 1842, XVI, *op. cit.*, 728; PP., 1843, XIV, *op. cit.*, 481.

[27] PP., 1817, VI, *Rept. S.C. of H.C. on the Police of the Metropolis*, 18, 19, 268; PP., 1833, XV, *Rept. S.C. of H.C. into Drunkenness*, 208; H. Taine, *Notes on England, op. cit.*, 11.

[28] PP., 1834, VIII, *Drunkenness*, 34, 35; PP., 1833, XV, *Public Walks*, 4n; PP., 1836, IX, *Arts and Principles of Design*, 115, 116, 147; PP., 1841, *National Monuments and Works of Art*, iv-vi, 156–97.

[29] *Railway Times*, 14 March 1841; *Railway Record*, 28 April, *Herapath's Journal*, 17 February 1849.

[30] P. BRR, 6W 1/4 *G. W. Minutes*, 8 and 29 August 5, 12, 19 and 26 September 1850.

[31] Daniel Wilson, *Lord's Day, op. cit.*, 196; C. J. Blomfield, *A Letter, op. cit.*, 13n.; L.D.O.S., *Minute Book I*, 6 September 1832.

[32] PP., 1847–48, *Rept. S.C. of H.L. on Sale of Beer and other Liquors on the Lord's Day*; W. Gawthorpe, *A Tract for the Times* (1849); L.D.O.S., *Quarterly Publication*, No. 17, p. 133, (October 1847).

[33] L.D.O.S., *ibid.*, No. 56, p. 448 (August 1854).

[34] PP., 1854–55, X, *First Rept. S.C. of H.C. on Sale of Beer Act*; PP., 1855, X, *Second Rept.*

[35] 3H, vol. 100, col. 459 (12 July 1848); J. T. Baylee, *A Word of Warning, &c.* (1860), 26–8.

[36] PP., 1854, XIV, *Rept. S.C. of H.C. on Public Houses, &c.*, 6, 7, 18.

[37] *Ibid.*, 110, 245–50; Joseph Livesey, *Life, op. cit.* clix, clxiii, 86, *A Letter to J. Wilson Patten, Esq.*, (1855), 6.

chapter six

1847–57

THE POLITICIANS

I   *Parliament*

The Sabbatarians obviously made a major effort to influence parliamentary opinion. The L.D.O.S. was one of the first pressure groups to operate in the reformed Commons and concentrated on M.P.'s because elections rendered them more vulnerable than the hereditary peers.

Following Agnew's lead, *The Watchman* had turned its readers' attention to elections during the 1830's, the L.D.O.S. had placed 'Addresses' in newspapers during the general elections of 1837, 1842 and 1852, and had alerted its auxiliaries.[1]

These tactics had had an impact on M.P.'s besides Roebuck. In 1848 the Radical Colonel Thompson believed that his anti-Sabbatarianism had cost him his seat. In 1851 Charles Hindley believed that Sunday legislation was about to become an election issue. In the same year Williams of Lambeth was accused of introducing his trade Bill to fulfill an election pledge.[2]

The parties had responded, too. The Tories had supported Agnew in 1837, and in 1838 their chief whip, Sir Thomas Freemantle, had criticised the Whig government for its coolness to Plumptre's Bill. An analysis of divisions on Hume's motion in 1840, Thornely's amendment in 1844, Locke's Bill in 1849 and Ashley's motion in 1850 reveals that most of the Tories voted for the Sabbatarians, with a very small number of anti-Evangelicals opposing them, whilst the Whigs and their allies were mainly anti-Sabbatarian but included a large Sabbatarian minority.[3]

The party leaders had no sympathy for the Sabbatarians. After Agnew's defeat in 1837 Lord Melbourne had opened

Hampton Court on Sunday afternoons, and after Hume's defeat in 1846 Lord John Russell had similarly opened Kew Gardens. Lord Derby, who led the Tories after 1846, was a former Whig who shared their attitudes, as he had shown over the Crystal Palace.

The leaders had adopted a neutral line, intended to avoid defeat in Parliament, whether caused by anti-Sabbatarian defectors, as had happened to the Tories in 1844, or by Sabbatarian defectors, as had happened to the Whigs in 1850. But Sabbatarian pressure seemed strongest and so the leaders bowed to it. As Chisholm Anstey, an Irish Liberal, put it in 1851, 'There was a rabid cry ... in favour of more Sabbatical legislation [which] happened to comprehend the middle class having votes.'[4]

The Tories were in a safer position, holding office only in 1852. Although they had to face the Crystal Palace crisis, Lord Derby was isolated from the clamour by sitting in the House of Lords and quickly gave way to the Sabbatarians. In addition, Lords Harrowby and Shaftesbury both refused the L.D.O.S.'s request to lead a parliamentary campaign against the Palace's projected Sunday opening.[5]

Derby's government contained three anti-Sabbatarians besides himself—Lord Malmesbury, an anti-Evangelical; Lord John Manners, a member of the Young England group; and Lord Stanley, his own son and heir. Only Lord Stanley took the issue to heart, but the country gentlemen among whom he sat were largely unmoved by any aspect of Sabbatarianism. Barely a handful of obscure members spoke on Sunday trade Bills (which were a metropolitan matter) and only Colonel Sibthorpe made a fuss about the Crystal Palace.[6]

Tory M.P.'s were content to follow the lead given by Henry Goulburn and H. M. Cairns (themselves rather untypical of their party at this time, having made their fortunes in commerce and the law and sitting for Cambridge and Belfast respectively), and so in 1856 voted by 226 to 1 (Lord Stanley, who was hardly a Tory at all) to keep the British Museum closed on Sunday afternoons.

The Whig coalition was in a different position, being in office and deeply divided on all aspects of the controversy; voting, for example, by 150 to 47 against opening. Hindley, Williams and Lord Robert Grosvenor (who introduced the Sunday trade Bills) were members of the coalition. They were opposed by its Radical members—Duncombe, Hume and Roebuck—who objected to religious prejudices dictating social policy, defended *laissez-faire* principles and claimed to protect the retailers and their working class buyers. Sir Joshua Walmsley was supported by his fellow Radicals, by the Catholic Irish Liberals and by advanced Whigs like Sir John Shelley and Lord Ebrington.

The Nonconformist Liberals were subject to competing pressures. They were separated from the Tories by a history of economic, political and religious discrimination, yet shared the Evangelicals' devotion to Fundamentalism. They were therefore attracted by the economic and political outlook of the Radicals, but repelled by their secularity. Social Sabbatarianism was to prove a valuable compromise.

In 1840 Hume had been supported by Mark Philips; by Joseph Brotherton, a teetotal Bible-Christian who sat for Salford; Joseph Fielden, the Methodist-Unitarian member for Oldham; and G. F. Muntz, a Baptist who represented Birmingham. In 1849 Locke had received the support of S. M. Peto, the Baptist railway contractor; John Bright, the Quaker leader of the Anti-Corn Law League; and William Heyworth and William Scholefield (both Unitarians) as well as Brotherton and Muntz. In 1850 Bright, Heyworth and Scholefield opposed Ashley; and W. J. Fox, a Unitarian minister, and George Hadfield, a Congregational solicitor (both prominent members of the Anti-Corn Law League), opposed Sunday trade Bills. James Heywood and William Murrough, another two Unitarians, supported Walmsley.

However, Edward Baines I had opposed Hume and in 1855 and 1856 Muntz had opposed Walmsley. He was joined by a new generation of Nonconformist Liberals who made impassioned speeches presenting the social Sabbatarian case. Prominent among them were Apsley Pellatt, the glass manufacturer; Frank Crossley, a carpet maker from Halifax; and W. E. Baxter, a Scotsman who had made his fortune in the Dundee jute trade. Each was a devout Congregationalist. They were backed up by two Whigs, Lord Kinnaird and Roundell

Palmer.[7]

The Home Secretary in most of the Whig governments of the period was none other than Sir George Grey. He was sympathetic to Sunday trade Bills, but in 1855 led Palmerston's government into difficulties by supporting Grosvenor, so backed down and in future was far more cautious. Palmerston was in favour of opening the British Museum on Sunday afternoons, and of Sunday afternoons bands, but placed his personal predilections behind the duty of preserving his government and party.

He had taken over the leadership at a time of great political confusion, when party lines were so fluid that it was necessary to conciliate all shades of opinion in order to maintain a majority, and to keep a careful eye on the extra-parliamentary scene. He valued Shaftesbury's advice on religious matters. He took Lord Harrowby into his government in 1855 as Lord Privy Seal and in 1857 as Chancellor as the Duchy of Lancaster. He knew that his Whig coalition was divided over Sunday trade Bills and the British Museum, containing almost all the anti-Sabbatarians and many of the most vociferous Sabbatarians.

He therefore played safe, quickly vetoing Lord Robert Grosvenor's Sunday trade Bill in order to allay working class discontent, and using his whips to keep the British Museum closed in order to avoid the risk of defeat at the hands of Sabbatarian defectors in alliance with the more united Tory party.

Above all he acted on his estimate of the strength of Sabbatarian opinion and its likely effects. In 1855 when he spoke against Walmsley's motion he commented that 'It is highly inexpedient that Parliament should by any vote set itself in opposition to that which is the religious feeling of the people'. He wrote to the queen in 1856 that 'This agitation [about Sunday bands] is likely to produce very inconvenient consequences in the House of Commons . . . but the matter is in itself not of sufficient importance to be worth the risk of a defeat'. Deference to the Sabbatarians was the obvious policy.[8]

II *The constituencies*

Palmerston told the queen that the Sunday bands agitation would cause trouble in borough seats because 'the Dissenters' were 'very violent' over the matter. Greville, the diarist, thought that the Cabinet backed down because it was convinced that the Sabbatarians were strong enough to unseat their opponents.[9]

Some M.P.'s shared Greville's prognostications. In 1855 Walmsley claimed that more M.P.'s would support him if their votes, and those of their constituents, were given in secret. In 1856 Lord Stanley referred to a circular issued by 'a society for the Due Observance of the Sabbath' which threatened M.P.'s who voted for Walmsley with 'public exposure'.[10]

The Watchman had once more directed its readers' attention to elections. *The Wesleyan Times* reported that William Biggs, a Radical who had seconded Walmsley, had been forced to resign his seat for Newport in the Isle of Wight, and predicted that the Sunday question would be a major issue in the next general election.[11]

Biggs had been forced out by a group of right-wing Whigs and replaced with a safer candidate, but a group of anti-Sabbatarian Radicals put up a rival, enabling the Tory to make the Sunday question the basis of his campaign, exploit the split amongst his opponents, and win the seat.[12]

The next general election, in 1857, was apparently a plebiscite on Palmerston's China policy, but Walmsley's contest at Leicester must be examined in detail. Walmsley was a convinced free-trader and a strong Radical. He was the son of a stonemason, had made a fortune in the corn trade and been made Lord Mayor of Liverpool, receiving his knighthood when the queen visited the city. In 1857 his fellow member for Leicester was John Biggs, William's brother, a manufacturer, thrice Mayor, proprietor of the *Leicestershire Mercury* and an equally strong Radical.[13]

Walmsley had been brought to Leicester in 1847 by the Ellis family, Quakers with a railway interest who led the right-wing Liberals. He had quickly proved too militant for them, acting as the figurehead of a popular coalition organised by Biggs consisting of ex-Chartists, poverty-stricken frame-work knitters and Radical Nonconformists. By 1857 Walmsley had lost the support of 'the best class of electors'.[14]

The Sabbatarian and social Sabbatarian cries were now used to break up the coalition by persuading the Nonconformists to desert Walmsley. John Ellis proposed John Dove Harris, a devout Congregational manufacturer, as a moderate Liberal in opposition to him. Dove Harris gained the support of all the Anglican and all but one of the twenty-nine Nonconformist clergy in the town, and his electoral address made the Sunday question the basis of his campaign. At the nomination Walmsley pledged himself to future neutrality on the issue, but Dove Harris decried his promise. Walmsley fell from the top to the bottom of the poll and lost his seat.[15]

J. F. Winks had led the Nonconformist clergy in their attacks on Walmsley. In 1842 he had led the Leicester Complete Suffrage Association and in 1848 had taken a prominent part in a meeting at which the Chartists had begun to move towards collaborating with the Radicals. Winks had worked with Thomas Cooper, who had arrived in Leicester in 1840 to edit the *Leicestershire Mercury*, before turning to Chartism and producing the *Midland Counties Illuminator*, and was to baptise Cooper on Whit Sunday 1859.[16]

The most militant members of the coalition stood by Walmsley. John Markham, who spoke for him at meetings and cross-questioned Dove Harris at the nomination, was a former Primitive Methodist preacher who had led the Leicester 'moral force' Chartists. John Collier, who similarly supported Walmsley, had been president of the Leicester Complete Suffrage Society and had chaired the meeting with the Chartists in 1848.[17]

William Baines, who 'gave his views as a Nonconformist' when speaking for Walmsley, was a notorious Congregational shopkeeper. In 1838 he had refused to pay Church Rate, been imprisoned for seven months and inspired his pastor, Edward Miall, to resign his charge at Bond Street Chapel and found *The Nonconformist*. J. P. Mursell, the one Nonconformist clergyman to refuse to support Dove Harris, had shared with Winks the leadership of the Leicester Complete Suffrage Association, was pastor to Harvey Lane Chapel and was also a decisive influence on Miall. In 1864 Mursell was to be made first president of the Baptist Union.[18]

Nonconformist clergymen usually voted for Radical and Liberal candidates: 'No other occupation was so partizan, so unfloating, so militant.' Their desertion of Walmsley was thus a notable event, but they had deserted an Anglican outsider for a local Nonconformist. Furthermore, on this issue they were an unusually sensitive section of the electorate, and it is unclear to what extent their example was followed by Nonconformist laymen. In fact Walmsley was defeated because right-wing Liberals deserted him for Dove Harris and because some Tories voted for Dove Harris with the sole purpose of unseating a Radical, Walmsley.[19]

Walmsley retained the support of the largely voteless lower classes, who cheered him at the nomination on Friday, at the poll on Saturday, pelted Winks with mud on Sunday—it was felt that only heavy rain averted a general demonstration against churchgoers—and groaned Dove Harris at the official declaration on Monday. The frame-work knitters and their wives feted Walmsley and his wife as they left Leicester.[20]

The remaining ten M.P.'s, each of whom was a Radical, Liberal or progressive Whig, who had voted for Walmsley's motion and faced a contest for an English seat in 1857, may be more briefly dealt with. Seven of them were defeated, although four of these supported Palmerston's China policy (as did Walmsley), and in three of their cases Sabbatarianism was used against them. It was not, however, the cause of their defeat, for a hidden feature of the 1857 general election was a strong right-wing movement in the constituencies, and Sabbatarianism was a minor feature of that phenomenon.

As a discerning Bolton Liberal put it 'various "dodges" are being restored to, to damage some of the candidates in the estimation of the electors. A cry is raised that Mr. Crook [the Liberal candidate] voted for "Sabbath desecration". This cry . . . is maudlin cant intended to mislead and damage Mr. Crook . . . a few votes are calculated upon for the Conservative.'[21]

The issue occurred in many other constituencies. In some London ones with a large electorate—those of Lord Ebrington, Sir de Lacy Evans, Sir J. W. Shelley, Sir Benjamin Hall and Lord

Robert Grosvenor—anti-Sabbatarianism was apparently popular. However, Holyoake thought that J. H. Parry, a Radical lawyer associated with William Lovett and sympathetic to the Chartists, failed to win Finsbury because his anti-Sabbatarianism made him deeply unpopular.[22]

Indeed, in the majority of other constituencies where the issue is known to have arisen—at Bath, Cheltenham, Huddersfield, Lincoln, Newark, West Kent, North Leicester, South Northampton, North Nottingham, North Lancashire and Oxford (where the novelist W. M. Thackeray stood unsuccessfully in a July by-election as a Liberal anti-Sabbatarian)—Sabbatarianism worked to the advantage of a Tory or to the disadvantage of a Radical, a Liberal or a Whig.[23]

In one case Sabbatarianism worked against a Whig member of the government, although in a curious way. At Bury in Lancashire Frederick Peel, Palmerston's Secretary at War, was defending himself against a Radical onslaught. R. N. Philips (brother of Philips, one of the first two M.P.'s for Manchester), a Unitarian anti-Sabbatarian, helped to win the seat for himself by the unscrupulous tactic of issuing placards associating Peel with the Sunday bands.[24]

Herein lay the importance of the Sunday question. It had been used to play upon the susceptibilities of Nonconformists in order to weaken Whigs, Liberals and Radicals. It alone rarely changed the way that Nonconformists voted, but may have been important in Leicester and Bury. Such episodes would certainly be remembered for a long time.

It is thus unlikely that the Sabbatarians had the electoral force attributed to them by Palmerston and Greville. They had swayed neither large numbers of votes nor constituencies, but had caused some trouble in a large number of constituencies and in two had swayed some votes. It was thus wise for those politicians who were indifferent to the subject to defer to the Sabbatarians in order not to antagonise them and risk alienating a few votes which might be vital. It was likely that, if M.P.'s responded to the mood in their constituencies, the Tory ranks would grow more Sabbatarian and the Whig leaders continue restrain the Liberals and Radicals.

Notes

1 *The Watchman*, 24 June 1835, 27 April 1836

2 3H, vol. 100, col. 452 (12 July 1848); vol. 116, col. 965 (18 June 1851).

3 3H, vol. 43, col. 887 (20 June 1838).

4 3H, vol. 116, col. 361 (30 April 1851).

5 L.D.O.S., *Minute Book V*, 5 November 1852.

6 3H, vol. 118, col., 1726 (29 July 1851).

7 3H, vol. 137, col. 917 (20 March 1855); vol. 140, col. 1053 (21 February 1856).

8 3H, vol. 137, col. 917 (20 March 1855); B. Connell, *Regina v. Palmerston* (1962), 222.

9 B. Connell, *ibid.*; L. Strachey and R. Fulford (eds.), *The Greville Memoirs* (1938), VIII, 228–9.

10 3H, vol. 113, col. 915 (20 March 1855); vol. 140, col. 1116 (21 February 1856).

11 *The Watchman and Wesleyan Advertiser*, 27 October 1852, 28 March 1855, 6 February 1856; *Wesleyan Times*, 4, 11, 25 February 1856.

12 *The Times*, 11 February 1857; *Hampshire Telegraph*, 14 and 24 January 1857.

13 H. M. Walmsley, *The Life of Sir Joshua Walmsley* (1879); A. Temple Patterson, *Radical Leicester, 1780–1850* (1954).

14 Asa Briggs (ed.), *Chartist Studies* (1967), 99–146; *Leicester Chronicle*, 28 March 1857.

15 *The Times*, 16 and 28 March, *Leicester Chronicle*, 14 and 21 March, *Leicestershire Mercury*, 14, 28 March, 4 April 1857.

16 Asa Briggs, *op. cit.*

17 *Leicester Chronicle* 21 and 27 March, *Leicestershire Mercury*, 28 March 1857.

18 Asa Briggs, *op. cit.*

19 J. R. Vincent, *Pollbooks. How Victorians Voted* (Cambridge, 1967), 5; *Leicester Journal*, 20 March 1857.

20 H. M. Walmsley, *op. cit.*, 336.

21 *Bolton Chronicle*, 25 March 1857.

22 G. J. Holyoake, *Bygones Past Redress* (1906), I, 182–4.

23 G. N. Ray, *Thackeray. The Age of Wisdom, 1847–1863* (1950), 250, 268–71; id., *The Letters and Private Papers of William Makepeace Thackeray* (1946), IV, 382–3.

24 *The Times*, 21, 26, 28 March 1857.

chapter seven
1847–57 (IV)
THE INTELLECTUALS

I   *Nonconformist social Sabbatarianism*

Between 1837 and 1847 most Nonconformists had remained
aloof from the Sabbatarian movement. When in 1847 J. T.
Baylee had set up a grandly named Metropolitan Committee in
an attempt to gain Nonconformist support for the L.D.O.S.'s
campaign against the Post Office he produced an imposing list of
Nonconformist sympathisers but gained practically no active
help.

The Nonconformist clergy had been faced with a genuine
ideological problem, as had their laymen in Parliament. Even
the Wesleyans, who often held both Tory and authoritarian
ideas, and did not regard themselves as Nonconformists, had not
been entirely happy with Agnew's Bill, and in the 1840's Edward
Miall's *Nonconformist* had stated its opposition 'to every legislative
attempt to secure the religious observance of the Sabbath'.[1]

However, the Wesleyans had embodied the Westminster
Confession's Sabbatarian statement in their Articles of Religion,
their domestic practices were Sabbatarian too, and *The
Watchman* and *The Wesleyan Times* supported the movement. The
other Methodist denominations followed the Wesleyans' lead
but with less force. The rank and file of the older, more definitely
Nonconformist Churches, the Congregationalists and the
Baptists, were at least as strongly Sabbatarian in their domestic
practices as they had been in the 1830's.[2]

In 1846 *The Watchman* had stressed the value of Sabbath
observance to the labouring classes and *The Nonconformist* had
defended the purely civil observance of the Sabbath on
humanitarian grounds. The Nonconformists were prepared for

social Sabbatarianism when it spread from the prize essays.[3]

The Hon. and Rev. Baptist Noel, who left the Established Church for the Baptists, championed social Sabbatarianism among that denomination. It very quickly took root among the most vigorously voluntary of the Nonconformist bodies, Miall's Congregationalists. The Rev. J. Angell James, who achieved fame as the leader of the denomination in Birmingham in the 1840's, and the Rev. Newman Hall, who came to prominence in London in the 1850's, both championed social Sabbatarianism.[4]

At the Congregational May Meetings in 1852 the Rev. J. Baldwin Brown, who wished to open the Crystal Palace on Sundays, was overcome by Angell James, Edward Baines II and Samuel Morley, a philanthropic industrialist. In 1854 and 1855, of course, Baines himself was to write on the subject and in any case used the *Leeds Mercury* to spread his views.[5] Edward Miall had supported opening the Crystal Palace, but by 1856 his readers were divided and he was constrained to oppose efforts to open the British Museum on Sundays on 'social' rather than 'religious' grounds.[6]

Thus by the middle 1850's the major Nonconformist Churches had accepted social Sabbatarianism, but were still reluctant to support the Sabbatarians. In 1856 the L.D.O.S. had set up its Metropolitan Committee to oppose Sunday bands. The Rev. W. H. Rule, secretary of the Wesleyan Sabbath Committee, who served on it, remarked, 'As for the leading Dissenting ministers they did indeed attend our meetings in sufficient numbers to argue against our movement on their own principle of not accepting legal obligation to the performance of any religious duty.'[7]

Indeed, during 1857 J. T. Baylee noted that 'The Congregationalists oppose the enactment of laws in reference to religion; a principle which they extend to the Lord's day. They regard legislation of this character as an interference with liberty, and conceive that human conduct, in religious matters, should be regulated by individual conscience, enlightened and instructed by the word of God, rather than by legal enactments.'[8]

Charles Haddon Spurgeon, the great Baptist preacher, was criticised by Sabbatarians for holding Sunday services in the

Surrey Music Hall, and although he abandoned the practice when the hall was used for Sunday concerts, in 1857 he threw doubt on the Sabbatarian belief that God punished Sabbath-breakers in this world when preaching in the Crystal Palace itself.[9]

II   *Opposition: sacred*

The Roman Catholic newspapers lost no opportunity to ridicule the Sabbatarians, and the Tractarians maintained that Sunday could only be preserved for religion by reviving the Church's holy days as national holidays.[10]

The heirs of Whately and Arnold also entered the fray. When in 1834 Arthur Stanley had gone up from Rugby to Balliol, he had supported a move to close the Union on Sundays, but soon changed his views under the influence of Benjamin Jowett. In 1856 Jowett noted, 'I took up *The Record* at the reading rooms . . . it points out for the edification of the Ministry that Providence whitewashed their misdoings by two large majorities immediately after Sunday bands were put an end to. I had rather believe in all the fables in the Talmud and Alkoran than this.'[11]

He had been anticipated by other leading Broad Churchmen, disgusted by the virulence of the Sabbatarian attack on the projected Sunday opening of the Crystal Palace. In 1853 the Rev. C. J. Vaughan, son of a Leicester clergyman, Arnold's favourite pupil, Stanley's best school-friend and later his brother-in-law, headmaster of Harrow School, published an anti-Sabbatarian pamphlet. So did F. D. Maurice, son of a Unitarian minister, an Anglican himself and professor of theology at King's College, London.[12]

Early in 1856 Henry Alford, appointed Dean of Canterbury in the following year, went into print; he was emulated by Baden Powell, yet another Oriel man, Savilian professor in Oxford, where it was said 'that he had the Sabbath on the brain'. He also had three wives and thirteen children, the twelfth of whom later founded the Boy Scouts.[13]

Most Broad Churchmen found it difficult to systematise their reaction against Sabbatarianism, and to produce an original interpretation of the Fourth Commandment, because they shared the meaning which the Sabbatarians themselves gave to 'holy' and to 'pleasure' and feared to set a precedent for attempts to reinterpret the other nine commandments.

However, they found it even more difficult to stomach many Sabbatarian attitudes. They therefore suggested that a new understanding of the commandment and of its requirements was permissible. Vaughan and Alford wrote that the *Old Testament* law had at this point been relaxed by the *New Testament* gospel, as shown in Christ's words 'The sabbath was made for man and not man for the sabbath'. Maurice feared that Sabbatarianism injured the spiritual life by implying that man might have six days for himself provided he gave one to God in return.[14]

Each pleaded for the moderation of inessential strictness in order to meet the problems of urban working class life, but made few practical proposals and did not recommend Sunday amusement or recreation. In 1852 Charles Kingsley repudiated Sabbatarianism and seemed to sympathise with opening the Crystal Palace on Sundays, but when writing to Maurice in 1856 he took a far more cautious line, emphasising the evils of Sunday drinking.[15]

Baden Powell, however, argued that the 'disclosure of the true physical history' of the origin of the world undermined the Creation account on which Sabbatarianism rested, and accused its protagonists of coming 'prominently into collision with the practical sense of the masses'. He translated his anti-Sabbatarian theology into a practical support for the provision of Sunday amusement and recreation.[16]

III   *Opposition: secular*

Present at the Sunday Trading riots in 1855 had been Robert Morrell and his wife, who, so he claimed later, had been the first to shout 'Go to church!' Morrell was a skilled Radical, a working goldsmith and jeweller to whom the riots brought home the whole issue of Sunday trade and recreation. He became convinced that the Crystal Palace and museums should be open on Sundays, so canvassed his workmates, found they agreed, and in the autumn of 1855 established the National Sunday League. Bradlaugh, who regarded his appearance before the commission as his first essay into public life, and never subsequently missed the opportunity to give a Sunday lecture, was a branch secretary. Holyoake aided the movement with a vigorously anti-Sabbatarian pamphlet and a short-lived magazine, *The Sabbath Debater*.[17]

Morrell gathered a group of equally skilled men on to the N.S.L. committee. Its treasurer, William Duthie, was a working diamond jeweller. Its secretary, John Heap, was the teetotal chairman of the council of the most famous of the mid-Victorian trade unions, the Amalgamated Society of Engineers; and George Howell stressed Heap's anti-Sabbatarianism when writing his obituary in the N.S.L.'s *Free Sunday Advocate*. By September 1856 they had raised 1,622 one-shilling subscriptions, and 151 donations from middle class supporters brought the total to almost £250. The M.P.'s Heyworth, Scholefield and Shelley lent their names to the society and Walmsley provided office space.[18]

In 1857 the N.S.L. set up the London Sunday Bands Committee, which replaced the military bands with private ones, surveyed the state of Sunday recreation in the provinces, and planned a nation-wide anti-Sabbatarian campaign, which was abandoned in order to concentrate on London.

The N.S.L. relied upon several middle class supporters. J. Baxter Langley, co-editor with Ernest Jones of *The People's Paper*, for which Marx wrote numerous articles, gave it free publicity and spoke at its meetings. W. H. Domville, a wealthy solicitor, who had already published several anti-Sabbatarian studies of the *New Testament*, gave it a lot of encouragement and some financial help. Robert Cox, educated at Edinburgh High School and University, in 1844 editor of the *Encyclopaedia Britanica*, and in 1857 of the *Phrenological Review*, which was owned by his uncle, George Combe, produced several anti-Sabbatarian tomes, providing theological ammunition for use against the Evangelicals. Baden Powell allowed the N.S.L. to reprint his work and became one of its vice-presidents. Morrell, Duthie and Heap wrote a series of pamphlets designed to prove that on the Continent innocent Sunday amusement and recreation did not lead to more Sunday labour than existed without them in England.

The N.S.L.'s brief incursion into the provinces raised up some of the Sabbatarians' own most redoubtable champions and revealed the anti-Sabbatarians' weakness. In Liverpool the N.S.L. was opposed by Canon Hugh McNeile, a notable slum parson, who in 1842 had helped the Tories win control of the city council and in 1868 was to be made Dean of Ripon by Disraeli. In Birmingham J. C. Miller, a prominent Evangelical clergyman, joined J. Angell James in attacking the Sunday postal services. Their efforts were opposed by G. M. Yorke, a Broad Churchman, and by Samuel Bache, a Unitarian minister. In 1856 George Dawson, Baptist minister to the Church of Christ the Saviour, preached three sermons calling for Sunday rest and Sunday recreation. Later in the year he accepted the position of president of the Birmingham Sunday League, which gained the support of the Unitarian Martineau family. In Leeds the anti-Sabbatarians were led by Radicals who challenged the influence of the clergy on the middle classes. In Manchester the anti-Sabbatarians were led by J. Panton Ham, a Unitarian minister, and by working class militants who poured scorn on Sabbatarian claims to represent the interests of the working classes. The anti-Sabbatarians were defeated: Sunday bands were suppressed in Liverpool, Birmingham and Leeds; and in Manchester the Botanical Gardens were opened only to subscribers.[19]

IV   *Ideology and the working classes*

Social Sabbatarianism had given the Nonconformists a way out of their difficulties, and had proved attractive to the Broad Churchmen and the Tractarians, Maurice, for example, refusing to allow Sunday amusement or recreation at his Working Men's College.[20] There remained a clash between the most determined Sabbatarians and their most secular opponents. The Sabbatarians still asked the State to regulate behaviour on religious grounds. In 1855, during the debate on Walmsley's first motion, Goulburn stated: 'The question at issue was simply this; would the opening [of the British Museum on Sunday afternoons] be conformable or not to the will of Him who framed the Sabbath?'[21]

In 1856, during the debate on Walmsley's second motion, Lord Stanley argued that the State had no right to regulate men's behaviour on religious grounds: 'He denied the right of any earthly tribunal or legislature to proscribe the relation which should exist between man and the Supreme Being'.[22] Roundell Palmer, a Tractarian lawyer, replied that whereas the State had no right to interfere with private actions within a man's household, and lacked the competence to distinguish between necessary and unnecessary labour, it had a duty to regulate national institutions according to the teaching of the Established Church.[23]

In fact, there could be no compromise between Goulburn's vision of a confessional State and Stanley's desire for a secular one, without social Sabbatarianism, which taught that irreligious acts had an anti-social result, and so should be avoided by the individual.

By this time all parties to the dispute were concentrating on the working classes. One of the Albertian essay adjudicators, the Rev. John Jordan, set the tone by establishing a short-lived magazine, *The Working Man's Charter*, whose title and content indicated that he, like Bickersteth and Shaftesbury, hoped to present the workers with an alternative to the political aspirations which had culminated in Chartism.

Baldwin Brown realised that the Churches had only a 'slight hold on the working classes' and feared that the Sabbatarians' attitude to the Crystal Palace would drive them beyond the pale of organised religion. He therefore recommended opening the Palace on Sunday afternoons, 'hoping that, by all the humanizing influences that are brought to bear on them [the working classes] we may regain a hold on them, and lead them'.[24]

Indeed, one of Walmsley's justifications for wishing to open the British Museum on Sunday afternoons had lain in 'the moral and religious influence which had been produced upon the minds of many who flocked to witness the glories of the late Crystal Palace. Among them were men who, sullen with suffering, were so ignorant as to confound order with oppression, and wealth with injustice; but yet those men, whose minds religious teaching had failed to soften, were subdued at the grandeur of the sights which they there beheld, and for the first time they learnt to reverence genius, intellect and property.'[25]

It is unlikely that the working classes were Sabbatarian if only because the essayists were untypical of their class, most being either skilled men or holding jobs in which a high degree of literacy was required. They were that cream of the respectable working class for whom the Nonconformists had a special appeal. As for the rest, even some Sabbatarians were candid enough to admit that they were at best indifferent to their ideas. In fact the L.D.O.S. employed the London City Mission to hand-pick pious labourers to produce at its meetings and to accompany deputations to the government. In 1854 it paid a guinea a week to a convasser who collected working class signatures for petitions to the House of Commons.[26]

It was hardly necessary to use such methods, for by 1857 the Sabbatarians seemed triumphant. Between 1847 and 1857 the L.D.O.S. had doubled its income from some £700 to some £1,500 a year and had paid off debts accumulated during the 1840's. In 1850 its Post Office campaign had produced 4,797 petitions bearing 643,357 signatures. Lord John Russell's defeat and Lord Palmerston's deference were a tribute to their effect.

The L.D.O.S. had already ceased to promote legislation of its own and its victories over the Post Office and public houses had been reversed, but its supremacy over the Crystal Palace and the British Museum was absolute. The party leaders had decided to maintain the *status quo*, refusing to close those institutions which were open lest they rouse the public at large, and refusing to open those which were closed lest they rouse the Sabbatarians.

In the country Sabbatarianism was marked by several paradoxes. Sabbatarians claimed to limit Sunday work, but proscribed Sunday amusement, whilst tending to neglect Sunday drinking. They had gained a political position which their grass-roots power did not justify. They claimed to act for and on behalf of the working classes, but were attempting to educate them in ideas and ways foreign to their existing leaders and habits.

These paradoxes remained undiscerned by most contemporaries and so did not weaken the Sabbatarians. Indeed, social Sabbatarianism had given them added strength, so that despite the stirrings of sacred and secular doubt and the growth of Radical opposition, the Sabbatarians so dominated the House of Commons that the Sunday afternoon opening of the British Museum was not voted on again for almost twenty years.

Notes

1 *The Watchman*, 23 June 1835; *The Nonconformist*, 19 August 1846.

2 Wesleyan Hist. Soc. Publications No. 2 (1897), *Articles of Religion 1, XXXII*.

3 *The Watchman*, 19 August 1846; *The Nonconformist, loc. cit.*

4 B. W. Noel (ed.), *The Christian Sabbath* (1850); J. A. James, *The Sabbath* (1850); Charles Hill, *Continental Sunday Labour* (1884), 62–3.

5 *Congregational Year Book* (1853), 96–7.

6 *The Nonconformist,* 27 October; 3 and 10 November 1852; 20 and 27 February 1856.

7 W. H. Rule, *Recollections, &c.* (1886), 230–1.

8 J. T. Baylee, *The History, op. cit.*, 212.

9 C. H. Spurgeon, *Our National Sins* (1857).

10 *The Tablet*, 23 February 1856; *Weekly Register and Catholic Standard*, 23 February and 1 March 1856; W. Grapel, *The Church's Holy Days* (1848); W. B. Barter, *Tracts in Defence, &c. (1851).*

11 G. G. Bradley, *A. P. Stanley* (1883), I, 132–3; E. Abbott and L. Campbell, *Jowett* (1897), I, 284–5.

12 C. J. Vaughan, *A Few Words on the Crystal Palace Question* (1853); F. D. Maurice, *Sermons on the Sabbath Day* (1853).

13 Henry Alford, *Two Letters to John Sterling, Esq.* (1856); Baden Powell, *Christianity without Judaism* (1856); William Tuckwell, *Pre-Tractarian Oxford* (1909), 198.

14 *Ibid.*

15 Mrs F. E. Kingsley, *Charles Kingsley* (1904 ed.), 138–40.

16 Baden Powell, *Christianity, op. cit., id., A Second Series of Essays* (1857), 104.

17 PP., 1867–68, XIV, *Rept. S.C. of H.C. on the Sale of Liquor on Sundays Bill*, 284; J. M. Robertson, *Charles Bradlaugh, op. cit.*, I, 52–60; G. J. Holyoake, *The Rich Man's Six, &c.* (1856), *The Sabbath Debater* (1856).

18 N.S.L., *Record*, No. 30, p. 15 (October, 1858).

19 Anon., *Sabbath Defence* (Liverpool, 1856); R. W. Dale, *J. Angell James* (1861), 461; G. Dawson, *The Christian Sunday, &c.* (1856); J. A. Langford, *Modern Birmingham* (1873), I, 431; A. B. Clifford, *The Sabbath Question, &c.* (Leeds, 1856); J. Panton Ham, *The Christian Sunday, &c.* (Manchester, 1856), A Working Man, *A Letter, &c.* (Manchester, 1856).

20 F. Maurice, *Life of F. D. Maurice* (1884), II, 290–1, 318–19.

21 3H, vol. 137, col. 915 (20 March 1855).

22 3H, vol. 140, col. 1074 (21 February 1856).

23 *Ibid.*, col. 1104.

24 J. Baldwin Brown, *The Sabbath, The Crystal Palace and the People* (1853), 3, 24.

[25] 3H, vol. 37, col. 915 (20 March 1855).

[26] R. K. Greville, *A Letter, &c.* (Edinburgh, 1850), 8; J. T. Baylee, *History, op. cit.*, 262; L.D.O.S., *Quarterly Publication*, No. 46, p. 448 (August 1854).

PART THREE

chapter eight

PROLIFERATION
1857–67

I　　　　　　　　　　　*New societies*

The crises of the 1850's stimulated the formation of several new societies concerned with the Sunday question. In April 1857 two pious solicitors, James Girdlestone and J. M. Lydall, and a leading London City Missionary, James Weylland, failed to convince the L.D.O.S. that it should work to extend its membership to non-Anglicans and to the working classes. They therefore founded the National Lord's Day Rest Association in order to promote a more widely supported movement. Their own Primary Address stressed the social advantages of Sabbath observance. They hoped to promote the election of Sabbatarians to Parliament and to demonstrate that the N.S.L. did not really represent the feelings of the working classes.[1]

In October 1857 the N.L.D.R.A. and the London City Mission set up the Cab and Omnibus Men's Sunday Rest Association. Its aim was to reduce Sunday labour, but its principal method was to distribute Bibles during tea meetings, so it did not win the confidence of the men and ceased to exist during 1866.[2]

In May 1858 Bishop Tait of London and Bishop Sumner of Winchester convened a meeting of prominent Anglican clergymen and laymen in the National Club and founded the Metropolitan Sunday Rest Association. The two bishops attracted the support of sixteen of their episcopal brethren as vice-presidents, and several highly respected moderate Evangelicals became members, notably the Revs. W. Cadman, W. W. Champneys and Thomas Dale. The interest of Lords Ebury and Chelmsford attracted eighteen other peers as vice-presidents too.

Tait arranged for his diocesan clergy to preach on the evils of
Sunday labour and issued a public letter drawing particular
attention to the evils of Sunday omnibus work. Under his
patronage the M.S.R.A. hoped to build up an alliance of
Churchmen, politicians and shop-keepers in order to reduce the
volume of Sunday trading in London.[3]

II   *The enthusiasts*

Most nineteenth century writers agreed with Dickens, who
thought Sabbatarianism typical of 'the extreme class of
Dissenters'. Charles Kingsley cast Alton Locke's mother as a
Calvinistic Baptist and a Sabbatarian.[4] Most historians have
confirmed their judgement. G. D. H. Cole and Raymond
Postgate and K. S. Inglis identified Sabbatarianism with the
Nonconformists. W. L. Burn likened Sabbatarianism to the
temperance movement and recognised that it was an important
issue which deserved further study. Chadwick noted that the
Sabbatarian leaders were Evangelicals but regarded the crises of
the 1850's as an early manifestation of the 'Nonconformist
Conscience'. He interpreted the general issue as a struggle
between the anti-Sabbatarian 'city' and the Sabbatarian
'country', and thought that the Victorian Sunday was eventually
secured by non-Sabbatarian means. Stephen Mayor, himself a
Nonconformist, saw Sabbatarianism as one of the most
characteristic features of lower middle class Nonconformity.[5]

Those historians who have studied the Victorian Sunday in
some detail have stressed the L.D.O.S.'s Anglicanism and
pointed to a more diffuse Sabbatarianism which had a wider
appeal, but have not produced an analysis of who were the
Sabbatarian and Sunday observance enthusiasts. Brian
Harrison has described the 1855 Sunday Trading riots, and his
article on religion and recreation in nineteenth century England
implies that the L.D.O.S. provided leisure time, that the
N.L.D.R.A. had working class support, and that both societies
had a philanthropic purpose.[6]

The L.D.O.S.'s first secretary, the Rev. J. T. Baylee, was a
Lancastrian graduate of Trinity College, Dublin. Those who

followed him were all Evangelical clergymen. Henry Stevens was previously curate at Bath Abbey Church, John Gritton a missionary in Ceylon, Frederick Peake a secretary to several Evangelical societies and J. B. Barraclough a parson in Lambeth.

Only Gritton's personality survives. He had been trained at Islington Missionary College and had absorbed the lowest of Low Church ideas. He wrote a prize essay on *Painted Windows*, which he believed to contravene the Second Commandment, and Hugh McNeile contributed a preface for the work's publication. In 1892 Gritton left the Anglican Church because the Privy Council failed to condemn all Bishop King's liturgical ways, henceforth producing an edition of the Prayer Book purged of Roman Catholic elements.[7]

The secretary of the N.L.D.R.A. from 1859 until his death in 1910 was Charles Hill, who had previously founded and run his own Christian Literature Institute. The honorary secretary to the M.S.R.A. was the Rev. Alfred Jones, Chaplain and Master of Aske's Hospital in Hoxton.[8]

Behind these stalwarts were the respectable Evangelicals. B.A. Heywood, a prominent figure in the Bath auxiliary and the N.L.D.R.A.'s solicitor, was a product of Repton School and Trinity College, Cambridge. G. F. Chambers, a prolific and vituperative Sabbatarian pamphleteer from 1857 until beyond the turn of the century, was a lawyer and a member of the Carlton Club. Robert Baxter, who had close links with the L.D.O.S., was a strong Tory whose son, Robert Dudley Baxter, was electoral statistician to Disraeli in 1867 and whose firm of solicitors, Baxter, Rose & Norton, was parliamentary agent to the Tory party.[9]

Below the respectable Evangelicals lay a group of men touched by the emotive force of Evangelicalism. For example, John Cockram, a cab driver who supported the N.L.D.R.A., had been converted by the Rev. Baptist Noel, written a prize essay on the Sabbath and used the prize money to found a firm, whose profits eventually enabled him to retire in comfort to a villa in Richmond.[10]

Such enthusiasts formed the backbone of the societies and drummed up support from among their social circles and the churches which they attended. However, at no time between 1831 and 1914 did the societies' total membership exceed 3,000, and although the L.D.O.S. raised £1,500 p.a. in the 1850's and the N.L.D.R.A. was to raise £500 p.a. in the 1880's the societies ran on a financial knife-edge.

The societies derived their impact from the appeal of their ideas, which were widely acepted; from the fact that the Churches existed in a form ideally suited to pressure group politics; from the dedication of able secretaries, who masterminded their operations; and from auxiliaries and enthusiasts, concentrated as before in the south of England.

Trollope gave an inimitable description of a clerical enthusiast in the Rev. Mr Slope, who featured in *Barchester Towers*, first published in 1857. Charles Hill described the laymen:

> There is no large class of men ... in France corresponding to those who in England and Scotland observe the Sabbath day and love it. These men are the backbone of Great Britain, the preservers of their country. They require no vast armies to keep them in order, no secret police to watch their movements. They do not attempt to influence the passions of the people against what is good; they are not Iconoclasts or Communists or Levellers. They are truly patriotic, striving to do their duty to God and to their Country. They are a national breakwater keeping back the rage and violence of the dangerous classes; and the Government will do wisely to pause before it takes any steps which would give offence to the men who would honour the Sabbath day.[11]

III   *The supporters*

During the 1850's and 1860's a certain polarisation took place amongst the bishops. Shaftesbury got Palmerston to nominate A. M. Villiers to Carlisle in 1856 and Robert Bickersteth (Edward's nephew) to Ripon in 1857. Both were Evangelical Sabbatarians. On the other hand, when in 1856 Tait was given London, Dean Wellesley of Windsor commended him to Prince Albert, an anti-Sabbatarian, precisely because he was neither an Evangelical nor narrow on the Sunday question. Tait had tutored Stanley at Balliol and in 1842 had succeeded Arnold at Rugby, where he made his name. Whilst in London he avoided the L.D.O.S. and patronised the M.S.R.A., giving a lead to the other bishops. His success in London eventually took him to Canterbury.

The queen acted on her own anti-Sabbatarian views. She ignored the protests of her devout lady-in-waiting, Louisa Noel, and travelled by train on Sundays. She later ensured that Tait's protégé, Davidson, also an anti-Sabbatarian, who was prepared for ordination by Vaughan, rose from Windsor through Rochester to Canterbury.

A similar trend towards moderation took place among the few aristocratic Sabbatarians. Shaftesbury is the best example. After having become unpopular in 1850 he had refused to lead an attack on the Crystal Palace and in 1856 had worked from behind the scenes to destroy the Sunday bands. Although his private opinions remained quite unrestrained, he was reluctant to attend the L.D.O.S.'s Annual Meetings, and only accepted the presidency of the N.L.D.R.A. at the second time of asking, subsequently refusing to take part in any of its campaigns.[12]

The societies built up their parliamentary support. The Wesleyan Sabbath Committee relied initially upon James Heald, the Tory M.P. for Stockport, the first member to refer to the prize essays as authentic expressions of working class opinion, and then upon a group of other Wesleyans. Most notable were the brothers Alexander and William McArthur, sons of an Irish manse, who made their fortune in the Australian wool trade, enabling Alexander to succeed Dove Harris as Liberal M.P. for Leicester and William to sit as Liberal Member for Lambeth, whence he became first Methodist Lord Mayor of London.[13]

The N.L.D.R.A. relied upon them too, but had its own spokesman in Thomas Chambers, a Congregational lawyer and Liberal M.P. for St Marylebone, who had made his parliamentary reputation by advocating the State inspection of nunneries. The N.L.D.R.A. also had close contact with Charles Reed, a Congregational printer and Liberal M.P. for Hackney, who in 1870 was to become first chairman of the London School Board.

The M.S.R.A. worked with Lord Chelmsford, a Tory lawyer who had the ear of Lord Derby, and with Thomas Hughes.

Hughes, the author of *Tom Brown's School Days*, had hero-worshipped Arnold at Rugby, followed in his footsteps to Oriel, taught boxing at Maurice's Working Men's College, and was also for some years one of the Liberal M.P.'s for Lambeth.

In 1858 the L.D.O.S. had established a link with H. M. Cairns, who was Tory Solicitor General at the time. In 1864 Lord Kinnaird put the L.D.O.S. in touch with Roundell Palmer, by then Whig Attorney General, who in 1865 gave a dinner at which several mechanics (provided by the London City Mission and fortified by a prayer meeting in the L.D.O.S. office) tried to win Gladstone's support. The L.D.O.S. relied upon Robert Baxter to supply it with information from the Tories and analysed the balance of opinion in the Commons after each general election.[14]

The societies could therefore count upon a band of principled adherents. In 1861 they destroyed the Department of Science and Art's plan to open the Glasnevin Botanical Gardens in Dublin on Sunday afternoons, embarrassing the Whig Lord President of the Council, Lord Granville, and the vice-president of the Committee of the Privy Council for Education, Robert Lowe. In 1863 W. H. Gregory, an Irish Liberal who had supported the plan, moved to similarly open the Edinburgh Botanical Gardens, but was opposed by the Lord Advocate, James Moncrieff, and by the Prime Minister, Lord Palmerston, who repeated the arguments which he had used in the 1850's and employed his whips to defeat the proposal.[15]

When in 1864, 1865 and 1866 Sir Coleman O'Loghlen, another Irish Liberal, introduced Bills to compel Irish railway companies to provide Sunday services, he was defeated by an unholy alliance of the railway interest in the country and the Sabbatarians, led by Cairns, in the Commons.[16]

IV   *Parliament and Sunday trade*

The most intractable parliamentary problem during the 1860's concerned Sunday trade. Most Sunday trade was caused because very long working hours and the habit of not paying any wages until late on Saturday night left the very poor with little chance but to shop on Sunday mornings. Its subsidiary causes were that the poor had neither the facilities to store food nor to cook it, that all classes relied upon small traders to supply refreshments (fruit, nuts, sweets, tobacco, etc.) on Sunday afternoons and that London in particular contained several flourishing Sunday street markets such as Petticoat Lane, Snow Hill and the New Cut in Lambeth, in some of which Jews took part after having observed their Saturday Sabbath.

The problem had three forms. The Sabbatarians were against all Sunday trading. The respectable shopkeepers wanted to ensure that their Sunday closing would not be taken advantage of by their numerous competitors, and so pressed the M.P.'s for Lambeth in particular to introduce legislation to compel small shopkeepers and stallholders to close on Sundays. Successful action of this sort would have caused hardship to the very poor.

Since 1830 a considerable change in attitude had taken place. Agnew's Bills had been the product of religious authoritarianism designed to promote Sabbath observance, part of which entailed prohibiting Sunday trading. Bills introduced by Peter, Fleetwood, Poulter and Plumptre had been paternalistic Sunday observance measures which allowed for the needs of the poor. All laid the penalty upon the actual seller.

Those introduced by Hindley, Harrowby and Grosvenor had been of a different type. They were promoted by London shopkeepers on their own account. They penalised not the shop man who sold goods (being intended less as a punishment for personal sin than as a deterrent) but levied fines upon his employer, generally made them cumulative, usually placed the responsibility for prosecution with the police and concentrated on non-perishable goods during the hours of morning service, leaving other times and goods regulated by the ineffective 1677 Act, thereby once more allowing for the needs of the poor.

Bills introduced by Lord Chelmsford and Thomas Hughes emanated from the paternalistic and shopkeeping traditions. In 1860 Chelmsford got his Bill through the Lords, but it fell foul of a technicality in the Commons and lapsed at the end of the session. In 1866 it was defeated at the third reading in the Lords, and shortly afterwards Chelmsford was taken from the back benches and made Lord Chancellor when Derby became Prime Minister, thus being constrained to abandon his efforts.

Chelmsford's Bills were supported by moderate and Whiggish Tories like Lord Harrowby and (when he enjoyed the freedom of opposition) Lord Derby; although it was noticeable that the spokesmen for the Whig Ministry, Lord Granville and Lord John Russell, were opposed to them in their original form. Middle-of-the-road bishops like Tait and Longley, and the Tractarian Wilberforce, supported them. They were, however, opposed on Sabbatarian grounds by Shaftesbury and by his protégé Bishop Villiers of Carlisle; and on *laissez-faire* grounds by Lords St Germans, Abingdon and Teynham, who, oddly enough, was a Baptist minister.[17] The M.S.R.A. was all too well aware of the problems involved. It was not satisfied with Chelmsford's first Bill, so during 1861 secured the L.D.O.S.'s agreement to work for a joint measure, and Robert Baxter drafted a metropolitan Sunday trading Bill. During 1862 the M.S.R.A. became impatient with the L.D.O.S., decided to extend the Bill's scope to the whole of England and renamed itself the Sunday Rest Association. However, early in 1863 its deputation to Sir George Grey, the Home Secretary, found that he refused to pledge his support for the Bill. Thus Arthur Mills, Tory M.P. for Taunton, a clergyman's son who had gone from Arnold's Rugby to Balliol before being called to the bar, declined to introduce it. No one else would, so the S.R.A. abandoned it and reluctantly supported Chelmsford's second Bill.

Chelmsford knew that the L.D.O.S. opposed his Bills and in 1866 attributed his earlier difficulties to their influence. The society's annual report had stated, 'Better it is to have laws on our Statute book witnessing against Sabbath desecration even if their penalities should not be enforced, rather than to allow those laws to be superseded by an expediency that ignores the Divine Authority of the day.'[18]

James Hayman, secretary of the Society for Promoting the Interests of the Trading Community, which had promoted and supported Sunday trade Bills since 1846, recorded how Agnew's efforts had left behind a legacy of anti-Sabbatarian feeling strong enough to destroy moderate Bills. Yet when that legacy had declined and the Home Secretaries Grey and Graham had supported Bills 'the opposition from the Lord's Day Society was such as to prevent the possibility of their becoming law'. He concluded that such was still the case.[19]

When dealing with the Lords themselves the L.D.O.S. cloaked its religious opposition to the Bills in the language of voluntaryism, informing members that 'the present state of public opinion . . . was such that far more good would be effected by leaving the cause of the Sabbath to the efforts of the clergy and persons associated with them . . . than by means of any compulsory interference with it by legislative action'.[20]

V   *Portents*

As early as 1859 the N.L.D.R.A. had realised that its attempt to rival the L.D.O.S. had failed. Most of the clergy whom it had attracted were Anglican, and many speakers at its meetings were prominent members of the L.D.O.S. It had not gained many working class members apart from a group of pious shopworkers associated with the Young Men's Christian Association, and was in financial difficulties.

In 1860 the N.L.D.R.A. changed its own name to the Working Men's Lord's Day Rest Association and presented itself to the public as the champion of the downtrodden Sunday workers. It then attracted the sympathy and pecuniary support of the Evangelical middle classes, enabling it to extend its work.

The W.M.L.D.R.A. challenged the N.S.L. to a series of public debates, employing Richard Whitmore, a London City Missionary who was a member of its own committee, as its representative. However, his services were dispensed with in 1864 because he referred to Christ as 'the Carpenter's son'.[21]

The W.M.L.D.R.A. then waged a dual battle to attract the working classes and to convince the public that they favoured social Sabbatarianism. During 1866 the society distributed 19,000 tracts at the Hyde Park Reform Demonstration, gave out up to 40,000 tickets of admission to single meetings, arranged for working class speakers to alternate with middle class ones at its meetings, guaranteed to pay for newspaper reports which emphasised the former, and issued lists of provincial branches which were got up by clergymen and scripture readers in correspondence with its committee.[22]

The heart of this battle lay in an attempt to win the minds of working class leaders. Those who had survived the demise of Chartism were often absorbed within one branch or other of middle class endeavour. Thomas Cooper was attracted by Maurice and inspired *Alton Locke* before becoming a Baptist. William Lovett joined Walmsley's Parliamentary and Administrative Reform Association. Ernest Jones, Bradlaugh and Holyoake attached themselves to the Radical wing of the Liberal party.

The leaders of the craft unions were often anti-Sabbatarian. John Heap was, as we have seen, associated with the N.S.L., and George Howell, who wrote his eulogistic anti-Sabbatarian obituary, led the Bricklayers. William Allan of the Engineers, George Odger (secretary of the London Trade Council) of the Boot and Shoemakers, and W. R. Cremer of the Masons (both for a few years members of Marx's International) were all strong anti-Sabbatarians.[23]

However, George Potter, often regarded as a labour militant because he opposed these leaders of the London 'Junta' and managed the Trade Union Congress of 1868, was a Sunday school teacher and a Sabbatarian, as he admitted to Roebuck when questioned before a select committee in 1867. Potter was forced to agree that working men who needed the protection of Sabbatarian legislation were unfit to receive the franchise.[24]

Baxter Langley was a member of the executive committee of the Reform League. Beales, the League's president, was even rebuked by the L.D.O.S. for allowing its branches to hold meetings on Sundays and promised to take the matter in hand. He refused to give Baxter Langley the League's full support when he fought Greenwich in 1865, but in the 1868 general election the League's candidates included several outspoken anti-Sabbatarians.

There was a division of opinion about Sabbatarianism among M.P.'s who supported the Reform League. For example, Dilke, an uncertain Anglican, and Mill, an agnostic, were strongly anti-Sabbatarian and patronised Odger; whilst Morley, the Congregational social-Sabbatarian, was about to extend his patronage to Arch.

The 1860's were a difficult decade for the L.D.O.S. It was afraid that the new societies would compromise its principles and detract from its influence on Parliament. In 1860 it refused to admit Nonconformists to its committee, but did co-operate with W. H. Rule and John Cumming. It followed the example of the new societies by emphasising the desecration produced by Sunday cabs, and broke new ground by setting up the Central Committee for Securing the Cessation of Sunday Excursion Trains in order to co-ordinate the efforts of its auxiliaries in the south coast towns.

The L.D.O.S. had detected a changed atmosphere and opinion among the educated classes which was antipathetic to its doctrine and practices. Whilst the Sabbatarians had fought their own battles during the 1850's other changes had taken place from which they could not for ever remain isolated.

Until the 1850's the Evangelicals had been the rising party within the Established Church, but the emergence of the Tractarians and Broad Churchmen had shaken their claim to act as the true interpreters of Anglicanism. After the publication of the results of the religious census in 1853 (which showed that barely 50 per cent of worshippers attended its services) the Established Church's claim to speak for the nation was itself shaken.

The whole Church had been taken aback in 1859 when Charles Darwin's *The Origin of Species* had appeared. In 1860 Bishop Wilberforce's wrangle with T. H. Huxley at a meeting of the British Association for the Advancement of Science in Oxford had revealed how sadly ill equipped were the Church's leaders to respond to such new ideas.

In 1859 too Sabbatarianism had been challenged by one of the most powerful intellects of the age, for Mill had included an attack on Sabbatarianism in his *On Liberty*: 'Another important example of illegitimate interference with the rightful liberty of the individual, not simply threatened, but long since carried into effect, is Sabbatarian legislation.'[25]

During the following year the Rev. James Augustus Hessey, the headmaster of Merchant Taylors' School, delivered the Bampton Lectures before the University of Oxford on the subject of *Sunday: Its Origin, History and Present Obligation*. He taught a Dominical theology and rebuked Mill: 'Such statements ignore, first, the Christianity of Government; secondly, the duty of

Government to promote, so far as it can, the welfare of its subjects in accordance with Christian principles.'[26]

The bishops were shocked again in 1860 by *Essays and Reviews* and in 1861 were unnerved by Colenso's challenge to the entire veracity of the Old Testament. Archbishop Sumner issued a declaration condemning *Essays and Reviews*, and Jowett and Baden Powell, who had used its pages to cast doubt upon the New Testament miracles, were prosecuted for heresy. Colenso was deposed and founded a secessionist Church in far-away South Africa. Maurice, who had publicised his unease about the traditional doctrine on eternal punishment as early as 1853, had long since been dismissed from King's College by a committee which included Bishop Blomfield and Sir Robert Inglis.

Each year seemed to see a fresh blow to orthodox religion. In 1863 came Renan's *Life of Christ*, and in 1865 J. R. Seeley's *Ecco Homo* and Lecky's *History of Rationalism*. The bishops tried to heal the wounds by calling the first Lambeth Conference in 1867. The Sabbatarians were intransigent. *The Record* printed a vitriolic review of Hessey's lectures and issued it as a special pamphlet. The L.D.O.S. took refuge in the Bible, their 'final court of appeal', and occasionally emerged to strike out at their enemies.[27]

Notes

[1] N.L.D.R.A., *Minute Book I*, 28 April, 26 May 1857.

[2] C.O.M.S.R.A., *Annual Reports*, 1858–65, *passim*.

[3] M.S.R.A., *Annual Reports*, 1859–75, *passim*; R. T. Davidson and W. Benham, *Archibald Campbell Tait* (1891), I, 264–5.

[4] Timothy Sparks (Charles Dickens), *Sunday*, op. cit., 8; id., *Little Dorrit*, op. cit., 67–72; Charles Kingsley, *Alton Locke* (1890 ed.), 3.

[5] G. D. H. Cole and R. Postgate, *The Common People*, op. cit., 307; K. S. Inglis, *The Churches and the Working Class in Victorian England* (1964), 71; W. L. Burn, *The Age of Equipoise* (Unwin paper ed., 1968), 278–80; O. Chadwick, *Victorian Church*, op. cit., I, 464; S. Mayor, *The Churches and the Labour Movement* (1967), *passim*.

[6] G. M. Ellis, '*The Evangelicals and the Sunday Question, 1830–1860. Organised Sabbatarianism as an Aspect of the Evangelical Movement*', unpublished Ph.D., Harvard (1961); Peter Fryer, *Mrs. Grundy: Studies in English Prudery* (1963), 20–118; David Brooke, '*The Opposition to Sunday Rail Services in North Eastern England, 1834–1914*', *Journal of Transport History*, VI (1963–64), 95–105; Brian Harrison, *The Sunday Trading Riots*, op. cit.; '*Religion and Recreation in Nineteenth*

Century England', *Past and Present*, No. 38 (December 1967), 98–125.

⁷ John Gritton, *Painted Windows* (1879); Anti-Sunday Travelling Union, *Our Heritage*, No. 25, 385, 89 (October 1901).

⁸ W.M.L.D.R.A., *Pearl of Days*, No. 277, p. 257 (May 1904); No. 339, p. 730 (March 1914).

⁹ Robert Baxter, *Narrative of Facts* (1833), *Liberalism Revolutionary* (1829); Robert Blake, *Disraeli* (1967 ed.), *passim*.

¹⁰ PP., 1895, VI, *S.C. of H.L. Lord's Day Act*, 163.

¹¹ Anthony Trollope, *Barchester Towers* (New York, 1963), 34–7; Charles Hill, *Sunday Labour*, *op. cit.* 73.

¹² L.D.O.S., *Minute Book IV*, 5 November 1852; Edwin Hodder, *Shaftesbury*, *op. cit.*, II, 304–7, III, 26–33.

¹³ 3H, vol. 104, col. 841 (24 April 1849); Wesleyan Methodist Conference, *Minutes XI* (1852), 464.

¹⁴ L.D.O.S., *Minute Book IV*, 26 February, 5 March, 30 November 1858; *ibid.*, V, 1 December 1863, 6 January 1864, 2 February 1865, 18 January 1866.

¹⁵ 3H, vol. 164, col. 759 (11 July 1861); vol. 171, col. 543 (8 June 1863).

¹⁶ 3H, vol. 175, col. 2102 (20 June 1864); vol. 178, col. 51 (22 March 1865); vol. 182, col. 243 (14 March 1866); *Herapath's Journal*, 10 January 1863, *Railway News*, 25 June 1864, *Railway Times* 17 March 1866.

¹⁷ 3H, vol. 158, col. 554 (3 May 1860); vol. 188, col. 929 (15 May 1866).

¹⁸ L.D.O.S., *Twenty-ninth Annual Report* (1860), 16.

¹⁹ James Hayman, *An Appeal to Tradesmen* (1863), 131.

²⁰ 3H, vol. 183, col. 1672 (1 June 1866).

²¹ W.M.L.D.R.A., *Minute Book I*, 26 May 1857, 3 May 1864.

²² *Ibid.*, II, 31 January, 14 February, 5 December 1866.

²³ George Howell, *Operative Bricklayers' Society Trade Circular*, vol. I, No. 3, p. 28 (November 1861).

²⁴ G. D. H. Cole and R. Postgate, *The Common People*, *op. cit.*, 395; PP., 1867–68, *Rept. S.C. of H.C. Sale of Liquor on Sundays Bill*, 231–2.

²⁵ J. S. Mill, *On Liberty* (Everyman ed., 1962), 146–7.

²⁶ J. D. Hessey, *Sunday*, *&c.*, (1860), 313, 328.

²⁷ The Record, *A Review of Dr. Hessey's Bampton Lecture* (1860); Henry Stevens, *The Sabbath and the Decalogue* (1866), 13.

chapter nine

TRIBULATION, 1867–82

Whilst Parliament had been enmeshed in the Sunday trading controversy during the 1860's, the Factory Inspectors had paid special attention to Sunday labour at blast furnaces. They praised devout masters who provided Sunday rest, but recommended legislation to prohibit Sunday blast furnace work by children, young persons and women.[1]

In 1867 the Tory Home Secretary, Spencer Walpole (nephew of the assassinated Prime Minister), introduced a Factory Acts Extension Bill. It forbade children, young persons and women from Sunday employment 'in or about a blast furnace'. As amended by a select committee guided by Lord John Manners (still an anti-Sabbatarian) the Bill extended that provision to 'any factory' and made special provisions for the Jews. The Bill was embodied in the Factory Acts Extension Act and the Workshops Regulation Act (both of 1867) which applied to establishments employing over fifty and between five and fifty persons respectively.[2]

Inspired by this achievement, Thomas Hughes tried to pass a Sunday trade Bill. In 1867, 1868 and 1869, supported in each year by the current Home Secretary—the Tories Spencer Walpole and Gathorne Hardy, and the Liberal H. A. Bruce—his Bill reached the committee stage in the Commons. It was defeated on each occasion because of opposition by members associated with the L.D.O.S. and by anti-Sabbatarian Radicals.

In 1869 Chelmsford decided to reintroduce his own Bill, and it passed the Lords in February 1870 because the Liberal Lord Chancellor, Lord Selborne, formerly Roundell Palmer, indicated that the government did not oppose it. Hughes took charge of it in the Commons and Bruce spoke for it at the second reading, which it passed on 6 July. Hughes then left for the U.S.A., where he had established an idealistic community called Rugby, leaving J. G. Talbot, a Tory Tractarian, to manage the committee stage on 3 August. Bruce advised him not to proceed any further and the Bill lapsed at the end of the session.[3]

Bruce was worried by the effect of the L.D.O.S.'s attempt to render a new Bill unnecesary by persuading magistrates in London to enforce the 1677 Act. In February 1871 Hughes introduced his Bill in a form applicable only to London, so the L.D.O.S. made a final effort to prove the worth of the 1677 Act by sending a donation to the Rev. J. B. Wright, who was using it to prosecute Sunday shopkeepers and stallholders. These prosecutions caused a storm of protest and led to a reaction in the Commons. At the second reading in April Bruce explained that he spoke for himself alone and in no way committed the government to support the bill, and so the measure was defeated. P. A. Taylor, a Radical who had eventually taken Walmsley's place at Leicester, introduced a Bill to repeal the 1677 Act, and Bruce introduced a Sunday Observation Act Amendment Bill on behalf of the government. This reached the statute book as the Sunday Observation Prosecution Act. It left the substance of the 1677 Act unchanged, but henceforward no prosecution could be instituted under it without the written consent of a chief police officer, two magistrates or a stipendiary magistrate.[4]

II   *Sunday lectures*

After taking part in debates with the W.M.L.D.R.A. Baxter Langley had sought a less transient way to spread his ideas. During 1865 he had arranged a series of Sunday lectures in St Martin's Hall, London. In 1866 T. H. Huxley gave a 'lay sermon' as part of a second series, provoking Robert Baxter to threaten the owner of the hall with prosecution under the 1780 Act. The lectures and 'sermons' ceased. However, in 1867 Lord Amberley (son of Lord John and father of Bertrand Russell) introduced into the House of Commons a Sunday Lecture Bill which would have exempted Sunday lectures from the scope of the Act. Despite the support of Bright and Mill the Bill was defeated.[5]

Baxter Langley found that the 1780 Act did not apply to meetings for religious worship, so formed his helpers into a 'free unsectarian church', registered it under the 1688 Toleration Act, ensured that sacred music was played at its 'services' and charged not for admission but for reserved seats. Thus when in 1868 Robert Baxter did prosecute he was unsuccessful.[6] Lady Amberley found 'services' which consisted of sacred music and lectures on cultural and scientific topics to be rather disappointing, but they had a considerable impact on the intellectual world and Matthew Arnold alluded to them in the preface to his *Culture and Anarchy*.[7]

By 1869 W. H. Domville, who had played an important part in organising Baxter Langley's lectures, realised that they were fated to remain but a minor part of the N.S.L.'s work. He therefore broke away and founded the Sunday Lecture Society. T. H. Huxley took the chair at the first meeting, and Domville explained that 'in teaching the facts of science, in order words in teaching the best knowledge which we may possess in all subjects, we ... shall assist in converting the masses into reasoning and reasonable beings, and shall thus get rid of some of the misery and wrong which we see around us'. The society's committee of lawyers and university men attracted a membership of some two hundred of London's intellectual middle class and arranged an impressive series of lectures.[8]

After Domville's secession the N.S.L. restyled the *Free Sunday Advocate* and concentrated upon organising Sunday railway excursions, but retained its links with the secular Radicals. In 1874 it shared the same address as Edward Truelove, an enthusiastic propagandist of birth control.

In 1875 the W.M.L.D.R.A. forgot the lessons of 1871 and gave its support to two prosecutions of the Brighton Aquarium Company, which charged for admission on Sunday afternoons. Amidst another outcry P. A. Taylor tried to repeal the 1780 Act and R. A. Cross, the Tory Home Secretary, rushed through a Remission of Penalties Act which enabled Home Secretaries to remit penalties due to its injudicious or vexatious use.[9]

The N.S.L. had supported the Aquarium Company, but

another group of its intellectual members, already worried by links with Truelove and his like, followed Domville's example and late in 1875 founded the Sunday Society, whose sole object was to open free libraries, museums and galleries on Sunday afternoons.[10]

In 1876 Truelove was prosecuted for obscenity and in 1877 Tory M.P.'s were to use his name, and those of Bradlaugh and Mrs Besant, who supported him and the N.S.L. , to blacken the latter's name. Thus in 1878 Lord Thurlow objected to Mrs Besant's remaining a vice-president of the N.S.L., but P. A. Taylor persuaded a general meeting to back her. Lord Thurlow transferred his support to the Sunday Society and in 1879 yet another group of intellectuals, led by Leslie Stephen, a leading mountaineer and savant, founded the Sunday Tramps in order to promote Sunday rambles. In later years G. M. Trevelyan was to become a member.[11]

The Sunday Society was widely supported. Arthur Stanley, since 1864 Dean of Westminster, the queen's favourite churchman, lent his name to it. So did Benjamin Jowett, since 1870 Master of Balliol College, Oxford. Their example was followed by several lesser Broad Churchmen. Haweis, whose services attracted crowds to St Marylebone; Voysey, who proved too Broad and was convicted of heresy; and Hansard and his curate Headlam supported it. The Roman Catholic Bishop of Salford, the Rev. T. A. Steinthal (a Manchester prohibitionist) and a handful of Ritualist, Baptist, Congregational and Unitarian clergymen were members, oddly united in their opposition to the respectable religious nation.

From among the politicians the society attracted the aged J. A. Roebuck, the Duke of Westminster, the Earl of Rosebery and a group of other Radicals, Whigs and Liberals. From the nation's intellectual elite the society gained Mill and Spencer, several authors, including Wilkie Collins, Charles Dickens and Anthony Trollope, a coterie of artists led by Holman Hunt, Millais and Rossetti, and a host of scientists. T. H. Huxley declined an invitation to become the society's president because of pressure of work; but Tyndall, the physicist, feared by many devout people for his scathing attacks on Christianity, became an enthusiastic member.[12]

Most of the Sunday Society's members belonged (like the Sunday Lecture Society's) to London's intellectual middle class. They published the *Sunday Review*, lectured to the Social Science Congress, set up branches in the provinces and tried to influence Parliament. They relied upon George Howard in the Lower and upon Lords Thurlow, a Liberal, and Dunraven, a Tory, in the Upper House.

III   *Impact*

The struggle over Sunday trade had revealed a change in the parties' attitudes towards authority. In 1869 Thomas Hughes, a moderate Liberal, argued that 'the people wanted . . . not less government, but more'. Richard Spooner, a strong Tory, feared that 'modern Liberalism seemed to value the individual citizen less than the police, which seemed to him to be reverting to despotism'. Indeed, P. A. Taylor, a keen Radical, went so far as to accuse Hughes of betraying the freedom-loving outlook of his party.[13]

Between them, the authoritarian Sabbatarians and the *laissez-faire* Radicals had almost destroyed the tradition of Sunday observance and of Tory paternalism, the 1867 Acts remaining as a memorial to it. The L.D.O.S. did not concern itself with the 1867 Acts until 1871, when it opposed provisions to make it easier for the Jews to take their Sabbath rest on Saturdays, arguing that only the Christian Sabbath should be observed in England. Its committee desisted 'at the strong representation of Lord Shaftesbury' (who had earlier thanked the government for the Acts) and produced a series of tracts designed to show the advantage of Sunday rest to workmen.[14]

The W.M.L.D.R.A. was associated in the public mind with the Sunday trading prosecutions. Consequently, little attention was paid to a select committee on Sunday postal labour which Charles Reed obtained in 1871, and the society found it hard to attract people to its meetings or to gain patrons.

The S.R.A. was similarly affected. It accepted Samuel Morley's advice to adopt a policy of moral suasion, called itself the Sunday Rest Association for Promoting the Voluntary Closing of Shops on Sundays, and gained the financial backing of the Evangelical banking families of Barclay, Bevan, Coutts and Hoare, but declined rapidly in the aftermath of the Brighton Aquarium prosecutions.[15]

Nonconformist social Sabbatarians were left in confusion. The Baptist newspaper, *The Freeman*, had opposed Sunday trade Bills because it thought them too Sabbatarian and likely to prove burdensome to the poor. The Wesleyan and Primitive Methodists were unsure whether to accept the Bills as pragmatic attempts to solve a difficult problem; or to oppose them because they fell short of the Divine Law; or, indeed, because they were contrary to *laissez-faire* principles. *The Freeman* had even supported Amberley's Bill, making comparisons with the Five Mile Acts, and defending the right freely to express opinions, however reprehensible, on Sundays as on other days.[16]

In 1871 the Wesleyan Sabbath Committee was the worst attended of the Conference Committees. After 1875 most Nonconformist annual assemblies ignored the Sunday question, occasionally passing formal resolutions against new proposals to open the British Museum on Sunday afternoons, and regarded the issue as an aspect of the decline in church attendance or of the temperance cause, rather than as a subject in itself.[17]

Faced with the Free Sunday Societies, some devout people laid less emphasis on the prohibition of Sunday amusements and more on the provision of substitutes. During the 1850's a religious magazine, *Sunday at Home*, presented non-biblical Sunday reading for the family; and in 1864 one of the aims of the new *Sunday Magazine* was to draw working men from Sunday newspapers. In 1867 Cardinal Manning supported Sunday recreation, in order to draw them from public houses. In 1868 Henry Solly, a leading Unitarian minister, allowed his Working Men's Club and Institute Union to give Sunday evening concerts. The L.D.O.S. warned him that he was contravening the 1780 Act by charging for admission, so he made entrance entirely free.[18]

Maurice's colleagues at the Working Men's College, Ludlow and Furnival, outraged his pious Sunday behaviour by arranging Sunday trips into the countryside. Ludlow regarded the N.S.L.'s Sunday activities as an antidote to drunkenness among the lower orders. Two years after Maurice's death in 1872 Furnival founded the Sunday Shakespeare Society, for the Sunday study of the bard's plays, whilst leading a Sunday excursion to Stratford upon Avon.[19]

In Liverpool the Rev. H. S. Brown, a Baptist acquaintance of Thomas Cooper, gave Sunday lectures to working men who attended his chapel. By 1879 things had gone far enough to allow the *Unitarian Herald* and the *Church Times* to support opening the British Museum on Sunday afternoons.[20]

IV   *The constituencies and the northern towns*

The W.M.L.D.R.A. had originally aimed to promote the 'election to Parliament of such Christian men as are understood to favour the Association' but from 1859 onwards had adopted the L.D.O.S.'s policy of trying to defeat leading anti-Sabbatarian candidates.[21] In the following years it intervened in several individual cases but did not make a major effort until 1867, when it traced Lord Amberley to South Devon. In the 1868 general election, the first to be held after the 1867 Reform Act, it opposed Mill at Westminster, Baxter Langley at Greenwich (where he was now supported by the Reform League) and attacked Bradlaugh, Sandwith and Dickson (standing as the League's candidates), who hoped to secure election for Northampton, Marylebone and Hackney. The L.D.O.S. opposed Dilke in Chelsea. In 1870 the W.M.L.D.R.A. opposed Baxter Langley in Colchester (where he stood on behalf of the Contagious Diseases Repeal Act Association) and in 1874 followed him back to Greenwich. In the same year it moved against P. A. Taylor at Leicester and E. H. Currie (the vice-chairman of the London School Board) in Tower Hamlets.[22]

The methods the Sabbatarians used were rather superficial. In 1868 the L.D.O.S. distributed 170,000 electoral tracts, but it did not investigate particular constituencies or ask its parliamentary supporters for advice. The W.M.L.D.R.A. posted up placards in constituencies reading 'If you want Sunday to be made a day of toil vote for . . .' and employed board men to perambulate the streets bearing similar messages, but did not spend more than £10 at any general election until 1880, and the sum spent then, £57 19s 6d, was minute compared with the lavish expenditure of most candidates.[23] Such methods failed to make the Sunday question an issue against Baxter Langley, Dilke or Mill, although in 1868 the W.M.L.D.R.A. wrote to congratulate W. H. Smith when he defeated Mill. The matter did cause trouble for Bradlaugh, Sandwith, Dickson, Currie and Taylor.[24]

Bradlaugh, Sandwith and Dickson were out-and-out Radicals who had few supporters, fewer financial resources and opposed official Liberal candidates; so the Sabbatarians' attempts to dissuade working men from voting for them, although poignant in the context of the struggle for working class representation, played but a small part in their defeat. More realistic candidates found that Sabbatarianism was but one of many factors working against them. Amberley was lost when the Tories publicised his advocacy of birth control. In Tower Hamlets the Nonconformist Liberal Association refused to support any candidate who favoured the Sunday opening of places of recreation and so discountenanced Currie, but the fact that he was a distiller influenced them too. It was claimed that Taylor's views caused Nonconformist Liberals in Leicester to plump for Alexander McArthur, who had been brought in to balance him, but he retained the support of many such voters and topped the poll.[25]

For many years the Sabbatarians had the provinces to themselves, but by 1875 the Sunday Lecture Society had branches in Bradford, Salford and Leicester; and in 1877 the Sunday Society decided to extend its own efforts in the provinces. Hitherto it had made a frontal assault upon the national galleries and museums, making much of the Sheepshanks Collection, which had been given to the nation in 1857, on condition that 'so soon as arrangements can properly be made' it should be open to view on Sunday afternoons. Now the society hoped that if large towns opened their galleries and museums on Sunday afternoons Parliament would be more likely to open the national ones.

During the next few years Sunday Societies were set up in Newcastle upon Tyne, Darlington, Leeds, Sheffield, Manchester, Liverpool, Birmingham, Wolverhampton, Yarmouth, Reading and Bristol. The provincial anti-Sabbatarians had the same basic characteristics as their metropolitan counterparts. They were members of the intellectual middle class, usually voted Liberal, and attracted support from Roman Catholic, Broad Church and Unitarian clergy, besides that of convinced Secularists.[26]

The first provincial struggle to open a municipal library on Sunday afternoons had taken place in Sheffield in 1858, but they did not become common until the 1870's. Birmingham and Nottingham are typical examples. In 1872 Jesse Collings, an ally of Joseph Chamberlain, the Unitarian leader of Birmingham Liberalism, became chairman of the city's Free Libraries and Art Galleries Committee. He decided to open both on Sunday afternoons in order to provide the working classes with an opportunity for self-education. He was supported by the local Labour Representation League, but the vicar of Edgbaston and Charles Vince, a Baptist minister, formed a Lord's Day Defence Committee to oppose him. The heat generated by their campaign survived Collings' triumph and gave the Tories an opportunity to attack Chamberlain, who had supported him, in the municipal elections.[27]

In 1877 anti-Sabbatarians founded the Birmingham Sunday Lecture Society and in 1880 hired the town hall from the Liberal council as a venue for their lectures. R. W. Dale, who had succeeded J. Angell James as the leader of Birmingham's Congregationalists, held to a non-Sabbatarian theology, but was a social Sabbatarian, and so waged a campaign against the council, breaking with the Chamberlain caucus, which he had previously helped to form.[28]

Similarly in Nottingham in 1880 advanced Liberals, led by the *Nottingham Journal*, proposed the Sunday afternoon opening of the town's library and museum, whereas Alderman Gripper, whose firm supplied the bricks to build St Pancras Station, the Congregational president of the local Liberation Society, led a campaign against it. However, the town's Nonconformist Association refused to support him, resenting the disruptive activities of Charles Hill, who had travelled up from London to agitate the issue, and fearing to detach Nonconformist voters from anti-Sabbatarian Liberals in the municipal elections.[29]

V   *Parliament*

The struggle in the constituencies and the northern towns was obviously intended to influence Parliament, but between 1856 and 1874 the Sunday afternoon opening of the British Museum was not put to the vote in either House. In 1869 W. H. Gregory had raised the issue, but Thomas Chambers and W. S. Allen, a Wesleyan, Liberal member for Newcastle under Lyme, barely had a chance to oppose him before the House was counted out.[30]

The Liberal government lost the general election of 1874 and Disraeli became Tory Prime Minister. Among the new members were Thomas Burt and Alexander MacDonald, miners' leaders from Morpeth and Stafford, the first working men to enter the House. Charles Hill wrote to ask for their support, but they replied that they favoured opening museums on Sunday afternoons.[31] Burt had been brought up a Primitive Methodist but had been influenced by Joseph Cowen, the Radical owner of the *Newcastle Chronicle*, a Unitarian, and was probably an agnostic. He had in turn influenced Macdonald. Both were Lib–Labs.

However, the W.M.L.D.R.A.'s cause was safe, for now a Tory government was to face the issue of the Sunday afternoon opening of the British Museum (hereafter referred to simply as opening, and its converse as closing) for the first time, and was to support the Sabbatarians. Disraeli had rebuked the zealous Tractarian rector of Hughenden for criticising his own Sunday travelling, but when Prime Minister in 1868 had dismissed Chelmsford and replaced him as Lord Chancellor with Cairns, who became his closest adviser and evolved a policy of bidding for the Evangelical vote.[32]

Despite the Tory defeat in 1868 Lord Blake regards the election of W. H. Smith as heralding the return of many of the naturally conservative classes to the Tory party. Many of them were Sabbatarians and leavened the party with the attitudes of Evangelicalism, of business and of the law. Smith came from a Wesleyan home and had hoped to study at Oxford and enter the Anglican ministry, but had gone into the family business instead. W. S. Charley, who spoke up for the W.M.L.D.R.A. during the Brighton Aquarium case, was a member of the

Church of Ireland, an Ulsterman who sat for Salford and reorganised the Tory party in Lancashire, before retiring from politics and the law to lecture against 'the higher criticism'.[33]

Between 1874 and 1880 Disraeli's government contained seven closers—W. H. Smith, Sir C. B. Adderley, G. J. Noel, Sir Hardinge Giffard (the Solicitor General, who prosecuted Truelove), Lord Sandon (who in 1880 became the third Earl of Harrowby) and, of course, Cairns himself. They did not immediately guide the government, because it also contained four openers—old Lord Malmesbury, the fifteenth Earl of Derby (formerly Lord Stanley), R. A. Cross (who, like Derby, had been educated at Arnold's Rugby) and Lord John Manners.

When on 18 May 1874 P. A. Taylor moved to open, only Beresford Hope, member for Cambridge University, a wealthy Tractarian who built and endowed All Saints, Margaret Street, claimed that the party as a whole was against him. When Taylor tried again in 1877, however, W. H. Smith opposed him 'both in his capacity as a Member of the House representing a very large constituency, and to some extent as a member of the Government'.[34]

The Lords debated the issue for the first time in 1878, when Lord Thurlow's motion to open was defeated by Cairns, who claimed that the working class constituencies in the large towns were against it, and declared that the government was too. When in 1879 Thurlow came forward again Disraeli (now Earl of Beaconsfield) ensured his defeat, believing that 'this proposed change is viewed with suspicion by the working classes'.[35]

In 1874 Taylor's speech had been inordinately long, for he tried to appeal to all sections of the House. He spoke of the Liberal ideal of individual freedom, and of the Nonconformist belief in toleration. He tried to allay fears that opening would lead to the 'Continental Sunday', arguing that it would not produce general labour but would place museums in competition with public houses. He hoped that the Tory party's dislike of Puritanism would lead it to support him.[36]

Members who replied made no attempt to deal with his actual arguments. Their speeches showed how well they had learned the slogans of the 1850's and how they were influenced by the struggle taking place outside the House. W. S. Allen countered

Taylor with a motion to open on weekday evenings. He scorned the openers—'foreigners, secularists and Republicans ... disciples of Mr Bradlaugh and Mr Holyoake ... the eccentricities and peculiarities of every Church in the three Kingdoms'. He attacked Baxter Langley, decried the N.S.L. and praised the W.M.L.D.R.A., claiming that it, the respectable Churches and the Sunday school teachers, knew that the working classes were against opening. Allen stirred the House by suggesting that on this issue the workers had no confidence in the Liberals and looked to the Tories.[37]

In 1877 Taylor referred to the precedent set by the Birmingham Free Library and Museum, and Alexander McArthur expounded the social Sabbatarian case in reply, but the greatest effect was made by Colonel F. M. Beresford, son of a rector of St Andrew's, Holborn, a staunch Tory. He told the House that the National Sunday League 'had amongst its supporters Bradlaugh, Truelove, Besant and others who were more or less implicated in the dissemination of indecent publications'.[38]

The number of signatures to petitions against opening had fallen from 629,000 in 1856 to 150,000 (over the Edinburgh Botanical Gardens) in 1863 to less than 100,000 in 1877. In 1874 and 1877 only seven members spoke on each occasion, and they were largely the same ones. But despite this apparent decline in Sabbatarian strength the links which they had established with the Tory party, at the level of men and of ideas, ensured that Parliament remained soundly, if less and less enthusiastically, against opening. In 1874 Taylor was defeated by 271 to 68, and in 1877 by 229 to 87.

Notes

[1] PP., 1864, XXII, *Children's Employment Commission, Second Rept.*, xii, xiii, 13; PP., 1865, XX, *ibid., Fourth Rept.*, 202, 206, 207; PP., 1866, XXIV, *ibid., Fifth Rept.*, xvi.

[2] PP., 1867, III, *A Bill for the Extension of the Factory Acts*, para. 7, sect. 1; PP., 1867, *Rept. S.C. of H.C. on a Bill, &c.*

[3] 3H, vol. 199, col. 834 (22 February 1870).

[4] L.D.O.S., *Minute Book V*, 27 January 1870, 23 February 1871.

[5] 3H, vol. 188, col. 99 (19 June 1867).

⁶ J. Baxter Langley, *Sunday Evenings for the People* (1867), *The Churches of the Past, Present and Future* (1867); P. Skottowe, *op. cit.*, 20.

⁷ B. and P. Russell (eds.), *The Amberley Papers* (1937), II, 21; J. Dover Wilson (ed.), *Matthew Arnold's 'Culture and Anarchy'* (Cambridge, 1969), 3, 213.

⁸ W. H. Domville, *A Report to a Preliminary Meeting, &c.* (1869), 13.

⁹ P. F. Skottowe, *op. cit.*, 19.

¹⁰ Sunday Society, *Report of the First Annual General Meeting* (1876).

¹¹ Annie Besant, *Autobiography* (1893), 249; D.Sommer, *Haldane of Cloane. His Life and Times, 1856–1928* (1960), 56.

¹² L. Huxley, *Life and Letters of T. H. Huxley* (1903), II, 344.

¹³ 3H, vol. 194, col. 560 (3 March 1869); vol. 208, col. 257 (25 July 1871).

¹⁴ L.D.O.S., *Minute Book V*, 30 March and 3 May 1871.

¹⁵ Edwin Hodder, *Samuel Morley* (1887), 420.

¹⁶ *The Freeman*, 9 May 1860, 5 April 1867; *The Watchman*, 23 May 1866; *The Primitive Methodist*, 27 July 1871.

¹⁷ *The Watchman*, 27 July 1871; *Congregational Yearbook* (1874), 54–61.

¹⁸ *The Sunday Magazine*, Pt. I, No. 1 (October 1864); PP., 1867–68, XIV, *S.C. of H.C. Sale of Liquor on Sundays Bill*, 113, 121; L.D.O.S., *Minute Book V*, 30 January, 27 February, 20 March 1868.

¹⁹ J. F. C. Harrison, *A History of the Working Men's College* (1954), 74–8, 112; J. M. Ludlow and Lloyd Jones, *Progress of the Working Classes* (1867), 249; F. Maurice, *Maurice, op. cit.* I, 319; John Munroe (ed.), *Frederick James Furnival* (1911), xii, lxxix.

²⁰ Thomas Cooper, *Thoughts at Fourscore* (1885), v; *Unitarian Herald*, 23 May 1879; *Church Times*, 9 May 1879.

²¹ W.M.L.D.R.A., *Minute Book II*, 12 August 1858.

²² H. B. Bradlaugh and J. M. Robertson, *Charles Bradlaugh, op. cit.*, I, 284; Josephine E. Butler, *Reminiscences* (1898), 25.

²³ W.M.L.D.R.A., *Minute Book II*, 11 February 1874.

²⁴ *Ibid.*, 17 December 1868.

²⁵ B. and P. Russell, *op. cit.*, II, 123–66; *East London Observer*, 31 January 1874; *Leicester Daily Mercury*, 2 February 1874.

²⁶ Sunday Society, *The Sunday Review*, July 1879, 215.

²⁷ J. Collings and Sir J. B. Lee, *Jesse Collings* (1920), 94; *Birmingham Daily Post*, 2 November 1872.

²⁸ R. W. Dale, *The Ten Commandments* (1871), 88–119, *The Town Council and the Sunday Lectures* (1881); J. A. Langford, *The Birmingham Sunday Lectures* (1881).

²⁹ *Nottingham Daily Guardian*, 4 March 1879, 3 March 1880; *Nottingham Journal*, 7 June 1880.

³⁰ 3H, vol. 195, col. 799 (14 April 1869).

³¹ W.M.L.D.R.A., *Minute Book II*, 11 February 1874.

³² Lord Blake, *Disraeli, op. cit.*, 544.

³³ *Ibid.*, 514; *Dictionary of National Biography*.

³⁴ 3H, vol. 219, col. 526 (19 May 1874); vol. 234, col. 1531 (8 June 1877).

³⁵ 3H, vol. 239, col. 882 (2 April 1878); vol. 245, col. 926 (5 May 1879).

³⁶ 3H, vol. 219, col. 526 (19 May 1874).

³⁷ *Ibid.*

³⁸ 3H, vol. 234, col. 1531 (8 June 1877).

chapter ten

FALSE DAWN
1882–96

I   *Henry Broadhurst*

In 1880 the electoral pendulum swung again, the Tories lost
the general election and Gladstone returned to power as Liberal
Prime Minister. His childhood was spent in an Evangelical home
and he was a strong Sabbatarian whilst a boy at Eton. Indeed,
he held typical Sabbatarian attitudes, in 1830 writing of Paris,
'The city was indeed a painful sight: in England matters are bad
enough, but by no means so far gone . . . I believe there is no
more exact criterion of the moral advancement of a people, than
the sanctity which they accord to the Christian Sabbath'. He
occasionally voted for Agnew, but spoke for Fleetwood's Bill
because it was more moderate than Agnew's. In 1840 he voted
against Hume's motion for opening and in 1844 obviously acted
on Sabbatarian grounds.[1]

In 1845 he feared to make a rapid visit to Strasbourg, 'which
must . . . be a mere sight, and so more like a spectacle than a
Sunday employment', but in subsequent years moderated his
views. He wrote letters on Sundays, and the manuscript of his
Vatican Decrees was dispatched from Hawarden on a Sunday
night. His theological approach to Sunday was not, as he
admitted, quite clear, but he thought that the substance of the
social Sabbatarian argument had influenced M.P.'s.[2]

Gladstone spoke on the Sunday question in the House on very
few occasions, no doubt recognising its vexatious potential. In
1871 he cautiously supported Charles Reed's motion to
investigate Sunday labour in the Post Office, explaining that he
was sympathetic to Sunday observance motions but did not
always support them, not being prepared to argue 'very strongly'

that all laws should conform to religious principles, yet agreeing with the need for the civil observance of a day's rest.[3]

Thus when in February 1881 Lord Dunraven moved to open, Lord Granville, the Foreign Secretary, said that the government would do nothing until it was certain that the country was in favour of change, but as an individual spoke and voted for opening. Selborne, Lord Chancellor again, remained silent but voted with the closers. Dunraven was defeated.[4]

In 1882 there was a new departure. When in February George Howard, himself a Liberal, moved to open he was opposed by A. J. Mundella, vice-president of the Committee of the Privy Council for Education, and member for Nottingham, which he instanced as a town whose working classes had recently voted for pro-closing candidates in local elections. Mundella did not make it clear whether he spoke for himself or the government, but the Liberal whips were used as tellers for the closers and Howard was defeated by 207 to 88. However, three members of the government—Bright, Dilke and Fawcett—voted with the openers, as did the leaders of the temperance interest, W. S. Caine, a Liverpool cotton broker, and Sir Wilfrid Lawson, an independent gentleman. Indeed, they had both spoken for opening, putting the Radical argument that if people had the opportunity to visit museums on Sundays they would be a little less likely to visit public houses.[5]

More remarkable than this split in the Liberal ranks was the fact that Thomas Burt had seconded Howard and that Henry Broadhurst had opposed him. Broadhurst was a Wesleyan who loved a cigar and carried a spirit flask. He had replaced George Howell as secretary of the Political Committee of the T.U.C. in 1875 and entered Parliament in 1880 as a Lib–Lab. After MacDonald's death in 1881 Burt and Broadhurst were the only two working class members in the House.[6]

Broadhurst was clearly a social Sabbatarian. J. G. Talbot was quick to congratulate him on 'an impressive . . . a touching speech'. Jesse Collings denounced him: Broadhurst 'stated that "labour should accommodate itself to the traditions of the country." He [Collings] did not wonder that that should have been cheered from the opposite side of the House, because a more Conservative and a more caste-retaining principle the strongest advocate of the difference between classes could not have advanced.'[7]

II   *Renewal*

Broadhurst seemed to confirm everything the Sabbatarians and social Sabbatarians had been saying about the working class since the 1850's. The W.M.L.D.R.A. immediately appealed to Samuel Morley and George Williams, a fellow Congregationalist (who was treasurer of the London Young Men's Christian Association, and in 1886 succeeded Shaftesbury as its president), for donations to carry out a postal survey of the officers of working class organisations such as trade unions and friendly societies, in order to demonstrate that the working class agreed with Broadhurst. The Sunday Society claimed that Broadhurst's views were unrepresentative, founded its own London Workmen's Sunday Committee, and in 1885 carried the battle to the annual conference of the T.U.C.[8]

The W.M.L.D.R.A. had found an effective new source of propaganda, benefited from a rapid increase in membership and enjoyed a period of prosperity lasting for some twenty years, expanding its magazine *The Pearl of Days*. In 1884 the L.D.O.S. felt confident enough to call a national conference, and as a result two new societies were founded later in the year.

Evangelical clergymen and enthusiasts from north London set up the Anti-Sunday Travelling Union, which in 1901 was to change its name to the Union Against Sunday Travelling. The Rev. W. L. Tweedie and Mr J. F. Wilson, a religious-book seller, already the honorary secretary of the Hastings and St Leonards L.D.O.S., established the Shareholders' Union for Reducing Sunday Labour on Railways.

Neither society was either strong or influential. The former had about 200 members, but they were very largely residents of London and near-by towns, and approximately two-thirds of them were women, who provided a readership for its magazine *Our Heritage*. The latter society consisted in reality of Tweedie and Wilson, who placed advertisements in religious newspapers in order to gather proxy votes and agitate the issue of Sunday trains at the railway companies' shareholders meetings.

The renewal extended to the provinces. The Dover L.D.O.S. waged a long campaign against the South Eastern Railway's cheap Sunday excursions. In Newcastle upon Tyne the Sunday school teachers set up an auxiliary and raised petitions against Sunday trams. In 1885 Sabbatarians in Bristol, led by James Inskip, father of Thomas Inskip, Lord Chancellor Caldecote, who was to support the L.D.O.S. in the 1920's and 1930's, fought to suppress Sunday bands.[9]

III   *The political Sunday*

Despite this renewal the most advanced elements in the Churches tried to win the working classes by relaxing their own Sunday manners. In 1883 the Working Men's College co-operated with the N.S.L. and set up a Sunday Evening Association to provide some cosy cultural relaxation for working men. Canon Barnett, in many ways Maurice's heir, criticised Sabbatarianism, organised Sunday concerts and lectures in the East End Settlements, and in 1895 became president of the Sunday Society.[10]

The Tractarians' more flamboyant successors, the Ritualists, had adopted anti-Sabbatarianism. Stanton, of St Alban's Holborn, lectured on Sundays to republican clubs in Bethnal Green, Dolling of Landport gave Sunday lectures to working men. Conrad Noel, a renegade member of the Sabbatarian family, was arrested and tried (and defended by Mrs Pankhurst's husband) after giving an open-air Sunday lecture.[11]

During the 1880's the Nonconformists developed the Pleasant Sunday Afternoon movement, whose very name was an oblique comment upon the existing Sunday and whose institution and progress were viewed with alarm by Sabbatarians. In 1888 Evangelical Sabbatarians in Bolton described P.S.A.'s, as they were known to their progenitors, as 'direct agents of secularization'.[12]

Within the Churches these men were leaders. The L.D.O.S. spurred the Bishop of London, Jackson, to reprimand Barnett for mounting his Whitechapel Sunday Art Exhibition in 1881, and in 1893 his Sunday morning lectures on history and science raised angry protests. Organisers of P.S.A.'s tried to explain away suspicions that 'The adjective "pleasant" by which these meetings are described ... [indicates] that the movement is merely another attempt to provide Sunday amusement for the working classes'. One minister was forced to resign when his congregation objected to the 'popular' format of his Sunday evening services.[13]

Outside the Churches they were followers. Barnett did not bring political discussions into his Sunday programme until it was absolutely necessary to do so in order to attract working men. Silvester Horne, a Congregational minister, later a Liberal M.P., who ran one of the most successful 'political' P.S.A.'s, hoped to counter Keir Hardie's attempt to 'sour the workmen'.[14] In 1891 John Trevor, a Unitarian minister in Manchester, founded the Labour Church, to make religion acceptable to the workers by challenging the connection between Nonconformists and the Liberal party.

They were in competition with the Labour pioneers. John Burns, who had abandoned a youthful Congregationalism, joined the N.S.L. and been influenced by Hyndman, led the unemployment demonstrations of 1886 and 1887 on Sundays. The stalwarts of the Independent Labour Party rejected the religion of their youth and used Sundays to spread their Socialist ideas. Hardie, a former member of the Evangelical Union Church; Snowden, a lapsed Wesleyan; Lansbury, a sometime Anglican; and Crooks, an ex-Congregationalist, graced street corners on Sunday mornings. Robert Blatchford, the Labour propagandist, wrote his first leading article as a defence of Sunday papers; and Lansbury learned his youthful militancy from *Reynolds' Newspaper*, taken by an otherwise strictly Sabbatarian grandmother.

IV   *Sabbatarian isolation*

Unfortunately for the Sabbatarians, the renewal of the early 1880's could not restrain the operation of the long-term forces that were isolating them from the intellectual, political and religious leaders of England.

The Sabbatarians were losing their influence over the politicians. Dilke, who in 1875 had spoken for a more drastic

limitation of the 1780 Act, commonly spent Sunday in the
Grosvenor Gallery or on the Thames. Rosebery, who in 1881
had spoken for opening, thought nothing of hiring a special
Sunday train for his guests. Curzon, who in 1896 was to vote for
opening, enjoyed Sunday parties.[15]

Edward, Prince of Wales, was the leader of society. He
admitted that he was broadminded on the Sunday question, but
behaved with discretion. When he travelled abroad he accepted
Arthur Stanley's advice to behave as foreigners expected an
Englishman would, and so abstained from Sunday shooting. At
Sandringham he provided the traditional Sunday luncheon of
roast beef and Yorkshire pudding and made a social ritual of
touring the estate in the afternoon. After dinner his guests played
party games, but abstained from bowls before the stroke of
midnight, 'it being considered an unseemly game for the
Sabbath'. During the 1880's, however, his passion for cards
became such that he played on Sundays as on other days,
ignoring Sabbatarian predictions of the certainty of Divine
retribution.[16]

Edward's adoption of the Saturday-to-Monday did much to
spread it, and the implication that the whole weekend was a
holiday, among the upper class, with the result that their Sunday
behaviour grew more and more casual. Similarly, as the
professions began to give up Saturday morning work they did
not reserve Sunday for religion as the Sabbatarians hoped but
followed the example of their social superiors.[17]

Some Nonconformists relaxed their Sunday manners. When
on holiday in the Alps Newman Hall went for Sunday walks,
arguing that he was unlikely to lead anyone into sin in such
remote spots, and spent a sociable Sunday afternoon with
Tyndall in the latter's chalet. The L.D.O.S. reacted to
relaxation by criticising some of the most renowned
Nonconformist leaders. It objected to Spurgeon's sermons being
telegraphed to Cincinatti on Sunday mornings, to Parker's
having religious magazines on sale at the City Temple on
Sundays, to the institution of P.S.A.'s at the Westminster
Chapel, and to Sunday temperance parades. In 1892 its *Quarterly
Paper* proclaimed that 'the bands of the Salvation Army have
done untold harm'. Such attitudes gained the L.D.O.S. a

reputation for extremism and also forfeited the sympathy of the Nonconformist leaders.[18]

The Sabbatarians could not rely on the bishops. In 1881 Tait, the Archbishop of Canterbury, had told the House of Lords that opening was a 'somewhat difficult and embarrassing question'. Those bishops who were strongly Sabbatarian—Ryle of Liverpool, Moule of Durham, Perowne of Worcester, Robert Bickersteth of Ripon, and Edward H. Bickersteth (Edward's son) of Exeter—knew that they were in a minority in the Church. Bickersteth of Ripon had chaired the L.D.O.S.'s A.G.M. in 1875 and Bickersteth of Exeter and Moule were vice-presidents of the W.M.L.D.R.A. and the Anti-Sunday Travelling Union, but as a whole the Sabbatarian bishops gave very little active help to the Sabbatarian and social Sabbatarian societies.[19]

V   *The House of Lords*

After Broadhurst's speech had made such an impact in the Commons the Free Sunday Societies concentrated on the Lords. In May 1883 Dunraven moved to open in an eloquent, if long and very detailed, speech whose arguments echoed Taylor's earlier efforts in the Commons. Shaftesbury and Cairns, who moved an amendment which requested opening on three weekday evenings in each week, put the Sabbatarian case and defeated him by 91 to 67.[20]

In March 1885 Thurlow surprised the Lords by announcing that the Trustees of the British Museum had themselves voted for Sunday afternoon opening. Shaftesbury, who was to have moved a weekday evening amendment, was too ill to attend, and Cairns, who was to follow him to his grave before the end of the year, made a dull speech full of facts and figues provided by the W.M.L.D.R.A., so did not impress the House. The vote was a tie, with 64 for the closers and 64 for the openers. In accordance with the custom of the House, Selborne, who was again Lord Chancellor, had the casting vote and gave it to the closers.[21]

After the demise of Shaftesbury and Cairns the third Earl of Harrowby led the closers and in March 1886 tried to pre-empt the issue by moving for weekday evening opening, but the government refused to commit itself. Later in the month Thurlow came forward again. Harrowby opposed him, claiming to speak for Lord Salisbury, the leader of the Tory opposition, who had previously voted with the closers, but was now on holiday in Italy. Unfortunately for the Sabbatarians Harrowby drifted into a wrangle with Granville, now Colonial Secretary, who gave his private opinion for opening in strong terms. The House followed his example and the openers triumphed by 78 to 62.[22]

The Sabbatarians represented an older generation. Shaftesbury (1801–85) and Cairns (1819–85) had absorbed their ideas in the era of Sabbatarian revival. Their speeches made it clear that they regarded themselves as defending traditional religious ideas and practices against the onslaught of modernity. While they lived their authority protected the Sabbatarian cause, but after their death Sabbatarian ideas were shown to have lost the appeal they had had for the Tory peers and, moreover, for the Lords in general.

In March 1886 Lord Stanley of Alderley, a Whig, who had left the openers and become a closer, told the House that Thurlow (who had suggested that continued closure enabled the rich to enjoy their own works of art but deprived the people of those owned by the nation) 'had caught from Mr. Arch and Mr. Chamberlain, by dining with them, their clap-trap about the wealthy classes'. The House, however, had voted for opening at the end of that very debate.[23]

New men and new ideas were certainly gaining ground. Early in 1886 Gladstone had appointed Thurlow Paymaster General and in August Salisbury had appointed Dunraven Colonial Secretary for the second time (the first being in the short-lived Tory government of 1885). Both were clearly 'new men'. Thurlow (1838–1916) wrote on social issues, publishing *Trades Unions Abroad*, and became chairman of the Salt Union, the best known of the late Victorian industrial combines. After Christ Church and the Guards Dunraven (1841–1926) became war correspondent for the *Daily Telegraph* and after resigning from Salisbury's government in 1887 devoted his fortune to ocean racing.

VI *The House of Commons*

The Liberal government did not consider itself bound by the Lords, and so the issue devolved once more upon the Commons, but did not arise there until 1891, when the Tories were in power again, albeit calling themselves Unionists. On this occasion the opening motion was put by H. L. W. Lawson, a Liberal Unionist, member for St Pancras West. Speeches by openers and closers alike centred not upon the merits or demerits of Sabbatarianism and social Sabbatarianism, but upon the opinions of public men both dead and alive, the precedent set by many northern towns, and the state of public opinion in London. Lawson had a majority of four to two among the back-benchers who spoke and looked forward to victory.[24]

During the previous decade the balance of power in the constituencies had shifted against the Sabbatarians. By the 1880 general election the W.M.L.D.R.A. had ceased to interfere in particular seats and contented itself with deluging the country with leaflets. In 1886 the L.D.O.S. decided to take no part at all, seeing that the Irish question would dominate the mind of the electorate.[25]

Whilst the Sabbatarians had relaxed their efforts, the anti-Sabbatarians had entered the electoral arena. In 1880 the Sunday Society took part in the election in order to challenge Disraeli's assumptions about the working classes, and in 1885 accepted Collings's advice to persuade candidates that Henry Broadhurst did not reflect their opinions.[26]

There were signs of a change in the balance of opinion in the Tory party in the country. In 1874 Taylor had pointed out that the party's newpapers had begun to support opening, and in 1886 Thurlow was able to show that the *Morning Post*, the *Daily Telegraph* and *The Times* backed him.[27]

A powerful impetus for change came from the Liberal Unionists who in 1886 had deserted Gladstone over his Irish policy. The majority of the Whigs favoured opening, the old-guard Radicals like Bright did so, and the newer generation like Collings and Chamberlain regarded it as a matter of social equity. The Tory party was also undergoing other subtle changes of composition, becoming not only more nearly conservative but more cultured as well.

A brief description of the leading openers in the Commons illustrates this. P. A. Taylor (1818–91) was a silk mercer, a supporter of Mazzini, and an advocate of the purest of *laissez-faire* principles. He resigned the representation of Leicester in 1884 and transferred his political sympathies to the Unionists in 1886. George Howard (1843–1911) was a skilled water-colourist and a trustee of the National Gallery. He entered the House as a Liberal in 1879 but became a Unionist in 1886, and succeeded to the earldom of Carlisle in 1889. H. L. W. Lawson (1862–1933), whose father had taken the *Daily Telegraph* over from Gladstone to Disraeli in 1879, entered the House as a Liberal in 1880, but subsequently drifted across to the Unionists.[28]

In 1891, unfortunately for Lawson, the Leader of the House, and leader of the Unionist front bench there, was W. H. Smith, nicknamed by *Punch* 'Old Morality'. Towards the end of the debate he rose to his feet and declared that he personally, and the government officially, were against opening. Thus Lawson was defeated by 166 to 36.[29]

VI   *Sabbatarian defeat*

Nevertheless events were moving against the Sabbatarians. W. H. Smith died later in 1891. During the general election of 1892 the W.M.L.D.R.A. failed to make the Sunday question an issue against Lawson at Gloucester. When Gladstone formed his last government after winning the election it included only two Sabbatarians, Henry Broadhurst and H. H. Fowler (later Lord Wolverhampton) the first solicitor and the first Wesleyan to enter the Cabinet. After offering him the Presidency of the Local Government Board and sending him to the queen to kiss hands, Gladstone commented wryly, 'Fowler gone to Windsor this evening, and . . . for once a Wesleyan Methodist will have to make his way back to town on a Sunday.'[30]

The anti-Sabbatarians now proceeded with some skill, in 1892 gaining the help of Davidson, now Bishop of Rochester. He had been appointed a trustee of the British Museum in 1884 and had then persuaded his fellow trustees to support opening, giving Thurlow his chance to surprise the Lords in 1885. In May 1892

Davidson presented to the Convocation of Canterbury a petition from the Sunday Society and secured a Committee on Sunday Observance under his own chairmanship. It reported in 1893, pointing out that the Lords had voted for opening in 1886, the T.U.C. in 1887 and the L.C.C. in 1889. However, most bishops opposed opening and the matter was shelved until 1894, when Davidson spoke in the most moderate tones. Frederick Temple opposed opening and E. H. Bickersteth sprang to the attack, predicting that if the Established Church condoned it working men would transfer their sympathy to the Nonconformists. Despite his eloquence the upper and the lower Houses followed Davidson, and two years later their example was referred to in the House of Commons.[31]

The Sabbatarians then made a tactical blunder. The Committee of the L.D.O.S. overruled John Gritton, who resigned, and late in 1894 used the 1780 Act to prosecute the Leeds Sunday Lecture Society. When the society was found guilty the Sunday Society formed a National Association of Sunday Societies in order to defend the Free Sunday Societies from similar actions. Although the verdict was actually reversed in the Court of Appeal, in 1895 Lord Hobhouse, president of the Sunday Lecture Society, introduced a Sunday Bill into the House of Lords, to try to prevent such prosecutions in the future.[32]

It was similar to Lord Amberley's Bill, limiting the scope of the 1780 Act by legalising payment for admission to educational and non-profit making Sunday lectures. It passed its first reading without debate but at the second on 25 March, Lord Cross (formerly R. A. Cross) suggested that its progress should be adjourned until a select committee had reported on the 1780 Act. Hobhouse accepted the suggestion.[33]

This committee gave the Peers their first chance to examine the officers of the Sabbatarian and anti-Sabbatarian societies. Neither Charles Hill of the W.M.L.D.R.A. nor Frederick Peake, the L.D.O.S.'s new secretary, made a good impression, rather letting down their side. Hobhouse later claimed that he had persuaded Charles Hill to support his Bill.[34]

During the general election of 1895 the Sabbatarians managed to influence only one seat, Shipley in Yorkshire, where the Tory candidate, J. Fortescue Flannery, enlisted the help of the L.D.O.S. and the W.M.L.D.R.A. in a successful attempt to defeat W. P. Byles, the sitting Liberal, member of a devout Congregational family which owned the *Bradford Observer*. A more typical result was obtained in London where the N.S.L. had made a major effort and impressed its views upon many of the predominantly Unionist members who were returned.[35]

Lord Salisbury gave Liberal Unionists places in his government. The Duke of Devonshire, G. J. Goschen, Joseph Chamberlain and Jesse Collings were all openers. All except Collings sat in the Cabinet, where they outweighed Lord Halsbury (formerly Sir Hardinge Giffard), and all except Devonshire, who was a member of the House of Lords, were prepared to vote for opening.

On 10 March 1896 Mr Massey-Mainwaring, a wealthy lawyer and art collector, the newly elected Tory Unionist member for Finsbury Central, moved to open the national museums and galleries on Sunday afternoons, care being taken that no attendant worked for more than six years per week and that conscientious objections were respected. On this occasion the atmosphere in the House was completely changed. Six other metropolitan members supported him, including John Burns, who implied that the working classes favoured opening, and Sir John Lubbock, who spoke for the trustees of the British Museum. Two Scottish members were with him too.[36]

Sir Mark Stewart, a Scottish Tory, the L.D.O.S.'s man, moved an amendment for week-night opening but was supported only by two crusty colonels, Messrs Sandys and Wardle, and by Lord Warkworth, whose maiden speech echoed their Sabbatarian effusions. Stewart had appealed for help to both front benches, but Sir William Harcourt, who led the Liberals in the Commons, had no sympathy for the Sabbatarians.[37]

The only member of the government to speak was G. J. Goschen, the First Lord of the Admiralty, who supported opening in, as he said, a purely private capacity. In effect the government allowed a free vote, nine of its members voting with the openers and eleven with the closers. The openers won by 178 to 93 and the result was received with cheers by an excited House. An analysis of the division shows that the openers included seventy-two Liberals, sixty-four Tory Unionists, twenty-two Liberal Unionists and twenty Irish Nationalists; whilst the closers consisted of seventy-two Tory Unionists, twelve Liberals and one Liberal Unionist.[38]

The Sabbatarians were beaten on their chosen ground. Neither the Churches nor the denominational newspapers supported their protests, and the government quickly arranged to open the British Museum, the National Gallery and Portrait Gallery, the South Kensington museums and the Bethnal Green Museum on Sunday afternoons.

Notes

[1] S. G. Checkland, *The Gladstones* (Cambridge, 1971), 85–6, 210; M. R. D. Foot (ed.), *The Gladstone Diaries* (Oxford, 1968), I, 420, II, 108.

[2] A. Tilney Bassett (ed.), *Gladstone to his Wife* (1936), 57, 62, 205; W. E. Gladstone, *Later Gleanings XI* (1897), 338–51.

[3] 3H, vol. 205, col. 209 (18 April 1871).

[4] 3H, vol. 258, col. 1478 (22 February 1881).

[5] 3H, vol. 268, col. 1148 (19 May 1882).

[6] *Ibid.*

[7] *Ibid.*

[8] Sunday Society, *Sunday Review*, October 1885, p. 37.

[9] *Dover Year Book and Calendar* (1866–89), *passim*; Newcastle upon Tyne Branch of the L.D.O.S., *Annual Report* (Newcastle on Tyne, 1881), *passim*; James Inskip, *The Sunday Band, &c.* (Bristol, 1885).

[10] Henrietta O. Barnett, *Canon Barnett* (1918), I, 96.

[11] Joseph Clayton, *Father Stanton* (1913), 28; *id.*, *Father Dolling* (1902), 36; Conrad Noel, *Autobiography* (ed. Sidney Dark, 1945), 49.

[12] *Bolton Chronicle*, 3 November 1888.

[13] Henrietta O. Barnett, *op. cit.*, I, 151, 337; A. H. Byles, *The Pleasant Sunday Afternoon* (1891), 5; J. W. Dixon, *Pledged to the People* (1896), 12.

[14] W. B. Selbie (ed.), *Charles Silvester Horne* (1920), 191.

[15] Roy Jenkins, *Sir Charles Dilke* (1969 ed.), *passim*; Kenneth Rose, *Curzon* (1969), *passim*.

[16] A. V. Baillie and H. Bolitho, *Arthur Stanley* (1930), 279; Christopher Hibbert, *Edward VII* (1976), 93; Kenneth Rose, *op. cit.*, 189.

[17] *Ibid.*, *passim*.

[18] C. Newman Hall, *Autobiography* (1898), 133, 138; L.D.O.S., *Quarterly Paper*, No. 121, p. 395 (November 1892).

[19] 3H, vol. 258, col. 264 (22 February 1881).

[20] 3H, vol. 278, col. 155 (8 May 1883).

[21] 3H, vol. 296, col. 825 (20 March 1885).

[22] 3H, vol. 303, col. 608 (12 March 1886), col. 1342 (19 March 1886).

[23] *Ibid.*, col. 1358 (19 March 1886).

[24] 3H, vol., 351, col. 1596 (20 March 1891).

[25] W.M.L.D.R.A., *Minute Book III*, June 1880.

[26] Sunday Society, *Sunday Review*, October 1885, p. 37.

[27] 3H, vol. 303, col. 1342 (19 March 1886).

[28] *Dictionary of National Biography*.

[29] 3H, vol. 351, col. 1596 (20 March 1891).

[30] A. Tilney Bassett, *op. cit.*, 258.

[31] *Acts and Proceedings of the Convocation of Canterbury*, 1892, 3, 4; G. K. A. Bell, *Randall Davidson, op. cit.*, II, 221.

[32] 4H, vol. 31, col. 342 (4 March 1895).

[33] 4H, vol. 31, col. 1523 (21 March 1895).

[34] PP., 1895, VI, *First Rept. S.C. of H.L. Lord's Day Act, passim*.

[35] L.D.O.S., *Minute Book VIII*, 25 October, 22 November 1894; W.M.L.D.R.A., *Minute Book V*, July 1895; *Shipley Times*, 20 July 1895.

[36] 4H, vol. 38, col, 617 (10 March 1896).

[37] *Ibid*.

[38] *Ibid*.

chapter eleven
THE SOCIAL GOSPEL
1896–1914

I   *Reformation*

After 1857 the Sabbatarians and social Sabbatarians had
made no additions to their stock of ideas and slogans, during the
1880's had ceased to excite the constituencies, and by the 1890's
had lost their hold on M.P.'s. The anti-Sabbatarians had also
lost much of their impetus, with the decline of high-minded
working class secularism and the concern of advanced
theologians with other problems.

During the 1860's the Churches' leaders had lost much of their
confidence in Fundamentalism. Not until the publication of the
Revised New Testament in 1881 did the bishops recover their
balance. Not until Darwin was buried in Westminster Abbey in
1882 and Frederick Temple published *The Relation between
Religion and Science* in 1884 did they exorcise the ghost of
evolution. Not until 1887 when Robertson Nichol issued *The
Expositor* and 1888 when Robert Forman Horton (both
Nonconformists) produced his *Inspiration and the Bible* was the
reliability of holy writ discussed in public.

Religious leaders had recovered their confidence, but in what?
Frederick Temple, who had been tutored by Davidson at Balliol,
had contributed to *Essays and Reviews* whilst head of Rugby
School, but in 1869 had received the bishopric of Exeter. By 1879
he no longer believed in the verbal inspiration of the Bible, but
was translated to London in 1885 and to Canterbury in 1897. He
was a leading advocate of the Social Gospel, as was his son
William, who eventually followed in his footsteps at Canterbury.
They found it a comfortable alternative to their theological
doubts. The Social Gospel and what may be called religious

liberalism often went hand in hand.

The Social Gospel, in the sense of maintaining that the working class's problems could be solved by the sensible application of the Ten Commandments and the Sermon on the Mount, and that the Churches had a special duty to mediate their teaching to the working class, had its origin in the 1850's with Maurice and his followers but did not grow until the 1880's. The Churches were shocked in 1883 by *The Bitter Cry of Outcast London*, frightened in 1886 and 1887 by the Socialist demonstrations and alarmed in 1888 when Mrs Besant led Bryant & May's match girls out on strike.

The Churches reacted quickly. Canon Barnett had opened Toynbee Hall in 1885. In June 1889 Canon Scott Holland of St Paul's founded the Christian Social Union, just in time for the dock strike which began in August, and in November contributed to *Lux Mundi*, the late-century equivalent of *Essays and Reviews*. In 1890 William Booth published *In Darkest England*, and within a few years the progressive leaders of almost every denomination had dedicated themselves to the Social Gospel.

Broadhurst's speech was a minor feature of this movement. During 1887 the Lambeth Conference set up a Committee on Sunday Observance and in 1888 Temple called a chapter meeting to discuss the subject. He presented a Dominical theology derived from Whately and Arnold, infused with a social concern emanating from Maurice. He deplored a current tendency towards Sunday amusement and recreation: 'There was a serious danger of the day being seized by the pleasure-lovers; and the money-lovers were sure to follow. Competition was tending to grow keener, and was only checked by the feeling that the day belonged to God. If this were removed there would be no check sufficient to keep from Sunday from being used by the employer of labour'.[1]

Manning, who sat with Temple on a committee to settle the dock strike, changed his mind about Sunday recreation, telling Broadhurst that Sunday was 'God's great gift to working men'. In 1890 the Catholic *Universe* followed Manning's example of condeming Sunday demonstrations, and in 1891 his influence ensured that the social value of keeping the Sabbath holy was mentioned in the papal encyclical *Rerum Novarum*. Whether or not these attitudes would make any contribution to solving the problem of Sunday labour remains to be seen.[2]

II   *Sunday labour: the Sabbatarians*

As far back as 1838 the London & Birmingham Railway had, as we have seen, refused Joseph Sturge's request to close its lines on Sundays, but it had resolved to limit its Sunday services to those of 'public necessity'. This left its employees who did work on Sundays in a difficult position: in 1846 its clerks complained that they were required to perform Sunday duty without extra pay.[3]

The Sabbatarian solution of the 1850's—no trains, no labour—had seemed a simple one, but pressure on the companies and on Parliament had failed. Trollope's Archdeacon Grantly had told the Sabbatarian Mr Slope, 'if you can withdraw the passengers, the company will withdraw the trains', but no amount of propaganda could persuade all Englishmen that it was a sin to travel by train on Sundays.[4]

During the 1860's the social Sabbatarians convinced *Herapath's Journal* of their case, and the London & North Western (of which the London & Birmingham was now part) set up a special committee to further reduce its own Sunday labour. In 1869 the Midland Railway's building contracts for St Pancras Station provided 'that no work shall be undertaken on Sundays' but continued, 'unless the Company's Engineer shall certify that it is absolutely necessary . . . the Company shall have the power to dismiss summarily any man found at work on a Sunday except on such a certificate'.[5]

Sabbatarians were incapable of dealing with Sunday labour on the railways, for their formula of 'acts of mercy and necessity' could obviously justify labour. This was a direct result of the Sabbatarians' being primarily concerned with sin rather than with social problems.

Readers of Mark Rutherford (W. H. White's) *The Revolution in Tanner's Lane* will recall how his wife objected to the act of Sunday trading, which was itself a sin, not to the real labour involved, and quietened her conscience by giving a tradesman a 'gift' instead of 'buying' goods on a Sunday. In the 1880's the

L.D.O.S. mounted a campaign against the Sunday use of the new automatic vending machines, regarding such use as sinful, although involving no labour.[6]

Frederick Peake, the L.D.O.S.'s secretary, explained its own attitude when examined before the Lords' select committee in 1895: 'Anything [on Sundays] that is not distinctly religious is wrong . . . We should hardly make it purely a question of "rest". We . . . seek the religious observance of the Lord's day as the primary thing, and the question of human rest . . . as a secondary matter arising out of that.'[7]

When attacking Sunday newspapers in 1899 the *Methodist Times* was to do so not because their production and distribution caused Sunday labour, but because their public sale and their contents tended to demean and secularise the atmosphere of the day, and made no objection to Monday papers because although they caused an enormous amount of Sunday work it was hidden from public view.[8]

III   Sunday labour: social Sabbatarians

In 1860 the W.M.L.D.R.A had decided to concentrate on Sunday railway and postal labour, but found it difficult to contact the Sunday workers themselves. In 1862 the London City Mission produced a Mr Mills who had been a pointsman with the London & North Western until his conversion: 'as he was at work a lady threw a tract out of a window entitled "Where are you going?". He read it and his mind was impressed by it and he did what he could to glorify God.'[9]

Mills provided information for a series of pamphlets, but his approach did not appeal to many railway workers. Thus although between 1866 and 1871 the embryonic railway unions made the demand for Sunday work to be paid at time-and-a-half a major part of their programme, the W.M.L.D.R.A. exercised no influence over them and early in 1872 Baxter Langley helped to found the Amalgamated Society of Railway Servants. In 1875 its executive planned a campaign on Sunday work and pay, and when the W.M.L.D.R.A. learned that Baxter Langley was involved it redoubled its efforts; but to no avail, for he consolidated his hold on the A.S.R.S.[10]

The W.M.L.D.R.A. had begun a Post Office campaign in 1864. In 1867 Thomas Chambers had raised the issue of Sunday postal labour in the Commons and in 1871, backed by 2,183 petitions bearing 200,000 signatures, Charles Reed had secured a select committee. As a result of its report the sixth-sevenths rule was reduced to two-thirds, and various other changes were made, in order to reduce Sunday labour. In 1887 the W.M.L.D.R.A. renewed its efforts and Dr G. B. Clark, the Liberal member for Caithness, secured another select committee. After the publication of its report Sunday postal services were quickly curtailed, again in order to reduce Sunday labour, so that in the following years many M.P.'s complained that the Sunday service was inadequate.

Social Sabbatarian pressure had an important result for the postal workers. Whereas in 1867 some 20,961 of the Post Office's 25,902 employees worked on Sundays, in 1894 only some 41,274 of 136,447 did so. By then, however, the government was far less responsive to the social Sabbatarians, for Charles Reed was dead and Dr Clark had lost his political respectability by virtue of championing the Boer government of the Transvaal.

Indeed, when examined before the select committee of 1887 Charles Hill showed very little knowledge of the working conditions of the men on whose behalf he purported to act, and when before the Lords' committee in 1895 admitted that half the W.M.L.D.R.A.'s members were clergymen or women and that the working classes as a whole were not interested in his work.[11]

In point of fact Broadhurst's speech had hidden the W.M.L.D.R.A.'s failure to establish real contact with the working class, and this had been further obscured from 1886 onwards when the society had accepted a suggestion by Lord Harrowby, then president, that selected trade union leaders be invited to follow him in the office.

IV   *Sunday labour: Lib-Labs*

Broadhurst's speech had revealed a division of opinion about the Sunday question within the T.U.C. He was opposed by Thomas Burt, Charles Freak (leader of the Boot and Shoe Makers), George Skipton (editor of the *Labour Standard* and leader of the London Trades Council) and by Will Thorne, one of the 'new' unionists who organised the unskilled workers.[12]

Broadhurst was supported, however, by William Abraham and Ben Pickard of the Miners, John Hodge of the Steel Smelters (all three of whom accepted invitations to serve as president of the W.M.L.D.R.A.), John Wilson of the Miners and Walter Hudson of the Railway Servants.

They all entered Parliament and may be regarded as the first generation of working class Nonconformists to do so. They had absorbed much of the social Sabbatarian propaganda current since the 1850's and although not expounding its mechanistic economic arguments were convinced that Sunday amusement was as contrary to the word of God and as detrimental to the working class as was Sunday labour itself. They were archetypical Lib-Labs.

William Abraham (1842–1922) was a Calvinistic Methodist by upbringing and supported the Liberals until his union backed the Labour Party in 1906. Ben Pickard (1842–1904), a Wesleyan non-smoker and teetotaller, known to his associates as the 'Iron Man', became first president of the Miners' Federation and between 1885 and 1904 sat in Parliament as a Liberal. John Wilson (1837–1914) was converted in 1868, accepted as a Wesleyan lay preacher in 1870, elected secretary of the Durham Miners in 1875 and entered Parliament as a Liberal in 1889. John Hodge (1855–1937) was a Scottish Presbyterian who set up the British Steel Smelters' Association in 1886, and was elected to Parliament for Labour in 1906, but served under Lloyd George during the first War and opposed his own Association's participation in the General Strike in 1926.

John Hodge sought to limit Sunday work for men in the iron and steel industry by arranging voluntary agreements between the employers and the employees. The problem seemed to be at its most intractable on the railways, where men frequently worked a twenty-four-hour Sunday shift in order to have the next Sunday off. In 1891 a select committee on the hours of railway labour saw a bitter wrangle between the general manager of the Great Eastern and Pickard and Wilson, neither of whom could appreciate how London's workers felt able to enjoy their Sunday rest on excursion trips, so depriving railwaymen of theirs. The committee's draft report recommended that Sunday rest be made more frequent for signalmen, and the report itself cited a Swiss Act of 1890 which gave each railway worker fifty-two holidays in each year, at least seventeen of which had to be on Sundays.[13]

V   Sunday labour: Radicals and Socialists

After 1871 the parliamentary struggle to reduce the hours of labour, on Sundays and on other days, was fought by advanced new Liberals, many of whom were anti-Sabbatarian. In 1871 Thomas Hughes had realised that he could do no more himself and supported Sir John Lubbock's Shops (Hours of Labour) Bill. Thus as the paternal tradition died out within the Tory party and was replaced by the non-interference outlook, some Liberals abandoned their *laissez-faire* principles for those of an interventionist social reform, which has since been called positive Liberalism.

As long ago as 1855 and 1856 Walmsley had justified some Sunday work because of its utility to the rest of the community. In 1859 Mill, who accepted the Sabbatarian and social Sabbatarian argument that if all workers worked on Sunday they would receive six days' pay for seven days' work, did so too and recommended the establishment of another weekly holiday for those who served the community on Sundays. In 1867 Frederic Harrison, the Positivist, had followed Walmsley's view, and Holyoake later adopted Mill's idea.[14]

During 1871 Lubbock secured a Bank Holidays Act, which, as amended in 1875, provided for statutory holidays on Easter and Whit Mondays, the first Monday in August and on 26 December (provided that it did not fall on a Sunday). In the 1880's and 1890's Lubbock worked on behalf of the shopkeepers to limit opening hours on all days in the week. Dilke did so on behalf of the shop assistants, and the National Shop Assistants' Union named its headquarters Dilke House.

During the 1880's Will Thorne was taken on by the Old Kent Road Gas Works in London, whose chairman, George Livesey, was a vice-president of the L.D.O.S., and regarded himself as a 'model' employer. Thorne had been taught to read by Marx's daughter, Eleanor, was deeply influenced by Tom Mann, and proved an energetic secretary of the Canning Town branch of the Social Democratic Federation, spreading its message at Sunday morning meetings. After Livesey's firm reorganised itself as the South Metropolitan Gas Company it intensified the work demanded on all days, so Thorne founded the National Union of Gas Workers and General Labourers. A short strike in August 1889 won the eight-hour day, but a later bid for double pay for all Sunday work was resisted by Livesey. Thorne made the mistake of calling out the men during the winter, so they were eventually starved back to work early in 1890. Livesey consolidated his victory by persuading the men to sign individual contracts and during the next ten years led the employers' resistance to the trade unions.[15]

Sunday labour for adult males remained widespread, partly because it was almost entirely without legislative limitation. The 1677 Act was very rarely used for this purpose. The 1822 and the 1836 Bread Acts (the 1794 and the 1821 Acts having been repealed) were no help to the bakery workers. Other workers were unprotected. The Royal Commission on Labour which reported in the mid 1890's showed that Sunday labour was particularly common in the iron and steel industry and in connection with railways and other forms of transport. The men themselves wanted to spend Sundays with their families, or to receive extra pay for Sunday work, as a compensation for them and as a deterrent for their employers.[16]

VI   *Turning points*

The first report of the Lords' committee on the 1780 Act seemed to favour the anti-Sabbatarians, but the openers' victory in the Commons caused Lord Halsbury to rally the Sabbatarians, and later in 1896 a second report opposed any change to the Act. Undaunted, Lord Hobhouse introduced another Sunday Bill in 1897. On this occasion Davidson, Frederick Temple (who had just received the see of Canterbury) and Maclagan (the aged Archbishop of York) protested that it was against the wishes and interests of the working class. Halsbury, still the Lord Chancellor, advised the House to reject the Bill, and it was defeated by 50 to 33.[17]

In 1899 a bitter circulation war between the Lawsons' *Daily Telegraph* and Northcliffe's *Daily Mail* led to Sunday editions. The Nonconformist *British Weekly* and *The Record* poured their wrath on the innovation, rousing the Churches, invigorating the denominational newspapers, and causing parliamentary questions to be put to Arthur Balfour, the Home Secretary. Temple spoke out in the strongest terms, and Joseph Parker (the Congregational leader) and Dr Clifford (the doyen of the Baptists) did so too. Thomas Burt and John Burns called on Lord Salisbury, the Prime Minister, to express their fears about the spread of Sunday labour. The Sunday editions were discontinued.[18]

During 1901 the government introduced a Factory Bill, whose provisions relaxed the 1867 Acts, which had been consolidated within the Factory and Workshop Act of 1878, allowing women to work on Sundays in creameries and young persons to work on Sunday nights at blast furnaces and paper mills. The L.D.O.S. found that Sir Mark Stewart, 'who possessed a herd of nearly 200 cows . . . [was] disinclined to support . . . resistance to the proposed legislation'. The society therefore asked Dilke to do so, and he drew Charles Gore (who had edited *Lux Mundi*, was a leader of the Christian Social Union, and about to be nominated to the bishopric of Worcester), an anti-Sabbatarian, into the struggle. Henry Broadhurst supported them, but to no avail.[19]

These crises brought about a revived interest in the Sunday question. The societies hoped to use it to extend their own influence and to halt what they regarded as a rapid decline in the standard of Sunday behaviour. The title of the Anti-Sunday Travelling Union's magazine, *Our Heritage*, expresses their defensive and nostalgic outlook. There had indeed been changes in the previous twenty years. The 'higher criticism' had reduced the faithful's confidence in the Bible. The Ritualist fashion of early communion had reduced churchgoers' respect for the rest of the day. Even clergymen were said to have encouraged Sunday excursions by bicycling to church. The institution of 'hospital' Sundays had given the day a less purely religious purpose; and the increasingly flamboyant Sunday behaviour of the rich was tempting the rest of the community to follow their example.

The Edwardian era was one of transition. When in 1905 C. F. G. Masterman wrote *In Peril of Change* he noted, 'The old religion . . . is . . . visibly dissolving . . . the older austerity is deliquescing into an increasing, if still half timid, determination to slough off the ancient restraints . . . the English Sunday of silence and spiritual exercises . . . belongs to a vanishing England.'[20] The rich had turned the Saturday-to-Monday into the long weekend, enlivened by the motor car. The middle class was using golf and tennis to turn Sunday into a holiday. The respectable members of the working class made 'Sunday tea' in the 'front room' a major social ritual.

However, in pious families Sunday retained much of its old rigour at the opening of the next reign. Osbert Lancaster recalled that in London the male members of his family wore a silk hat and a frock coat for church and had doubts about the propriety of Sunday travel. At his grandfather's in the country weekday reading was put away and suitable 'Sunday reading' brought out; but there were some relaxations, a homberg and a dark suit being thought allowable for morning service, and croquet being permitted in the afternoon. Tennis might not be played because 'the court was visible from the road and the vicar feared that the spectacle of the gentry at play might lead the villagers into sin', whereas croquet might, because the lawn was hidden from view and the game would thus imperil only the participants' souls. Clock-golf 'remained a bone of contention', Osbert's aunts believing 'that it was in some way a "worldlier" sport and therefore unsuited to the Lord's day'.[21]

VII   *The Social Gospel: the Churches*

It is clear that the Edwardian Sunday had more in common with that of the 1850's than with that of our own time, and there is no doubt that it impressed children and foreign visitors alike as one of the peculiarities of English life, but many of the country's religious leaders were uneasy about what they interpreted as the trend of the age.[22]

During 1902 the Rev. W. B. Trevelyan published his *Sunday*, giving a Dominical theology and recommending a careful and

considered relaxation of Sunday behaviour. Later in the year the
Rev. F. Meyrick rebuffed Trevelyan in his own *Sunday Observance*,
presenting the Fundamentalist Sabbatarian case and defending
social Sabbatarianism by quoting extensively from William
Arthur.[23]

Later in the year Thomas Kingscote founded the Lay
Movement for Worship and Rest, marking a new phase in the
course of the Sunday question. His elder brother, R. H. H.
Kingscote, had been aide-de-camp to Reglan in the Crimea and
after a varied career became Paymaster to Edward VII, gaining
Thomas an appointment at court as gentleman usher in 1908. In
June 1901, however, Thomas Kingscote called a meeting in the
choir vestry of St Peter's, Eaton Square, and outlined his ideas
on Sunday observance. As a result a band of volunteers issued
circular letters asking the upper classes to give a lead to the
nation and gained several hundred promises of support.

What the Lay Movement was formally established in 1902 its
members were requested to sign 'pledge cards' agreeing to
sanctify Sunday and to give Sunday rest to their servants. A trio
of old-fashioned Evangelical M.P.'s—Colonel Williams, Sir John
Dorrington and Sir John Kennaway (shortly to be Father of the
House)—supported the Lay Movement; and the publicity which
it gained enabled the L.D.O.S. and the W.M.L.D.R.A. to put
their own ideas before the public too.

In 1905 Kingscote invited the Rev. H. Bickersteth Ottley to
become the Lay Movement's hon. chaplain. Together they
raised the state of the nation's observance of Sunday at the next
meeting of the Canterbury Diocesan Conference. Davidson, now
Archbishop, made a distinction between Sabbath and Sunday
observance, opposing the former but supporting the latter. The
distinction had enabled him to promote opening in 1896 and to
attack Hobhouse's Bill in 1897. He now rallied to the defence of
the English Sunday and set up the awkwardly named National
Sunday Observance Advisory Committee.

Bickersteth Ottley was invited to be its hon. chaplain too, and
the Bishop of Croydon became its chairman. In 1906 he
presented its report to the Convocation of Canterbury, stressing
that something must be done to protect the English Sunday,
preferably in co-operation with the Nonconformists. On 6

March the report itself was published by the S.P.C.K. and received widespread attention, prompting one of the earliest experiments in ecumenical cooperation.[24]

Davidson took the report to heart, called for his clergy to preach on the matter during July and in October held meetings at Caxton Hall and the Mansion House, using them to draw together the English Churches. He himself represented the Anglicans; Fr Bernard Vaughan, a renowned preacher on social issues and brother of the late cardinal, the Roman Catholics; and Dr Scott Lidgett, president of the Free Church Federal Council, the Nonconformists. Lord Avebury (formerly Sir John Lubbock) attended on behalf of several shopkeepers' organisations and Frederick Rogers did so on behalf of what was described as the National Committee of Organised Labour.[25]

The meetings resolved to set up a nation-wide Sunday movement under the guidance of a committee, so in March 1907 Davidson, Vaughan and Scott Lidgett issued a *Message to the Nation* and in November Davidson chaired a working meeting in the Jerusalem Chamber of Westminster Abbey. This was attended by many men previously unconnected with the Sunday question, such as the Rev. Percy Dearmer and Mr Thomas Bowick of the National Hygenic League, but Thomas Kingscote and Bickersteth Ottley emerged as hon secretaries to the committee which was established.

Bickersteth Ottley was the driving force behind the Churches' new interest in the Sunday question. He had been born in 1853, son to the Rev. Edward Ottley of Richmond, Yorkshire, and of a daughter of Robert Bickersteth, Bishop of Ripon. He had won a scholarship to St John's College, Oxford, taken a first in Classical Mods. and in 1874 begun his clerical career with a curacy at the prestigious Evangelical stronghold of All Souls, Langham Place. After serving in a wide variety of parishes he had received Norwood in 1898. He showed considerable organising ability, had a powerful mind and was a prolific author on the theme of 'religion and the world'. It was rumoured that he had refused two offers of colonial bishoprics. During 1907, however, his health broke down and he resigned Norwood, accepting yet another honorary position, as Canon of Canterbury, and devoting his remaining energies to the Sunday question. His aim was to combine the forces of religion and labour, and to achieve that end he had not only guided events within his own Church but had kept a close watch upon the trade unions and the politicians.[26]

VIII   *The Social Gospel: the workers*

During 1906 the railway unions formed the All Grades Movement and pressed for improved pay and conditions, among other things demanding that all Sunday work be paid at least one and a half times the normal weekday rate.

The secretary of the Amalgamated Society of Railway Servants was Richard Bell. He was a Wesleyan and had accepted the presidency of the W.M.L.D.R.A. in 1899, entering the House of Commons under the auspices of the Labour Representation Committee in 1900. He became chairman of the L.R.C. in 1902 and was chairman of the T.U.C. in 1903 and 1904, but refused to sign the Labour Party's constitution in 1905 and resigned all his political and union positions in 1909, protesting against what he saw as the Labour movement's drift to Socialism.

He acted as spokesman for the railway workers before a series of arbitration boards. Whilst questioning the manager of the London & North Western in 1907 he discovered that its porters were paid 17*s* 6*d* for a six-day week, with nothing extra for working on alternate Sundays, yet had 2*s* 6*d* deducted if they took a Sunday off. The manager regarded the men as servants whose duties obliged them to work a seven-day week when required, and drew a parallel with agricultural labourers who performed 'necessary' work.[27]

Bell dwelt on the obtuse attitudes revealed by this case, but based his claim for extra pay for Sunday work on the arguments evolved in the 1890's, that it would compensate the men for losing a rest day and deter the employers from requiring Sunday work. At first the arbitrators were rather unimpressed, but the oft-repeated plea of 'family life in danger' aroused their compassion, and they granted the unions' wishes on Sunday pay.

However, the railway clerks and office staff were not included

in the arbitration awards. They were still required to work on
Sundays without extra pay and now found their position
especially galling. Those employed by the L.N.W. complained to
the company, but with no success, for the Railway Clerks'
Association was ill organised and feared to compromise its
respectability by militancy. In 1910 sympathetic Labour M.P.'s
publicised the issue by combining with Sabbatarian M.P.'s from
Ulster to amend a Bill promoted by the Midland Railway
Company, compelling it to close its Irish golf courses on
Sundays.[28]

The T.U.C. had discussed Sunday labour in 1901, 1903, 1904,
1907, 1908 and 1909, and was to do so again in 1911 and 1912.
In March 1906 a group of Labour M.P.'s, including Snowden
and Hudson, had introduced a Textile Workers' Saturday and
Sunday Holiday Bill, gained a select committee and in July
brought forward a more detailed second Bill. In 1912 George
Barnes, Will Crooks, Keir Hardie, George Lansbury and Will
Thorne promoted a Weekly Rest Day Bill intended to apply to
all workers.[29]

Meanwhile Lord Avebury had continued his efforts on behalf
of the shopkeepers. In 1905 he introduced a Sunday Closing of
Shops Bill and gained a select committee which reported in
1906. The report revealed conditions akin to those of the 1860's,
complete with thriving Sunday morning street markets. The
L.D.O.S. opposed the Bill but the W.M.L.D.R.A. and a host of
shopkeepers' associations and trade unions gave evidence in its
favour. Avebury therefore reintroduced it in 1906, 1907 and
1908, but without success. Eventually the Liberal government
included the substance of his Bill in its own Shops Bill of 1911,
but the Sunday clauses aroused so much opposition (from
Sabbatarians, small traders, Jews and advocates of *laissez-faire*)
that they were deleted, and so formed no part of the Shops Act of
1912.[30]

However, Avebury had inspired others. In 1906 four Scottish
M.P.'s had introduced a Sunday Trading (Scotland) Bill. In
1908 two Liberal M.P.'s, C. Goddard Clarke and C. E. Price
(previously a partner in M'Vitie & Price, the biscuit makers)
had introduced a Weekly Rest Day Bill on behalf of the National
Hygenic League. Both Bills had failed, but the government

decided to ask its consuls to supply details of foreign Sunday legislation. It transpired that since the early 1890's almost all European countries apart from Britain had placed legal restrictions on Sunday labour.[31]

Emboldened by this knowledge, Lord Hill introduced another Weekly Rest Day Bill on behalf of the League and Sir John Kennaway introduced a Sunday Shops Bill of his own. In 1911 E. A. Goulding, Tory Unionist member for Worcester City, introduced a Railway Clerks' Weekly Rest Day Bill and in 1913 Lord Henry Cavendish Bentinck introduced a general Weekly Rest Day Bill. He was supported by a group of old-fashioned Tory Evangelicals and by Walter Hudson and Arthur Henderson, leader of the Iron Founders' Union, a Wesleyan lay preacher.

Only the Tory Unionist M.P. for Holborn, Mr Remnant, was successful. In 1906 he had embarked on a campaign to provide the police with a weekly rest day (preferably and usually on Sundays). Despite government obstruction on the ground that the proposal would necessitate a larger and thus more expensive force, he secured an Act for the English police in 1910. The Scots, apparently more thrifty than Sabbatarian, did not gain one until 1914.

X   *The Imperial Sunday Alliance*

Unusually, events abroad now impinged on the English religious scene. In 1861 Alexander Lombard, a Protestant banker, had established the Geneva Committee for the Sanctification of Sunday, and in 1877 had founded the International Federation for the Observance of Sunday. Since then the Federation, which derived its support from Continental Protestants, had held several congresses, some of which English Sabbatarians had attended, on their return frequently lamenting the laxity of their erstwhile brethren. In 1908, however, a congress was held in Edinburgh and, although the Continentals stressed the social rather than the religious aspect of Sunday observance, the proceedings proved more suited to the Englishmen's taste.[32]

The Edinburgh congress inspired Bickersteth Ottley to found

the Imperial Sunday Alliance later in 1908. In 1909 he took up
the National Hygenic League's defeated Bill, redrafted it and
decided to make a campaign for its passage the basis of a nation-
wide Sunday movement. He hoped to build on Davidson's
initiative in order to achieve his own aim of drawing together the
forces of religion and labour.

The L.D.O.S. did not co-operate. It had already called 'This
determination to settle the whole matter on the basis not of
Divine Law but of personal convenience, with a flavouring of
humanitarian sentimentality . . . a most threatening danger'.
The W.M.L.D.R.A. held aloof, not liking to oppose the
L.D.O.S. In 1904 the Wesleyan Conference had noted the
revived interest in Sunday observance and in 1907 had welcomed
the *Message to the Nation*, but gave no help to the Alliance.
Similarly, the Baptist Conferences of 1906, 1912 and 1914
stressed the need for stricter Sunday observance, but rendered
no practical help.[33]

In 1909 the Convocation of Canterbury resolved to support the
Alliance and set up a committee chaired by Paget, Bishop of
Oxford, to work out how best to do so. It reported back in the
following year, recommending that every diocese should
establish a committee of its own in order to back the Alliance.
However, Paget (who had contributed to *Lux Mundi*) was no
Sabbatarian and remarked that Sunday should be used for
'reasonable, healthful and appropriate enjoyment'. The
committee's recommendation was lost sight of amidst a welter of
wrangles led by Evangelicals.[34]

The Alliance was supported by Walter Hudson and by
Frederick Rogers, whom it described as its Labour Secretary.
Rogers was a most interesting man, reflecting many aspects of
the Sunday question. He had been born into a poor family in
1846, brought up as a Baptist by his mother, influenced in his
youth by the Rev. J. A. Picton, a radical Congregationalist, and
in the 1890's converted to Anglo-Catholicism by A. H. Stanton,
the curate of St Alban's, Holborn. During the previous decade
Rogers had helped inspire the foundation of Toynbee Hall and
subsequently maintained a close association with it, supporting
its ideals in his political and literary writings.

He was a skilled craftsman by trade and in 1892 became

president of the Vellum Binders' Union, representing it at the
T.U.C. in 1892 and from 1895 to '98. In 1899 he was asked to
become secretary to the National Committee of Organised
Labour, a pressure group campaigning for old-age pensions, and
his work on its behalf gained him a national reputation. Thus in
1900, when he represented the Vellum Binders at the founding
conference of the Labour Representation Committee, he was
elected to the trade union section of its executive and became its
first chairman, serving as treasurer two years later.

Rogers was neither a Socialist nor a Lib-Lab, but a humane
social reformer, and between 1901 and 1906 lost sympathy with
the Socialist–Liberal opposition to the 1902 Education Act,
coming to regard 'party' politics as at best vexatious and at worst
inimical to real social progress. Thus in 1911 he accepted
Conservative nomination as an alderman on the London County
Council and although claiming to be non-party usually voted
with the Conservative municipal reformers, in what he took to be
the national interest. When asked to submit an entry to *Who's
Who* he did not mention his former connection with the L.R.C.
In 1914 he gave wholehearted support to the British war effort
and toured the country making recruiting speeches, but injured
his health and was to die in 1915, his funeral service being held
at the Anglo-Catholic church of St John the Divine,
Kennington.[35]

It cannot therefore be said that the Alliance fulfilled
Bickersteth Ottley's expectations. It derived its force almost
entirely from the amorphous feelings of the latest revival, that
something really must be done. It had only ten branches outside
London, its devout clerical supporters were largely Anglicans
and almost three quarters of its membership of two thousand-
odd were women. The eleventh Baron Kinnaird (who used his
influence to keep the Football Association free of Sunday games)
supported the Alliance, but he was insufficiently enthusiastic to
relieve the financial problems which followed the publication of
the *Sunday Guardian*.

The *Sunday Guardian* represented almost all the approaches to
Sunday Observance during the previous sixty years. It contained
an element of Sabbatarianism, an infusion of social
Sabbatarianism and was pervaded by the paternal Sunday

observance tradition as interpreted by the liberal churchmen. In short, it represented that amalgam of old and new which was the Social Gospel.

The *Sunday Guardian* campaigned to persuade local authorities to use the 1909 Cinematographic Films Act to suppress Sunday cinema performances, and the Alliance's supporters intervened in the L.C.C. elections over the issue. The *Sunday Guardian* sought out groups of Sunday workers and explained how only complete public abstention from Sunday amusement combined with legislative action could help them. The magazine's most obvious achievement was to adapt religious slogans to the phraseology of the early twentieth century. Sunday was essential to the survival of Christianity, and its observance entailed incalculable spiritual and social advantages. In a highly competitive society it gave men in all walks of life an opportunity to calm their shattered nerves and to cultivate their family life. Sunday rest would render the working classes happy and content, reducing unrest and keeping strikes at bay. For the workers themselves, Sunday was 'the great leveller of accidental distortion of human life . . . it teaches the workman that, in virtue of his Christian birthright, he is not a mere "numeral" in the ranks, he is a man'.[36]

Bickersteth Ottley judged in the spring of 1914 that the time had come to have the Alliance's Weekly Rest Day Bill introduced into the House of Commons, for he had been unable to allay Sabbatarian opposition and his own campaign was beginning to lose impetus. Neither the remonstrances of *The Record* or of *Our Heritage* were able to persuade to L.D.O.S. to call off its attempt to defeat the Bill. The Wesleyan Sabbath Committee criticised it as a lax and imperfect measure. Most denominational newspapers gave it very little coverage and adopted a cautious attitude; but only the *British Congregationalist* opposed it, preserving the outlook of *The Nonconformist* by criticising 'legislative interference'.[37]

On Friday 22 May 1914 E. A. Goulding moved the second reading of the Alliance's Bill. 'Paddy' Goulding was the right man for this difficult job. He was an Evangelical but was not known as a 'religious' member, for his popularity stemmed from his business connections and the receptions which he gave for political aquaintances in his luxurious house near Henley.

Despite this, his advocacy of the Bill was met by the implacable
opposition of a band of Unionists led by H. L. W. Lawson and
Sir Frederick Banbury. They employed a cacophony of
Conservative hyperbole, claiming that the Bill could usher in
bureaucratic tyranny, restrict personal liberty and play havoc
with the nation's economic life. Mr Stanier opposed it on behalf
of the National Union of Farmers. Mr Lionel Rothschild
expressed his sympathy but opposed it on behalf of the Jews. Mr
Lunon did so on behalf of the Gaelic Athletic Association, which
feared for its Sunday games; despite Redmond, the leader of
Irish, having allowed his name to appear on the back of the
Bill.[38]

The measure was loyally supported in principle by an older
strand of Toryism led by Lord Henry Cavendish Bentinck and
Colonel Williams (who had broken with the L.D.O.S. on the
issue); and by Walter Hudson and J. H. Thomas, the
railwaymen's leaders. Mr Ellis Griffith, Under-secretary of State
at the Home Office, said that he had seldom heard a Bill so
soundly abused and suggested that since it was so badly drafted
a second reading would not be justified unless its sponsors
agreed to send it to a select committee which could examine the
whole question. Goulding later tried to clarify the position but
Griffith had left the House and Robertson, the Parliamentary
Secretary of the Board of Trade, the only official who remained,
felt unable to speak without him. Consequently Goulding moved
to a vote and the Bill was lost by 119 to 109.[39]

It was defeated by a combination of Irish Nationalists who
were Roman Catholics and Conservative Unionists who were
advocates of non-interference. They outvoted a coalition of older
Tories, Liberals and Labour men who regarded it as a modest
measure of social reform. The division lists reveal that fifty-four
Irish Nationalists, forty-four Conservative Unionists, nineteen
Liberals and one Labour member voted against; whereas sixty-
eight Liberals, twenty-four Tory Unionists, thirteen Labour
members and one Irish Nationalist voted for. The Labour
members were Duncan (secretary of the Independent Labour
Party), Bowerman (secretary of the Trades Union Congress),
Will Crooks, Philip Snowden, George Barnes, John Hodge, J. H.
Thomas, F. W. Jowett (founder of the Bradford Labour

Church), J. Parker, T. Richardson, S. Walsh, G. J. Wardle and J. Williams (who had once been a Nonconformist minister).

The ambiguities and irrelevancies of Sabbatarianism and social Sabbatarianism were highlighted by the growth of the Social Gospel and of positive Liberalism, which had come together in the Imperial Alliance's Weekly Rest Day Bill. However, the Churches remained more interested in proscribing Sunday amusement than providing Sunday leisure, as was shown by the force of their attack on Sunday newspapers and their unenthusiastic response to the Rest Day Bill. Moreover Labour M.P.'s voted for it neither because of a clearly articulated social nor a devoutly held religious outlook, but because they remained under the influence of 'the religion learned at their mother's knee'. As W. C. Steadman, leader of the Barge Builders' Union, and secretary of the Parliamentary Committee of the T.U.C. from 1904 to 1911, had told the Commons in 1900, 'You may imagine that because I sometimes go and agitate in Hyde Park or elsewhere on the Sabbath, I have no regard for that day. I treat the Sabbath as a serious day. Thank God I had good parents who brought me up in the Church of England, and I still adhere to the faith of that Church.'[40]

Notes

[1] E. G. Sandford, *Memoirs of Archbishop Temple* (1902), 59.

[2] Henry Broadhurst, *Henry Broadhurst. The Story of His Life* (1901), 299; *Universe*, 3 and 10 May 1890.

[3] P., BRR., HL 2/R25/34.

[4] Anthony Trollope, *Barchester Towers, op. cit.*, 46.

[5] *Herapath's Journal*, 13 June 1868; P., BRR., LNW 4/105 and 185, Instructions on Sunday Labour; L.D.O.S., *Quarterly Publication*, No. 66, p. 761 (July 1861), No. 67, p. 783 (January 1862); Jack Simmons, *St Pancras Station* (1968), 36.

[6] M. Rutherford (W. H. White), *The Revolution in Tanner's Lane* (1971 ed.), 82–3; L.D.O.S., *Minute Book VIII*, 19 February 1885, 25 November 1886.

[7] PP., 1895, VI, *First Rept. S.C. of H.L. Lord's Day Act*, 110, 128–9.

[8] *Methodist Times*, 30 March 1899.

[9] W.M.L.D.R.A., *Minute Book I*, 5 February 1862.

[10] *Ibid.*, II, 2 February 1872; P. S. Bagwell, *The Railwaymen* (1963), 38–40, 52–4; G. W. Alcock, *Fifty Years of Railway Trade Unionism* (1926), 196–8.

[11] PP., 1887, VIII, *S.C. of H.C. on Sunday Postal Labour*, 27–31, 43–51, 73–4;

PP., 1895, VI, *First Rept. S.C. of H.L. Lord's Day Act*, 133–40.

[12] Sunday Society, *Sunday Review*, October 1885, p. 37.

[13] PP., 1890–91, XVI, *S.C. of H.C. on Railway Servants (Hours of Labour)*, xiv, 481.

[14] 3H, vol. 137, col. 915 (20 March 1855); vol. 140, col. 1053 (21 February 1856); J. S. Mill, *On Liberty*, *op. cit.*, 146; Frederick Harrison, *Sundays and Festivals* (1867), *passim*; G. J. Holyoake, *Bygones*, *op. cit.*, II, 205–7.

[15] Will Thorne, *My Life's Battles* (n.d.), 35–40, 51–122; PP., 1893–94, XXXIV, *Royal Commission on Labour*, 91–219.

[16] *Ibid.*, *passim*.

[17] PP., 1895, VI, *First Rept. S.C. of H.L. Lord's Day Act*, passim; PP., 1896, *Second Rept.*, iv.

[18] *British Weekly*, 20 April 1899; *The Record*, 28 April 1899; M. Adamson, *Joseph Parker* (1902) 43, 329; G. W. Byrt, *John Clifford* (1947), 13, 25; E. G. Sandford, *Temple*, *op. cit.*, 335.

[19] L.D.O.S., *Minute Book VIII*, 21 June, 19 July 1901; G. L. Prestige, *Charles Gore* (1935), 153, 180; Henry Broadhurst, *Life*, *op. cit.*, 252–3.

[20] C. F. G. Masterman, *In Peril of Change* (1905), 323.

[21] Osbert Lancaster, *All Done From Memory* (1963), 42, 89–91.

[22] F. C. Rose (ed.), *French Visitors to Britain, 1800–1926* (1964), 184–5.

[23] W. B. Trevelyan, *Sunday* (1902); F. Meyrick, *Sunday Observance* (1902).

[24] *Acts of the Convocation of Canterbury* (1906), 298–300.

[25] G. K. A. Bell, *Davidson*, *op. cit.*, I 506.

[26] Imperial Sunday Alliance, *Sunday Guardian*, September/October 1908, p. 82.

[27] P., BRR., *London and North Western Arbitration Minutes*, 443.

[28] *Ibid.*, HL 2/R25/34, GW 7/81; 6H, vol. 17, col. 1272 (14 June 1910).

[29] George Lansbury, *My Life* (1928), 116.

[30] PP., 1905, VIII, *Sunday Closing of Shops Bill*; PP., 1906, XIII, *Rept. Joint Select Committee Sunday Closing of Shops Bill*.

[31] PP., 1906, V, *Sunday Closing (Scotland) Bill*; PP., 1909, LXXI, *Rept. . . . Foreign Sunday Legislation*.

[32] Andrew Elliot, *The World's Rest Day* (Edinburgh, 1908).

[33] L.D.O.S., *Occasional Paper*, No. 129, p. 19 (December 1900).

[34] *Acts of the Convocation of Canterbury* (1910), 157–68.

[35] Frederick Rogers, *Labour, Life and Literature: Some Memories of Sixty Years* (1913), *passim*; Joyce Bellamy and John Saville (eds.), *Dictionary of Labour Biography* (1972).

[36] I.S.A., *Sunday Guardian*, No. I, p. 2 (November 1910).

[37] *The Record*, 29 May 1914; *Our Heritage*, No. 72, p. 86 (April 1914); *British Congregationalist*, 21 May 1914.

[38] 6H, vol. 62, col. 2223 (22 May 1914).

[39] *Ibid.*

[40] 4H, vol. 82, col. 184 (27 April 1900).

PART FOUR

chapter twelve
SUNDAY DRINKING
1855–1914

I   *Sabbatarians v. teetotallers*

It is now possible to see how, despite the triumphs of the
1850's, the Sabbatarians had lost their grip on the Victorian
Sunday, but before the Victorian Sunday itself can be fully
appreciated it is necessary to examine the issue of Sunday
drinking after 1855. The Sunday Trading riots and the repeal of
the Wilson Patten Act made most Sabbatarians wary of any
further attempt to close public houses on Sundays. Nothing was
done until 1861, when temperance enthusiasts in Hull founded
an Association aiming to prohibit the sale of alcoholic liquor
between 10.00 p.m. on Saturdays and 6.00 a.m. on Mondays.

They persuaded one of Hull's M.P.'s, J. A. Somes, to
introduce a Sunday Closing Bill but failed to establish a national
society. In 1866 a group of Anglican temperance supporters in
Lancashire took up the matter and launched the Central
Association for Stopping the Sale of Intoxicating Liquors on
Sundays (C.A.S.S.I.L.S.). By 1868 the four founders, the Rev.
Dr J. Garrett, Thomas Clegg, Robert Whitworth and Thomas
Bazley, had attracted a diverse body of supporters: Cardinal
Manning, the Rev. Charles Garrett, a teetotal Wesleyan; the
Rev. Dawson Burns, a Baptist prohibitionist; the Rev. S. A.
Steinthal, an anti-Sabbatarian prohibitionist; and the Rev. T. A.
Stowell, a Sabbatarian. The Association advocated the total
closing of public houses on Sundays for 'the special reason that
on that day the working classes are not employed in their
ordinary labours, and they are therefore peculiarly exposed to
temptations'.[1]

The L.D.O.S. had been reluctant to associate itself with the

Hull Association, but in 1861 supported Somes's Bill, which was defeated by 278 to 103. In 1864 he introduced a second Bill, but modified it to allow off-sales, so losing the support of the Hull Association without gaining that of the Commons, the Bill being defeated by 123 to 87.

In 1866 the Central Association hoped to introduce a total Sunday closing Bill, but Able Smith introduced one of his own which allowed both off-sales and mealtime opening. The L.D.O.S., however, gave its continuous support to both Somes's modified Bill and to Abel Smith's: so was called upon to explain why it opposed partial closing Sunday trade Bills but supported partial closing public houses Bills. It answered that Sunday trade Bills legalised 'directly or indirectly' that which was already illegal by the terms of the 1677 Act, whilst Abel Smith's Bill made illegal that which was at present legal. Such sentiments read strangely when compared with the society's earlier determination to proceed in 'accordance with the command of God'.[2]

There was a considerable difference of outlook between Sabbatarians and teetotallers, who provided the driving force behind the Hull Association and behind C.A.S.S.I.L.S.; as had been presaged by the select committees of 1854 and 1855. In Parliament T. B. Horsfall, Richard Newdegate and J. G. Talbot, each of whom favoured total closure of museums on Sundays, opposed attempts to close public houses similarly. On the other hand, Sir Wilfrid Lawson, W. S. Caine and Samuel Smith each favoured the Sunday opening of museums and the total closure of public houses. The former Tory group defended the role public houses could play in working class life; the latter Liberal group wished to reduce the role alcohol did play.[3]

The Sabbatarian enthusiast J. M. Weylland did not ask for the Sunday closure of public houses: 'there are social difficulties in the way of closing all day on Sunday . . . Public morals demand that the houses should be closed, and public convenience, in some cases, is against it.' He buttressed his argument by explaining how total Sunday closing would be so unpopular with the working classes as to cause riot and tumult; and that would have been unwelcome to Sabbatarians who claimed working class support.[4]

It may be that Weylland was sufficiently realistic and flexible in attitude to see the impracticability of suddenly restricting this aspect of working class life and sufficiently sensible to confine his efforts to closing museums and galleries in which the working classes really took, despite Radical hopes and aspirations, but a meagre interest. Yet he did not extend the argument about a day of rest, or about the dangers of six days' pay for seven days' work, from the issue of Sunday recreation to that of Sunday drinking, or apply it to the publicans and their servants who were working a seven-day week. Underlying his position lay the assumption either that Sunday drinking was of greater social desirability and utility than Sunday recreation, or that Sunday drinking was not sinful in itself whereas Sunday recreation was. Such attitudes reflected a very important distinction between the Sabbatarian and the teetotal movements.[5]

II   *The Central Association*

The size of the Association's finances and the scale of its operations indicate that it had more in common with temperance than with Sabbatarian organisations. Its system of local agents, whose numbers rose to five by 1880, helped gain national coverage, but the fact that its headquarters were in Manchester probably reduced its ability to influence Parliament, and it was never strong in London. In the early years its clerical support was similar in distribution to that of the L.D.O.S.—rural areas, with a concentration in the south and in small towns—and indeed some local Sabbatarian Societies sent subscriptions; but that pattern fell away and was replaced by clerical support from more urban areas. The bulk of this clerical support—unlike that of most temperance societies—was Anglican, although on the executive committee the Anglicans were slightly in the minority. In fact during 1866 and 1867 Nonconformist teetotallers and prohibitionists who were in sympathy with the militant United Kingdom Alliance had taken over the leadership.

The Central Association therefore stressed both Sabbatarian and temperance reasons for Sunday closing. Canon Stowell attracted the support of Bishop Wordsworth (author of the hymn to Sunday, 'O, day of joy and light') and Bishop Magee, the best-known episcopal critics of the militant teetotallers. The Rev. Steinthal, linked to the National Sunday League and the Sunday Society, gained the support of the equally critical John Morley, an agnostic. The Association persuaded each of them to write one of its Sunday Closing Leaflets.

III   *Politics*

The one immediate and ultimate aim of the Association was, of course, to secure a measure along the lines of the Forbes Mackenzie Act, but political circumstances were against it. The moderate Tory tradition that had produced Wilson Patten had withered as the temperance movement fell further under the control of teetotal Nonconformist Liberals. Nor could the latter move their own party while it contained a principled *laissez-faire* group. After the Sunday Trading riots neither party was prepared to risk placing any further drastic restrictions upon Sunday drinking hours. Debates at the second reading in 1863, 1864 and 1868 (although only in the latter year was the Bill approved by C.A.S.S.I.L.S.) showed all the arguments which were used in subsequent years.

Somes, like Lawson, began by entering his protest against the charge of being actuated by a blind and bigoted zeal for the observance of the Sabbath, but knew the main objection he had to overcome was the charge that he was 'influenced by a desire to trench upon the liberties and enjoyments of the working classes'. Both he and Lawson denied that the Wilson Patten Act had anything to do with causing the Sunday Trading riots. Somes told the House how 4,101 petitions contained the signatures of workers and their wives and daughters, and his main argument rested on the plea that, by rescuing that class from temptation, crime and disorder would be reduced.[6]

Members were unconvinced. Speakers from virtually all parts of the House forcefully explained how the Bill would restrict the liberties of the working classes. The tactically minded Tory Ker Seymour was both realistic and cynical: 'speaking as a legislator, there were worse things than drunkenness, and one worse thing was to have a rankling feeling of discontent among the people at class legislation being indulged in at their expense'. Roebuck accused the Sabbatarians and the teetotallers of coming together in 'two muddy streams' in order to carry 'out their own individual views respecting the enjoyments of others . . . What [they] wanted was to turn this nation into a sour, ascetic, hypocritical people.'[7]

In 1863 Sir George Grey had produced a comprehensive case against the implementation of Somes's Bill, but as early as 1868 the official Whig–Liberal attitude had changed. Gladstone accepted the Radical Hibert's suggestion for a partial Bill combined with the issue of six-day licences, explained that he was not convinced that drunkenness had declined, mentioned the possibility of local option—which had been proposed by the Tory Newdegate and the Radical Ayrton in 1863—and told how he had been impressed by a deputation of respectable working men but asked for a select committee to assess working class opinion on the Bill because 'he should look with great suspicion upon any movement for restrictive measures of this sort, if the movement were confined to the members of the upper and middle classes; and he was certainly, though it might sound somewhat paradoxial, unwilling to do good to the working classes against their will'. Gladstone was followed by Gathorne Hardy, the Tory Home Secretary, who after recounting a host of difficulties and dangers surrounding the Bill as it stood, accepted Gladstone's suggestion, persuaded Abel Smith to accept it, and allowed the Bill to pass the second reading. The committee divided on sharply partisan lines—restrictionists versus non-restrictionists—and the latter, led by the Liberal Knatchbull Hugessen, overruled Able Smith's efforts in order to produce a majority report which declared that any further restriction of Sunday licensing hours would bring the law into disrepute.[8]

IV   *Local option*

The Central Association seemed to want all or nothing. Several of its erstwhile parliamentary supporters—Rylands, J. W. Pease and C. H. Wilson—embarrassed it by advocating partial Sunday closing. When in 1872 Bruce's Licensing Act reduced Sunday opening time by two and a half hours the

Association was unsure whether to welcome it as a first step or to condemn it as an ignoble compromise.[9]

A greater threat lay in Gladstone's hints in 1868 of local option. Harcourt implied in 1880 that he would willingly see the problem solved on the basis of local option and in 1881 a Welsh Sunday Closing Act was passed; but by supporting abortive Bills for Cornwall, Durham, Yorkshire and the Isle of Wight the Association dissipated its energies. When in 1884 Harcourt instanced Cornwall and Durham as counties in which Sunday closing might be possible if it was supported by a majority of the people C.A.S.S.I.L.S. deprecated 'such a so-called settlement.'[10]

Salisbury declared himself favourable to local option in 1885, and the Association felt able to announce that the Sunday closing movement had 'entered a new phase in its history' when in 1888 clause IX of the Unionists' Local Government Bill empowered county councils to regulate Sunday opening hours. After the government had announced its intention of withdrawing the clause the Central Association began a campaign to transform the Bill into a total Sunday closing measure and, probably in return for co-operation in withdrawing clause IX, W. H. Smith (the Leader of the House) agreed to provide time to debate the second reading of the Association's Sunday closing Bill.[11]

The disgruntled secretary of the Local Government Board, C. T. Ritchie, failed to amend the Bill by suggesting that the matter be dealt with on a county basis and it passed its second reading, but in committee the Radical Labouchere carried an amendment in favour of local option which 'was supported not only by the recognised enemies of Sunday closing, but also by some of its friends'.[12]

The Central Association soon recovered from the initial disappointment of this rather confused result and retained high hopes of victory, but although its own Bill passed its second reading in 1889 no other Sunday closing Bill reached its second reading until 1897, and the Liberals (who took local option to heart) seriously embarrassed the Association by enshrining it in their Liquor (Local Control) Bill of 1893.[13]

V   *Total Sunday closing*

The Central Association mounted a major campaign for its own solution. Its first method was a major educational and propaganda campaign whose literature elaborated religious, social and industrial reasons for Sunday closing—many of which (as its opponents said) could equally well have been used to advocate seven-day closing. In the Association's opinion Sunday closing would free the Lord's day from an evil influence, remove a rival to churches, chapels and Sunday schools, defer to the conscientious scruples of religious men, free all publicans from Sunday labour, remove a source of temptation from the weak, remove a source of early death and self-induced poverty; preserve public order, give the police a day's rest, remove an illogicality from the law, improve industrial efficiency, help counter foreign competition, and release money to stimulate the economy. The latter three points were stressed in order to appeal to the business mentality which seemed to prevail in the House of Commons, and because C.A.S.S.I.L.S. itself received the support of businessmen such as Samuel Smith, the Liverpool shipbuilder, and J. C. Stevenson, the South Shields chemical manufacturer, who took charge of the Association's Bills in the Commons.[14]

The second method was to substitute electoral action for the mass presentation of petitions, and so C.A.S.S.I.L.S. lost no time in asking its supporters to carry the fight to the ballot box by making Sunday closing a test question. It issued electoral tracts by the quarter million, hoped to have some influence in every constituency, saw the value of concentrating on by-elections, and certainly tried to prepare for the 1906 general election with more thoroughness than any other, issuing cartoons which showed how the Sunday opening of public houses drew the fathers of England from the places of worship which their families attended.[15]

The third was to stress the quality of its supporters. In 1885 the Central Association announced that it gave 'voice to the aspirations of the working class' and was backed by that portion of them who 'because they wish to become the better-to-do class . . . are asking that the door of the public house may be closed all

day on a Sunday'. The emergence of Lib-Labs such as George
White gave some substance to the Association's claims. He told
the Commons that Sunday drinkers composed that 'section of
men who were destructive of the industrial pre-eminence of the
nation, a burden to the class to which they belonged, frequently
the main instrument to breaking down their trade union efforts,
and in other ways a general detriment to the advancement of the
working classes'.[16]

These efforts were designed to avoid the faults of petitions
(which indicated that the Central Association's support came
mainly from the northern English Nonconformists) by
impressing upon M.P.'s that the demand for Sunday closing
came from all areas and all classes, especially those enfranchised
in 1884. They had an equivocal effect. As early as 1868 Roebuck
had told the Commons that the publicans were a more powerful
electoral force than the temperance movement, but the
Association's efforts helped bring about the identification of
Liberalism with temperance and Toryism with the drink trade
which had already intensified during the late 1870's. Even that
result had unfortunate effects, for it caused 'the trade' to
redouble its own propaganda—so much so that in 1900
C.A.S.S.I.L.S. itself thought both parties feared the
publicans—and left the Association almost completely
dependent upon the Liberals who, as it well knew, included
powerful opponents of total Sunday closing.[17]

VI   Decline, compromise, failure

The Central Association had declined financially in the late
1880's and drastically reduced the scale of its operations. It
revived in the late '90's during an upsurge produced by the
Liberals' 1893 Bill, the Churches' United Temperance
Committee, and the Royal Commission of 1897. In 1900 the
Association implied 'that it would accept partial closing as an
interim solution'. It overhauled its organisation, took an office in
London, cultivated Lib-Labs and I.L.P. men and even set up a
special Parliamentary Committee. But the time for compromise
had already passed by. Asquith saw to it that the doomed
Licensing Bill of 1908 contained but partial Sunday closing

clauses, and although in 1909 the Association introduced a similar Bill of its own it never had any chance of success because Asquith was suspicious of, and the Unionists were opposed to, its provisions.[18]

The Central Association had failed because (unlike the later Sabbatarians) it did not merely defend the *Status quo*, but (like the anti-Sabbatarians) tried to bring about a change involving deep-seated principles and interests. By 1870 its supporters consisted of militant Radicals and Liberals who wanted the State to use its power to destroy a religious, moral and social evil. Unfortunately, the Liberal party still contained a large *laissez-faire* group, and the Tory party was well aware of the issues involved.

In the 1830's and 1840's moderate Tories had detected a link between excessive drinking and public order, and the Sabbatarians between public houses and working class radicalism. But the 1855 Sunday Trading riots and the replacement of tap-room chin-wagging with high-minded secularism and Nonconformity had produced a new political outlook.[19]

Ker Seymour and his like knew that it was far safer for the working classes to drink beer on Sundays, and to gain political capital by defending their right to do so, rather than to educate themselves in museums, libraries and art galleries or absorb the stuff of this new Liberalism: 'What,' asked the Tory M.P. Mr Wharton in 1882, 'are these poor people to do on the Sunday? Are they to go to a number of conventicles which are turned into political agencies for the dissemination of Radical principles?' That defence of the right to Sunday drinking, with its echoes of King James and of Hippolyte Taine, is a theme to which we must return in the Conclusion.[20]

Notes

[1] E. Matthews, *Lecture to the Social Science Association*, 1871; C.A.S.S.I.L.S., *Report of the Conference Held in Manchester* (1866); *Manchester Guardian*, 15 October 1868.

[2] C.A.S.S.I.L.S., *First Annual Rept.*, (1867), 8–12; L.D.O.S., *Quarterly Publication*, No. 69, p. 787–9 (January 1862), No. 78, p. 936 (July 1867).

[3] 3H, vol. 139, col. 1551 (31 July 1855); vol. 171, col. 296 (3 June 1863); vol.

175, col. 174 (6 May 1864); vol. 207, col. 384 (21 June 1871); vol. 286, col. 1397 (2 April 1884); vol. 334, col. 977 (27 March 1889); 3H, vol. 171, col. 304 (3 June 1863); PP., 1877, XI, *First Rept. S.C. of H.L. on Intemperance*, 236.

⁴ J. M. Weylland, *The Man with the Book* (1872) 207.

⁵ 1877, XI, *S.C. of H.C. on Intemperance*, 358.

⁶ 3H, vol. 171, col. 277 (3 June 1863).

⁷ 3H, vol. 175 col. 171 (6 May 1864); vol. 190, col. 1847, 1857 (18 March 1868).

⁸ 3H, vol. 171, col. 309, 317, 319 (3 June 1863); vol. 190, cols. 1852, 1857 (18 March 1868); PP., 1867–68, XIV, *Rept. S.C. of H.C on the Sale of Liquor on Sundays Bill*, iii–v.

⁹ 3H, vol. 171, col. 1857 (3 June 1863).

¹⁰ 3H, vol. 253, cols. 909–11 (25 June 1880); vol. 286, cols. 1431–3 (2 April (1880); C.A.S.S.I.L.S., *Eighth Annual Rept.* (1875), 11; *Eighteenth Annual Rept.* (1885), 16.

¹¹ C.A.S.S.I.L.S., *Nineteenth Annual Rept.* (1886), 18; 3H, vol. 327, col. 1145 (25 June 1888).

¹² 3H, vol. 332, col. 319 (14 December 1888); C.A.S.S.I.L.S., *Twenty-second Annual Rept.* (1889), 11.

¹³ *Ibid.*, *Twenty-seventh* (1894), 12; 4H, vol. 46, col. 87 (10 February 1897).

¹⁴ Samuel Smith, *Four Good Reasons for Sunday Closing* (C.A.S.S.I.L.S. Sunday Closing Leaflets), No. 8, p. 3 (1883).

¹⁵ James Cropper, *The New Electorate and Sunday Closing*, *ibid.*, No. 27, 1 (1885); *Sunday Closing Reporter*, No. 82, p. 185–6 (December 1905).

¹⁶ W. Young, *How Sunday Closing is Opposed* (1885), 2; *id.*, *A Sham Handbill* (1885), 1–2; 4H, vol. 146, col. 1547 (25 May 1905).

¹⁷ 3H, vol. 190, col. 1856 (18 March 1868); C.A.S.S.I.L.S., *The Sunday Reporter*, No, 65, 11 (March 1900).

¹⁸ *Ibid.*, *Thirty-fourth Annual Rept.* (1900), 14; 4H, vol. 195, col. 638 (30 October 1908).

¹⁹ J. T. Baylee, *Statistics and Facts*, *op. cit.*, 17.

²⁰ 3H, vol. 272, col. 1035 (19 July 1882).

conclusion

I

The Victorian Sunday was thus far more than a perplexing part of so many biographies and novels. It was a major feature of nineteenth century life. However, most existing interpretations, like those of its seventeenth-century predecessor, contain certain inadequacies. In particular, it is clear that Sabbatarianism was not the creation of the Nonconformists and that Sabbatarians were not intimately associated with the temperance movement.

Chadwick's interpretation in terms of 'city' versus 'country' contains an element of truth, for the major challenge to Sabbatarianism came from London and the great northern towns; but although Sabbatarianism was strong in rural areas, it was strongest in the respectable middle class of the small towns and suburbs in the south of England.

His supposition that the Victorian Sunday was secured by non-Sabbatarian legislation is an apposite one, for the Licensing Acts and several minor Acts had a significant effect, and legislation entirely unconnected with Sunday protected it from pressure by providing the people with greater weekday leisure and opportunities; but the most characteristic features of the Victorian Sunday were produced not by legislation but by personal conviction and social custom.

Similarly, W. L. Burn's comment that Sabbatarianism was a test case on the issue of authority and liberty is a perceptive one, for that is exactly what it was; and he rightly points out that the Victorian Sunday was not merely a Protestant phenomenon, since it influenced devout Catholic families as well. However, his suggestion that it was not found by almost everyone to be boring and repressive is beside the mark, for given the nature of the social discipline which the Sabbatarians inculcated it had an inevitable tendency to become so.

Harrison is correct in suggesting that the 1855 Sunday

Trading riots indicated working-class hostility to the Evangelicals, but his study of religion and recreation overestimates the Sabbatarians' interest in providing leisure time and underestimates their desire to control it, besides exaggerating the volume of their working-class support and the philanthropic nature of their motives. Of greater significance in this context, though, is the contribution which the Sabbatarians made to the remoulding of working-class behaviour before the 1850's and to the modification of their attitudes afterwards.

The Victorian Sunday was produced by the middle class, which had evolved a religious phenomenon, Sabbatarianism, that was attuned to its own condition. Edward Miall had glimpsed the truth of the matter: 'British Christianity is essentially the Christianity developed by a middle class soil'.[1]

Between 1530 and 1914 the Sabbatarians shared common problems and characteristics. When the Tudors swept away Roman Catholicism they established an authoritarian Protestant State, made the Bible more widely available than in England previously or on the Continent subsequently, and put more pressure on Sundays by reducing the number of saints' and holy days.

Sabbatarians were generally property owners who were literate but read mainly the Bible, possessed political influence but exercised authority over their inferiors, and often suffered economic hardship but received little protection. Sabbatarianism arose out of their religious preconceptions, but freed them from competition, enabled them to spend their Sundays in comfort, and gave them a chance to discipline and to instruct the lower orders, for whom (like the aristocracy) the doctrine and its practices had less appeal and purpose.

The nineteenth century enthusiasts were an insecure class, threatened from above and below. Their religious outlook lacked the tolerance of the upper and the common sense of the lower class. They were prey to extreme ideas and notions, and Sabbatarianism gave them a fixed and immutable standard with which to judge the rest of their countrymen.

Most Sabbatarian literature was concerned mainly with biblical matters, because Sabbatarians believed that behaviour should conform to God's will; so their task was to demonstrate what that was and then to secure obedience to it; hence the title of Daniel Wilson's book—*The Divine Authority and Perpetual Obligation of the Lord's Day.*

The Sabbatarians regarded themselves as a chosen people who had a duty to enforce God's law within their families and upon the nation. They and their ideas had more in common with Old Testament times than with our own. Sabbatarianism was a sign and a symbol which confirmed their status and separated them from the rest of the community. It had much in common with pre-Christian ideas that abstinence on what Weber calls 'taboo days' entailed Divine rewards, whereas indulgence provoked vengeance; and seemed redolent with an atmosphere of propitiation or sacrifice. The early Evangelicals might well have pondered over Wilson's declamation that 'the Sabbath was the Lord's tribute . . . the acknowledgement He requires for all His blessings, temporal and spiritual'; for did this not incline to Salvation by works rather than faith alone?[2]

Thus Sabbatarianism was related to social and to religious conditions, and there is also a chronological link between it and years of national emotion and tension; the Civil and the Napoleonic wars, the early 1830's and the Crimean and the Boer wars, for instance. Similarly, there was a major religious revival in the late 1850's, and the Churches' renewed interest in the Sunday question around 1900 coincided with the notorious Kensite outbreak of 1898 and the Welsh revival of 1905.

II

Sabbatarianism was concerned with Sin—men's relations with God and obedience to His Law—rather than with morality or social reform. Sabbatarianism taught that personal and national Sabbath-keeping or -breaking would produce a divine reaction. Social Sabbatarianism was an attempt to demonstrate that essentially religious acts would produce a social reaction too: sinful Sunday amusement resulted in anti-social Sunday labour.

This outlook led to the priorities which at first sight appear so paradoxical but which were the inevitable outcome of Sabbatarianism: its comparative unconcern with Sunday labour, its prohibition of Sunday recreation; its criticism of Sunday travelling and its relative indifference to Sunday drinking. However, the Victorian Sunday was formed by these priorities.

In the depression-stricken countryside of the 1880's no harvest work was done on Sundays, but the migrant Irish labourers were thought to be heathens because they sang and danced after returning from Mass. Protestant English farmers' children were taught to ' "remember that thou keep holy the Sabbath day." Of course the manservant and the maid-servant had to milk the cows, that was necessary work [but] . . . Nobody ever read a newspaper or whistled a tune except hymns . . . on Sundays.'[3] No wonder the Sabbatarians quoted the Fourth Commandment as given in Exodus and ignored the version in Deuteronomy (5 : 14) 'that thy man servant and thy maid servant may rest as well as thou'.

The most characteristic feature of Sabbatarianism and of the Victorian Sunday which it produced was the attempt to proscribe Sunday amusement and recreation, and over the course of the century this had had different effects on each class. By encouraging church and Sunday school attendance, and drawing a picture of domestic comfort, the Sabbatarians had given the lower classes a standard at which to aim. But by doing so they had undermined the festal Sunday tradition in accordance with which the lower classes already cleaned and dressed themselves on Sundays. They wanted a day of abstention, whereas the workers kept a holiday, a feast not a fast.

The abstemious Sunday was better suited to those who spent the week in easy circumstances than to those who laboured for their bread. The Sabbatarian standard and the Victorian Sunday were essentially middle class phenomena. They produced a day which had a funereal character, notorious for its symbols—the hushed voice, the half-drawn blind and the best clothes. When adopted by the lower classes these symbols produced the respectable poor. Neville Cardus, the (Manchester) *Guardian's* cricket correspondent, remembered William Attewell, in 1912 cricket professional at Shrewsbury School: 'Each Sabbath, after our mid-day meal, he put on a hard stiff collar. I recollect his struggles with it. "Cuss it," he would protest, "but ah mun do it; it's the Lord's Day." '[4]

The Sabbatarians probably hoped to make the abstemious Sunday a pattern for the whole week, much as, in Samuel Butler's words, 'The Clergyman is expected to be a kind of human Sunday', but, short of that, the problem which successive generations of adults faced—how to spend Sunday—was highlighted in the lives of children. 'Paradoxically, Sunday was the moral danger zone, because to play games . . . would have been shocking . . . Even two services could not be stretched right across the gap.' The solution was to supplement them with the Bible and a vast genre of 'Sunday reading'. Occasionally perhaps Bunyan and the religious classics, but frequently inconsequential stories: '. . . the book was called "*Three Wet Sundays*". It was obviously a Sunday book . . . but it seemed to be about some children who talked of nothing but the Israelites for three wet Sundays.'[5]

If Mark Twain may be taken as having an English counterpart, this produced a strange morality: 'Tom said . . . we would all go home and meet next week and rob somebody and kill some people. Ben Rogers said he couldn't get out much, only Sundays, and so he wanted to begin next Sunday; but all the boys said it would be wicked to do it on Sunday, and that settled the thing. They agreed to get together and fix a day as soon as they could.'[6]

Of course, some adults continued to spend Sunday travelling. The Sabbatarians dwelt upon Sunday railway accidents with a peculiar fascination. When in 1861 a Sunday excursion came to grief in the Clayton tunnel on the London–Brighton line, the worst railway accident to that date in Britain, Sabbatarians saw the hand of God at work. When in 1879 a storm swept away the Tay Bridge, taking with it a regular Sunday train carrying seventy-five passengers, the whole country shuddered.

The evils of Sunday drinking could not be displayed so dramatically. Even when 'Mark Rutherford', who had relinquished the Sabbatarian culture, described the drunkenness of third-class passengers on a Sunday excursion train he subscribed to Sabbatarian melodrama by having his wife catch typhoid on the trip. As late as the 1890's trains on the newly built District Railway, in which the Wesleyan financier R. W. Perks had a major interest, stopped in 'church time' from 11 a.m. to 1.00 p.m. on Sundays.[7]

III

The Sunday question had obviously had a complex impact upon political life. Agnew had valued the Reform Bill because it strengthened the pious middle classes, and Anstey had confirmed that opinion, noting that Parliament usually ignored the voteless lower classes. When the latter did speak out, as in the 1855 Sunday Trading riots, or when the Sabbatarians went too far, as in the prosecutions of the 1870's, governments of both parties acted to allay the disturbance and to redress the balance. The aristocratic party leaders were content to 'hold the ring' and to maintain domestic tranquility: reversing, for example, the Sabbatarians' victory over the Post Office and public houses, but allowing them to hold their chosen ground on museums. It is a testimony to the inherent Sabbatarian paradox that collection and delivery continued and public houses remained open but museums remained closed on Sundays.

Trollope, who worked for the Post Office, satirised Ashley's transient victory in *The Three Clerks*, writing of a snap division in a thin House with the whips absent. In a later novel, *The Prime Minister*, he analysed aristocratic attitudes: 'It was Sunday afternoon . . . There had been a question as to the propriety of Sabbath archery, in discussing which reference had been made to . . the growing idea that the National Gallery should be opened on the Lord's day. But the Duchess would not have archery. "We are just the people who shouldn't pre-judge the question," said the Duchess.'[8]

The party leaders were wise to be wary when dealing with the Sunday question in the Commons, for it could complicate already difficult circumstances. In addition to the major issues, they could never be sure that some Sabbatarian zealot was not about to inflame religious opinion. During 1851 the eccentric Tory Colonel Sibthorpe had alarmed the Whig Cabinet by rooting out and publicising by means of parliamentary questions the fact that a professional photographer had been allowed into the Crystal Palace on Sundays to photograph the exhibits.[9]

Although the leaders had overestimated the electoral impact

of the Sunday question—by overestimating the Sabbatarians'
own weight, over-exaggerating the Nonconformists' electoral
action and taking partisan advice—their policy of avoiding
difficulty over a side issue was tactically correct. The leaders also
responded to changes in the composition and outlook of their
parties. After the demise of the high Tory opponents of
Sabbatarianism the House of Commons was a battleground
between authoritarian Sabbatarian Tories and the *laissez-faire*
anti-Sabbatarian Radicals, who fought over the great nineteenth
century issues of freedom and liberty.

Most of the M.P.'s who so fought were members of the middle
class but reflected a subtle division within it. Most of the early
Sabbatarians were connected with commerce, the law and the
Established Church, each of which valued State regulation and
authority; whereas the anti-Sabbatarians were frequently
industrialists, utilitarians or Unitarians, many of whom were
deeply suspicious of the State.

The social Sabbatarians stood uneasily between. The
strongest were Wesleyans who retained something of their
founder's own authoritarianism and his sympathy for the
Establishment. For Nonconformists social Sabbatarianism was a
valuable compromise, and many of them regarded it as a
genuine form of social concern, although the most militant were
never happy with it. Edward Miall was an M.P. from 1852 to
1857 and from 1869 to 1874 but refrained from speaking on any
aspect of the issue.

By 1879, when Disraeli spoke for the Sabbatarians, the Tories
supported the *status quo*—voting to keep galleries, libraries and
museums closed, and to keep public houses open on Sundays.
Far better to champion the loyal Sabbatarians, the drinking
classes and the publicans; and to oppose the Radicals who
wished the working classes to educate themselves on Sundays
and to join them within the Liberal Party.

Between 1880 and 1914 this situation changed dramatically.
The authoritarian Tories gave way to the non-interference
Conservatives. The social-Sabbatarian Liberals either became
Unionists or adopted the new interventionist positive Liberalism.
The Radicals disappeared, some becoming Unionists and others
accepting the new Liberalism. Thus in 1914 the Conservative

and Unionist party was able to present itself as the defender of English liberty and to stigmatise the Liberal party as its major threat.

Neither the Tories and Conservatives nor the Radicals and some of the social-Sabbatarian Liberals were really concerned with immediate social effect of their ideas. The Tories hoped to maintain the existing structure of society. Some of the social-Sabbatarian Liberals sought an escape from their ideological problems. The Radicals wanted to give the people a choice between Sunday education, drinking and worship. The Conservatives opposed all regulation, unless it was to their own advantage. Each group excluded from its outlook merely humanitarian feelings. In the mid-nineteenth century they had almost destroyed the paternal Sunday observance tradition and in the late nineteenth and early twentieth retarded the growth of positive Liberalism, movements whose proposals would have had a beneficial social effect.

In 1860, when trying to conciliate the Radical M.P. for Finsbury, Thomas Slingsby Duncombe, who in 1842 had presented the Chartist petition, Lord Chelmsford admitted that he was opposed both by the religious and by the secular worlds. Lord Selborne was so concerned to justify his own social-Sabbatarian compromise between the two that he devoted ten pages of his autobiography to the matter. Few men were as balanced as Hugh Lupus Grosvenor, the Whig Duke of Westminster, who supported the Sunday opening of museums, the Sunday closing of public houses and fought for the legislative protection of shop assistants.[10]

IV

The impact of the Sunday question on religious and intellectual life was closely related to these political changes, for all three aspects of the issue were inseparable. By the late 1850's social Sabbatarianism had appeared to solve many of the acute religious problems involved, but the Sabbatarians feared that if the Radicals succeeded in their fight for opening, than they would facilitate the spread of ideas which would weaken Fundamentalist Protestantism.

During the 1860's and 1870's anti-Sabbatarianism was led by men disatisfied with contemporary religion, who regarded themselves as agents of intellectual enlightenment, sometimes falsely. Baxter Langley refused to follow his father's footsteps as an Anglican clergyman and established the Sunday Lectures; but Cox did edit the *Phrenological Review* and the Amberleys dabbled in spiritualism, as did so many of their class and generation.

The Free Sunday Societies attracted the cream of England's intellectuals. On the one hand were clergymen such as Benjamin Jowett and Arthur Stanley, who doubted the traditional formularies; and devout laymen such as Charles Dickens and Anthony Trollope, who desired a more humane religion. On the other were those whose scientific interests inclined them to agnosticism, such as Charles Darwin and T. H. Huxley (who coined the word); and those whose rationalism led in the same direction, as it did for Grote and Mill.

The Sabbatarians and their allies competed with the anti-Sabbatarians for the leadership of the working classes. After the collapse of Chartism the workers were deeply influenced by secular Radicalism and by anti-Sabbatarianism, but George Potter's entry into political life heralded a change. As the products of the Sunday schools rose to prominence in the trade unions and entered Parliament as Lib-Labs it became clear that the social-Sabbatarian propaganda of the mid-century had had a considerable effect.

Contemporary religion was changing, too, within the Established Church under the influence of a quite remarkable series of men from Oriel College and Rugby School, and later of the religious liberalism which some of them promoted. The religious liberals are often regarded as brave and forward-looking men, for they alarmed their clerical contemporaries and set the tone for much of twentieth century Anglicanism, but this interpretation needs qualification.

They were supremely moderate men. In 1889, for instance, Frederick Temple hoped not that the men would win the dock strike, but that it would end peacefully. They belonged to the professional classes who held industry and trade in a certain contempt, and patronised the lower orders without

compromising their own social position. They had avoided
Sabbatarian authoritarianism and social-Sabbatarian
individualism, but had not produced an original standpoint of
their own. Their theological roots remained with Whately and
Arnold and their social concern hardly advanced beyond
Maurice, for its other main element was the paternal Sunday
observance tradition as interpreted by Lord Chelmsford and
Thomas Hughes.

Bishop Westcott of Durham was an unusually firm exponent
of the social relevance of Christianity. He had been taught at
King Edward's School, Birmingham, by James Prince Lee, who
had begun his teaching career under Arnold at Rugby and
became first Bishop of Manchester. Westcott himself had taught
under Vaughan at Harrow and been Davidson's house master
there. In 1894 he was president of the Christian Social Union,
and when he told its members that 'We claim for Christian law
the ultimate authority to rule social practice' he spoke from the
same logical position as the militant Sabbatarians, but
interpreted the law in a more humane way. This form of
paternalism both preceded and survived *laissez-faire*, when it was
misleadingly and mistakenly called Christian Socialism, to act as
the basis of the Social Gospel.[11]

That movement grew in parallel with positive Liberalism,
which was an abandonment of and an advance beyond *laissez-
faire*. During the 1880's perceptive laymen and clergymen
detected the new phenomenon. In 1884 Herbert Spencer
published *The Man Versus the State*, warning of the decline of the
'old' and the rise of the 'new' Liberalism which was extending
parliamentary control, ostensibly for altruistic social motives. In
1889 the Rev. W. Campion, writing on 'Christianity and
Politics' in *Lux Mundi*, assessed the current 'rebound from the
minimising views of the function of the State'.[12]

The co-operation between religion and labour which the
Social Gospel facilitated between 1900 and 1914 was the
culmination of the cross-class alliance that the Sabbatarians and
social Sabbatarians had promoted for decades, but it was made
possible only by the intellectual deficiencies of each side.

The religious liberals had produced a peculiarly amorphous
faith, if such it was. In 1906, when he was ordained by Davidson,

Paget having refused to do so, William Temple believed without qualification in neither the Virgin Birth nor the Resurrection. Although president of the Workers' Educational Association from 1908 to 1924, and a member of the Labour Party from 1918 to 1925, he thought of the working classes in terms reminiscent of social-Sabbatarian propaganda. In 1925 when Bishop of Manchester he expressed his own concern for the apalling social conditions in the diocese by leading a campaign against the Sunday opening of cinemas—helped by Hewlett Johnson, the future 'Red Dean' of Canterbury, himself the product of an Evangelical and Sabbatarian home. Such was the Established Church's social message.[13]

Similarly, within the Labour Party, although the Lib-Labs had been replaced by the stalwarts of the I.L.P. and L.R.C. many of them, notably Henderson, Lansbury, Snowden and Thomas, and the lesser known Jowett and Walsh, had supported the Weekly Rest Day Bills. They were but the latest generation of English working class leaders without an adequate guiding ideology, as was shown by the failure of their governments in 1924 and 1931 and their subsequent escape into either collaboration with the classes they effected to destroy or the rarified heights of idealist rhetoric.

V

Most Victorians were unaware of the issues involved in the Sunday question. Their Sunday behaviour responded to underlying movements of custom and outlook rather than to argument. The culture which produced the Victorian Sunday had been eroded by the attitudes which emerged in the 1870's and challenged by the secularity and materialism of the Edwardian era.

The First World War completed the process, putting new pressures on Sunday and shaking belief in a God who intervened in the affairs of men. Its economic aftermath weakened the Sabbatarian class and the coming of a mass electorate reduced its political influence; and the people at large were given the incentive and the opportunity to abandon traditional restraints.

It is from the people, bound by custom and legislation, that the twentieth century Sunday is derived. By 1914 the Acts of 1677 and 1780 had both been supplemented by legislation placed on the statute book so unobtrusively that it had never been the cause of controversy. In 1839 a Metropolitan Police Act had given the metropolitan police power to direct traffic away from churches during divine service. In 1845 a Gaming Act had made illegal the Sunday playing of billiards and bagatelle in public halls. In 1847 a Town Police Clauses Act had given the provincial police similar power to their colleagues in London. In 1850 a Sunday Fairs Prevention Act had forbidden Sunday fairs, in 1866 a Naval Discipline Act forbade courts martial to sit on Sundays, and in 1872 a Pawnbrokers Act forbade their shops to open on Sundays.

During the 1920's the L.D.O.S. fought a hard rearguard battle, encouraging supporters to ensure that these Acts were enforced by the police and to institute prosecutions themselves under the 1677 and 1780 Acts. The society ensured that the Empire Exhibition was closed on Sundays, and T. W. H. Inskip's support strengthened its hand, but a plethora of court cases led to demands for changes in the law.

In 1930 the Hairdressers' and Barbers' Sunday Closing Act regulated a trade which in the case of Palmer *v.* Snow (1900) had been judged to be outside the scope of the 1677 Act. In 1931 a spate of prosecutions of Sunday cinemas, brought by common informers in order to secure the substantial penalties stipulated by the 1780 Act, produced a crisis. The government rushed through a Temporary Regulation Act and in 1932 passed the Sunday Entertainments Act. This allowed cinemas to open on Sundays, subject to a form of local option and certain other conditions, and legalised Sunday concerts, museums, galleries, zoos, gardens, lectures and debates, indemnifying them from prosecution under the 1627, 1677 and 1780 Acts.

In fact the 1930's saw a revolution in Sunday law. In 1921 the League of Nations' International Labour Organisation had formulated a convention on the 'weekly rest day' and in 1933 began to put pressure on countries which had not implemented it. Thus the Home Office resolved to place English Sunday law on a rational basis, mobilised the Sunday observance tradition, overcame the surviving Sabbatarian and *laissez-faire* purists, and promoted a series of interventionist social reforms. Later in 1933 the Children and Young Persons Act restricted the Sunday employment of children aged under fourteen. Then in 1936 the Retail Meat Dealers Act and the Shops Act closed almost all shops on Sundays. In 1937 the Factory Act repealed the Factory and Workshop Act of 1901, prohibiting the Sunday employment of women and young persons in factories, and allowing fewer exceptions.

The most marked change in Sunday behaviour in the 1930's was the very rapid decline in church attendance. This was blamed on the open-air cult and the wireless, in particular on the broadcast of religious services, which it was said encouraged churchgoers to stay at home. The most notable Sunday broadcasts of the decade were the Archbishop of Canterbury's address after the abdication crisis in 1936 and the Prime Minister's announcement of the declaration of war in 1939.

The Second World War had similar general effects to the first, and the consequent threat to Sunday caused the L.D.O.S. to redouble its own defence of the 1677 and 1780 Acts, which it had succeeded in retaining on the statute book. In 1947 the Convocations of Canterbury and York issued a booklet, *Your Sunday in Danger*, and in 1951 the L.D.O.S. waged such a powerful campaign against the Sunday opening of the Festival of Britain that a special Act was passed asserting its legality. In 1953 John Parker, a Labour M.P., failed to get the 1780 Act repealed, and in 1955 the British Council of Churches issued a paper on *Sundays Observance and Legislation*. In 1957 it turned to *Sunday Observance and Overtime*.

During the next year, 1958, Cuthbert Bardsley, the Bishop of Coventry, planned to hold a Sunday Festival of Music and Ballet in the carefully tended remains of his bombed-out former cathedral. He was forced to cancel it following a campaign led by the L.D.O.S. This episode stirred up considerable controversy in the Churches. When in 1964 the Anglican Church began to promulgate its revision of the Canons of 1603 the Canon 'Of Sundays . . .' did not mention Sunday recreation, but did reflect the phraseology of the sixteenth and nineteenth centuries—'The Lord's Day, commonly called Sunday, is ever to be celebrated as a weekly memorial of our Lord's resurrection and kept according to God's holy will and pleasure, particularly by attendance at divine service, by deeds of charity, and by abstention from all unnecessary labour and business.'[14] Dennis Howell, subsequently Labour Minister for sport, reacted to the Coventry episode by moving for a select committee to examine the Sunday observance laws. Harold MacMillan's Conservative government did not want to embroil itself in the issue, and refused his request.

In 1960, however, the Wolfenden Committee on Sport and the Community (appointed by the Central Council on Physical Recreation) countenanced Sunday football provided it was not commercially organised and did not take place during normal hours of worship. The government responded in 1961 by setting up the Crathorne Committee on the Law on Sunday Observance, which reported in 1964, favouring liberalisation of the 1780 Act but opposing Sunday sports which involved the payment of players or which took place during morning service. In 1966 Lord Willis introduced into the House of Lords a private member's Bill based upon the committee's recommendations, but it did not reach the statute book.   Behind the scenes the legislative revolution begun in the 1930's had continued. The Statute Law Revision Acts of 1948 and 1966 had repealed some early Sunday laws, and the Repeals Act of 1969 itself repealed almost all the remainder except for the 1780 Act. Finally at the close of 1971 Lord Strabolgi, a Labour peer, and Lady Lee, widow of Nye Bevan, introduced their Sunday Cinema and Sunday Theatre Bills. Lord Windlesham, Minister of State at the Home Office, indicated that the Conservative government adopted a position of 'benevolent neutrality' and the Bills passed both Houses without debate, receiving the royal assent the following year.

The Sunday Cinemas Act of 1972 amended the 1932 Sunday Entertainments Act, making it easier and simpler for cinemas to open on Sundays; and the Sunday Theatres Act allowed theatres to open on Sundays, if they were licensed under the 1968 Theatres Act, and indemnified them from prosecution under the 1780 Act.

Sunday law in 1980 therefore owes comparatively little to the legislation of previous centuries. The 1831 Game Act, the 1833

Elections on Sundays Act, the 1845 Gaming Act (as updated in 1963) the 1847 Town Police Clauses Act and the 1872 Pawnbrokers Act are of minor significance. Sunday law is squarely based on the 1950 Shops Act (which repealed and amalgamated the 1936 Acts), the 1961 Factory Act (which repealed and incorporated the 1937 Act—itself, of course, derived ultimately from the 1867 Acts) and on the ubiquitous 1780 Act as modified in 1932 and 1972.

The Shops Act promotes the Sunday quiet of town centres and the Factory Act ensures the Sunday rest of women and young workers. It may be true that in these respects the late twentieth-century Sunday is more strictly observed than in Victorian times. In a similar way there are now neither Post Office deliveries nor collections on Sundays, because the management decided that they were unprofitable and the men later refused to have them back. The sound and fury of the Sabbatarians has thus accomplished less in these respects than the factory inspectors and the Home Office, sharing in the paternal Tory and the positive Liberal traditions, and the Post Office's commercial common sense.

However, adult male Sunday labour is still regulated not by legislation but by custom and in service industries such as the railways (whose work rhythm still necessarily runs counter to that of the community at large) remains commonplace. Whether or not trade unions have reduced it by securing 'double time' is an open question, for it has led lower-paid men to compete for Sunday work.

Perhaps the greatest change has taken place in the customs which influence Sunday leisure. There are now few homes in which churchgoing is the accepted practice and fewer in which Sunday reading is required. Even churchgoers have abandoned their Sunday suits and the majority of people dress ever more casually. Virtually only the Sunday dinner survives as a relic of an earlier age. Sunday afternoon is used more and more frequently for organised sport, the M.C.C. having sponsored Sunday matches and the royal family having patronised Sunday equestrian events. Nowadays only the Football Association confines its games to Saturdays.

Many people consider that the most obvious mark of our

Sunday is the licensing hours, themselves partly outside the scope of this study. The knowledge that Sunday is a largely work-free day which can be used for recuperation still no doubt encourages many people to drink to excess on Saturday night; and when Christmas Day and New Year's Day fall on Sundays some magistrates are reluctant to give 'extensions' for music and dancing lest they aid and abet the breaking of the 1780 Act and put the police in a difficult position. On Sunday itself public houses remain closed in church time.

In many respects, therefore, the Sabbatarian paradoxes which formed the Victorian Sunday have been redressed, but the English Sunday retains the mark of its origins. Amidst a welter of ill-defined attitudes and confused opinions it remains, according to one's own circumstances, a day of boredom and gloom, of calm and reflection, or of enjoyment and pleasure. Many of those who care nothing for religion regard it as an oasis amidst the desert of contemporary civilisation.

The 'Sunday question' is no longer of any importance politically, and the desire of some Labour M.P.'s to repeal the 1780 Act is more than adequately balanced by the L.D.O.S., which still exists, remaining faithful to Daniel Wilson's principles and deriving its support from Evangelicals, members of Fundamentalist Churches and from Scotland. Its 'sister' societies have all disappeared. Only the W.M.L.D.R.A. and the Imperial Sunday Alliance survived beyond 1918, the former being absorbed by the L.D.O.S. shortly after the First War and the latter shortly after the Second. Among the anti-Sabbatarians, most fell foul of the First, the National Sunday League succumbed to the Second and only the Sunday Tramps was remembered by the 1960's.[15]

By and large, therefore, the situation is as Baldwin Brown and the Broad Churchmen feared. The Churches have not regained a hold on the working classes, and the gulf between orthodox belief (if it exists nowadays) and many of the self-designated intellectual class is probably wider than it was. The content of religion has changed so much that even devout people find it hard to believe that Christian leaders and thinkers of previous centuries spent so much of their time with the Fourth Commandment, and in such a manner.

But the Sabbatarians were partly responsible for that result. Their unreflecting identification of their own beliefs and practices with the essence of Christianity had alienated many men from the Churches. Similarly, their insistence on the authority of the Bible alone, and the social Sabbatarians' emphasis on the social utility of religion, left even the faithful confused and lost in an age which shared neither their assumptions nor conditions. After 1914 most Christians therefore ignored the Sunday question, so that now the Sabbatarians are a minority even among Fundamentalists, social Sabbatarianism is forgotten, and the religious liberals have brought about the collapse of the post-Catholic system of Fundamentalism.

William Temple and C. H. Dodd tackled the deficiencies in Fundamentalist Sabbatarianism several decades ago. Their scholarly expositions reconciled the static nature of the seventh day (which marked the rest after Creation) with the dynamic nature of the first (which signified the Resurrection) by following Augustine and evolving a concept of 'creative rest'. In addition, Temple implied that if Sunday were a day of true spiritual joy it might also serve what the twentieth century Church calls the 'human spirit'. They built upon and caused the intensification of a trend which had begun in Europe and North America in the early 1930's, to investigate the origin of Sunday in the early Church, and that trend has produced some interesting and scholarly work.[16]

However, most of the 'popular' religious leaders and thinkers, rather than helping to construct a spiritually satisfying and intellectually convincing alternative to Fundamentalism, have usually revamped the Imperial Sunday Alliance's Social Gospel as a new brand of humanitarian Christianity—ignoring the important questions of religious belief and practice and of civil authority and behaviour which the Sabbatarian controversy raised. Until such basic questions are tackled and answered the Churches can regain neither their confidence nor their influence.

Notes

[1] A. Miall, *The Life of Edward Miall* (1884), 151.

[2] M. Weber, *The Sociology of Religion* (1966), 39; Daniel Wilson, *The Lord's Day*, *op. cit.*, 184.

[3] Alison Uttley, *The Country Child* (Penguin ed., 1970), 222, 206.

[4] Neville Cardus, *Autobiography* (1975), 67.

[5] Samuel Butler, *The Way of all Flesh*, *op. cit.*, 24; Claud Cockburn, *I Claud* (Penguin ed., 1967), 33; Alison Uttley, *op. cit.*, 126.

[6] Mark Twain, *Huckleberry Finn* (Penguin ed., 1970), 19.

[7] M. Rutherford (W. H. White), *Autobiography and Deliverance* (1969 ed.), 260–7; C. Mackenzie, *My Life and Times. Octave Two* (1963), 263.

[8] Anthony Trollope, *The Three Clerks* (World's Classics ed., 1925), 85–7, *The Prime Minister* (World's Classics ed., 1961), Pt. I, 227.

[9] 3H, vol. 116, col. 361 (30 April 1851).

[10] G. T. H. Duncombe, *Thomas Slingsby Duncombe* (1868), III, 215–19; Roundell Palmer, Earl of Selbourne, *Memorials* (1896), Pt. I, vol. II, pp. 276–86; G. Huxley, *Victorian Duke* (1967), *passim*.

[11] B. F. Westcott, *Christian Social Union Addresses* (1903), 2.

[12] H. Spencer, *The Man versus the State*, *op. cit.*, *passim*; Charles Gore (ed.), *Lux Mundi* (1892 ed.), 322.

[13] Hewlett Johnson, *Searching for Light* (1968), 71.

[14] S.P.C.K., *The Canons of the Church of England* (1969), 10.

[15] W. Vaughan Thomas and A. Llewellyn, *The Shell Guide to Wales* (1969), 8.

[16] William Temple, *Readings in St. John's Gospel* (1939), I, 108–10; C. H. Dodd, *The Interpretation of the Fourth Gospel* (1953), 320–4; W. Rordorff, *Sunday, &c.* (1968).

appendices

Scotland

John Knox was a radical Reformer who followed Luther and Calvin, Frith and Tyndale in attacking the Sabbatarian elements in contemporary Catholicism. During his ascendance in Scotland the Presbyterians reduced the status of Sunday and abolished the Church's saints' and holy days. After his death in 1572 embryonic English Sabbatarianism spread into the lowlands and into the towns of Scotland, receiving legislative recognition in 1579, and being well established there by 1644. Following the formulation of the Westminster Confession, fully fledged Sabbatarianism quickly took root too, being embodied in an Act of 1661, then spreading northwards and westwards as the Highlands were opened up after the '45, during which time the doctrine lost its original force and vigour in the Lowlands.[1]

Towards the end of the eighteenth century militant Sabbatarianism revived as the Evangelicals extended their influence into Scotland, and in 1834, when they gained control of the General Assembly for the first time, the Church of Scotland issued a resounding Sabbath observance proclamation and gave its support to Sir Andrew Agnew. In 1839, after his parliamentary efforts had roused opinion, the Scottish Society for Promoting the Due Observance of the Lord's Day was set up in Edinburgh. Its members hoped to abolish all Sunday railway traffic from Scotland.[2]

However, Scottish Sabbatarianism was strongest in the north and west, and after the formation of the Free Kirk there in 1843 the Sabbatarians were divided denominationally and ideologically. The Free Kirk was the very epitome of voluntaryist ideas, and its supporters soon questioned the use of legislation to ensure Sabbath observance.[3]

Thus in 1848 when the Evangelical Alliance was divided over this aspect of Sabbatarianism and its Scottish members founded the Scottish Sabbath Alliance the Free Kirk was reluctant to participate and in 1849 had a Sabbath Committee of its own. Dr Chalmers, the Kirk's founder and leader, expounded what was virtually a social Sabbatarian position. The year 1849 was, however, also significant for the fact that the outcry caused by Locke's railway Bill caused

Henderson, of Prize Essay fame, to set up the Glasgow Working Men's Sabbath Protection Society.[4]

It was believed in England that Scottish feeling caused the government to procure the defeat of Locke's Bill, and in the 1850's and 1860's successive governments showed themselves willing to defer to what they regarded as the strength of Scottish opinion on the subject. In fact the Scottish societies usually exerted direct pressure on Parliament only when specifically Scottish matters were involved, as in 1863 when W. H. Gregory had attempted to have the Edinburgh Botanical Gardens opened to the public on Sundays, and it is doubtful if the religious public acted without their stimulous.[5]

Yet during these very years Scotland shared to a minor degree in the rise of non- or anti-Sabbatarian theology which was championed by some of its most able Christian leaders—Wardlaw the Congregationalist and Macleod, Queen Victoria's favourite clergyman.[6]

During the late century Scotland shared too in the decline in coherence and strength which weakened English Sabbatarianism but tried to recoup its strength under the stimulous of the revival which came with the new century. Then the Lord's Day Alliance of Scotland published articles in the I.S.A.'s *Sunday Guardian*. With characteristic conservatism and vigilance they looked back to the great days of Agnew and criticised Asquith for reviewing Boy Scouts on a Sunday. The Alliance servered its connection with the I.S.A. because the latter did not share its own Sabbatarian principles and took no part in supporting the I.S.A.'s Weekly Rest Day Bill.[7]

In the twentieth century Sabbatarianism has survived longer in Scotland than in England. In 1923 the inhabitants of Clydeside presented the Duke of York (later King George VI) and Elizabeth Bowes-Lyon (now the Queen Mother) a clock on the occasion of their wedding: on six days of the week it played marches, but on the Sabbath it was silent. In the following year the royal couple were criticised for shooting on Sundays during their African tour. Such attitudes have survived to the present day, but they are concentrated in particular among the 'Wee Frees' of the far west and north, regions which are most akin in their essential characteristics to the days of Sabbatarian emergence and growth.[8]

Thus Scottish and English Sabbatarianism have both similarities and differences. They experienced similar chronologies of growth and decline and appealed primarily to much the same class of people—ministers of religion and small commercial and agricultural proprietors of a rather limited intellectual and cultural outlook. In a very obvious way, nineteenth century Scottish Sabbatarianism was subject to the same theoretical stresses and strains as its English counterpart: the members of the Free Kirk corresponding in this respect to the English Nonconformists—Sabbatarian in their private practices, unwilling to impose religious obligations by legislation, and separated by a deep gulf of outlook and position from most of their parliamentary representatives, who might certainly find themselves in a difficult position if they were Liberals.

They differed in so far as the English had developed Sabbatarianism and the Scots adopted it—and because it flourished all the more strongly in Scotland, was more powerful and pervasive, met much less organised opposition and survived longer. It did so because the urban, industrial and cultural conditions which had developed in England and challenged its supremacy there were quite slow to spread northwards, and they have not yet become diffused throughout the whole of Scotland.

Notes

[1] J. K. Carter, *op. cit.*, *passim*; R. D. Brackenridge, 'Sabbath Observance in Scotland, 1644–1834', unpublished Ph.D. thesis Glasgow University, 1963.

[2] Thomas McCrie, *Agnew*, *op. cit.*, 345–50.

[3] John Bridges, *Sabbath Defence Tactics*, *op. cit.*, 5–6; anon, *The Sabbath and the Railway* (c. 1848), *passim*.

[4] E. Stearne (ed.), *The Religious Condition of Christendom* (1852), 122–35; James Bridges, *Agnew*, *op. cit.*, 15; Thomas McCrie, *Agnew*, *op. cit.*, 346.

[5] *The Watchman and Wesleyan Advertiser*, 4 April 1849; *The Nonconformist*, 2 May 1849.

[6] R. Wardlaw, *The Sabbath, A Tract for the Times* (Glasgow, c. 1850); N. Macleod, *The Lord's Day, &c.* (Glasgow, 1867).

[7] I.S.A., *Sunday Guardian*, No. I, 14–16 (November 1910), No. II, 25 January/February 1911), No. III, 39 (March/April 1911).

[8] David Duff, *Elizabeth of Glamis* (1973), 70, 94.

II   *Wales*

Between 1530 and 1780 the Established Church in Wales was moribund, its bishops and its clergy English-speaking, out of touch with the Welsh people, to whom the Bible was not widely available in their native tongue. Sabbatarianism neither grew nor flourished in these circumstances.

After 1780 the gentry, from among whom most of the Church's clergy were drawn, resisted the Evangelicals; and the peasantry and the middle class became strongly Nonconformist, or 'Chapel', as it was usually put in Wales.

The Welsh Nonconformists were devoutly Sabbatarian in theology and scrupulously so in their private lives. In his classic *How Green was my Valley* Richard Llewellyn described how cooking was allowed on Sundays only in special circumstances and the 'Sunday dinner' therefore eaten on Saturday. Despite this, the Nonconformists did not create an organised Sabbatarian movement. They were deeply influenced by Voluntaryism and spent much of their energy fighting the Establishment.[1]

Thus because the Evangelicals were weak and the Nonconformists preoccupied and, indeed, because there was no secular anti-Sabbatarian movement in Wales, the principality was not concerned with the Sunday question, except as part of the temperance movement.

Wales is memorable because its Nonconformists produced the biblical scholar C. H. Dodd, who has left a description of a Sunday in the 1880's which may fittingly serve as an epilogue to this account of the Victorian Sunday.

Sunday was the high festival of our religion. Work and play alike were taboo. You might walk in the garden and admire the flowers, but to pull up a casual weed was reprehensible. If in dressing on Sunday morning I had the misfortune to detach a responsible button, I had to prove beyond doubt that its absence was an affront to decency before my mother could feel justified in stitching it on. To take a bath on Sunday was not thought of. To shave was a misdemeanour. Shortly before my time a minister of our chapel had, so my grandmother told me, been arraigned by his deacons for this crime. He found indulgence on the plea that his beard was exceptionally dark and of strong growth. My father, until well on in middle life, shaved on Saturday night in preparation. When in due course I myself started to shave, I was rebuked for my untimely zeal to show a shining Sabbath face. To write a letter on Sunday was a secular occupation, which could be justified only by genuine necessity. No books might be opened but 'Sunday books', and that category was rigidly defined. No music but 'sacred music' might be sung or played. It is true that the problem of classifying instrumental music as sacred or secular was never quite satisfactorily solved. I remember being pulled up for playing on the piano a 'piece' which my music teacher had certified as suitable for Sunday, because, apparently, my father associated its melody with some secular words. No toys of any kind were permitted. I recall a very curious exception. One of our mild indoor amusements was the mounting of 'scraps' in an album. One year Christmas fell on a Sunday. This was a depressing conjunction, for we might only look at our presents and then put them aside 'till tomorrow'. But among them we found an assortment of 'scraps' in the form of Bible pictures, and these we were allowed to cut out and mount even though the day was a Sabbath. My vivid recollection of this early episode shows how exceptional the indulgence appeared. I have no doubt that it cost my parents much anxious casuistry, and represented a very imaginative and sympathetic thought for us.

The activities of Sunday were practically restricted . . . to going to chapel twice and to Sunday School in the afternoon. A short walk after service was permitted, but it must not exceed half-an-hour or so. I well remember head-shaking over some young person of our communion who had been seen 'going for a walk on Sunday afternoon'. The gravity with which the formula was pronounced left no doubt that this was the first step in the *facilis descensus Averno*.[2]

Notes

[1] R. Llewellyn, *How Green was my Valley* (1973 ed.), 9.
[2] F. W. Dillistone, *C. H. Dodd: Interpreter of the New Testament* (1977), 29–32.

III   *Statutes*

The following is a chronological list of the major Acts of Parliament relating to Sunday observance in England, and a brief summary of their main provisions. It does not include licensing Acts. It is not intended as a manual of Sunday observance law. For that the reader should consult P. F. Skottowe, *The Law Relating to Sunday* (1936), H.M.S.O., *Chronological Table of the Statutes* (1976) and, of course, *Statutes at Large*.

12 Rich. II, c. 6. *Weapons and Unlawful Games*, 1388. Prohibited Sunday tennis and football, and encouraged Sunday archery. (Repealed, Continuation of Acts, 1624).

27 Hen. VI, c. 5. *Sunday Fairs and Markets*, 1448. Prohibited Sunday fairs and markets, except on 'the four Sundays in harvest'. (Exception withdrawn by Fairs and Markets Act, 1850, and repealed by Statute Law Repeals Act, 1969.)

5 and 6 Ed. VI, c. 1. *Act of Uniformity*, 1551. Enjoined the duty of attending the Sunday services of the Church of England. (Repealed, S.L.R. Act, 1969.)

5 and 6 Ed. VI, c. 3. *Holy Days and Fasting Days*, 1551. Allowed Sunday work in time of harvest and 'if necessity shall require'. (Repealed 1553, re-enacted 1604, repealed, S.L.R. Act, 1969.)

1 Chas. I, c. 1. *Sunday Observance Act*, 1625. Declared illegal Sunday bear and bull baiting, interludes and common plays. Declared illegal travelling out of one's parish to take part in legal Sunday games. (Repealed, S.L.R. Act, 1969.)

3 Chas. II, c. 3. *Sunday Observance Act*, 1627. Prohibited Sunday travel by carriers and drovers, etc., and Sunday killing and selling by butchers. (Repealed, S.L.R. Act, 1969.)

29 Chas. II, c. 27. *Sunday Observance Act*, 1677. Prohibited Sunday work and trade; excepting acts of necessity and mercy, sale of milk, dressing of meat in inns, cookshops and victualling houses. Limited Sunday legal proceedings and restricted Sunday travelling. (Repealed, S.L.R. Act, 1969.)

10 Will. III, c. 13. *Billingsgate Act*, 1698. Allowed the Sunday sale of mackerel before and after divine service. (Repealed, Sea Fisheries Act, 1868.)

11 Will. III, c. 21. *River Thames Act*, 1698. Allowed forty Thames watermen to ply for hire on Sundays. (Repealed, River Thames Act, 1827.)

9 Anne, c. 23. *Hackney Coaches and Chairs Act*, 1710. Allowed Hackney coaches and chairs to ply for hire on Sundays. (Superseded, Hackney Carriage Act, 1831.)

30 Geo. II, c. 25. *Militia Act*, 1757. Exempted Sunday as a drilling day. (Superseded, Militia Act, 1803.)

2 Geo. III, c. 15. *Fish Act*, 1762. Allowed fish carts to travel freely on Sundays. (Repealed, S.L.R. Act, 1948.)

5 Geo. III, c. 13. *Westminster Tolls Act*, 1765. Charged tolls on vehicles travelling in and about Westminster on Sundays; to finance street cleansing, lighting and paving. (Repealed, S.L.R. Act, 1948.)

21 Geo. III, c. 49. *Sunday Observance Act*, 1780. Declared places open for public entertainment on Sundays, to which admission was by money, tickets sold for money, refreshments sold at special prices or subscription, to be deemed a disorderly house. Owners, managers, conductors and assistants at such places, and the advertisers, printers and publishers of placards, etc., were liable to fines of £200 and £50 which were recoverable by a common informer who brought a successful prosecution. (Although amended, remains on the statute book.)

34 Geo. III, c. lxi. *London Bakers Act*, 1794. Applied to London and places within a twelve-mile radius of the Royal Exchange. Allowed

bakers to work on Sundays from 9.00 a.m. to 1.00 p.m. when they might sell bread and bake meat, puddings and pies for customers who brought them in and fetched them away. (Repealed, S.L.R. Act, 1871.)

43 Geo. III, c. 96. *Military Service Act*, 1803. Allowed Sunday drilling, but persons with religious scruples could drill on another day in lieu. (Incorporated in Defence of the Realm Act, 1806.)

1 and 2 Geo. IV, c. 50. *Bread Act*, 1821. Applied outside the metropolitan area. Allowed bakers to work from 9.00 a.m. to 1.30 p.m., to deliver and to prepare for Monday baking, in addition to selling bread and baking meat, pudding and pies. (Repealed S.L.R. Act, 1861.)

3 Geo. IV, c. cvi. *London Bread Act*, 1822. Applied the 1821 Bread Act to London and the metropolitan area, with a doubled scale of fines. (Repealed, Baking Industry Act, 1938.)

7 and 8 Geo. IV, c. lxxv. *River Thames Act*, 1827. Allowed boats, etc. to ply for hire freely on Sundays. (Repealed . . .)

1 and 2 Will. IV, c. 22. *Hackney Carriage Act*, 1831. Allowed Hackney carriages to stand and ply for hire on Sundays on the same terms as on weekdays. (Repealed, Revenue Act, 1869.)

1 and 2 Will. IV, c. 32. *Game Act*, 1831. Declared illegal Sunday killing and taking of game. (Strengthened by Salmon and Fresh Water Fisheries Act, 1923, which declared illegal Sunday salmon fishing.)

3 and 4 Will. IV, c. 31. *Elections on Sundays Act*, 1833. Directed that elections of officers of corporations and other public bodies required to be held on Sundays must in future be held on the Saturday preceding or the Monday following. (Remains on the statute book.)

6 and 7 Will. IV, c. 37. *Bread Act*, 1836. Applied the 1822 London Bread Act to the rest of England. (Repealed, Food and Drugs Act, 1938.)

2 and 3 Vict. c. 47. *Metropolitan Police Act*, 1839. Allowed the metropolitan police to direct traffic away from churches during the hours of divine service. (Repealed, S.L.R. Act, 1973.)

8 and 9 Vict., c. 109. *Gaming Act*, 1845. Declared illegal the public playing of billiards and bagatelle on Sundays. (Fines updated by Betting, Gaming and Lotteries Act, 1963.)

10 and 11 Vict., c. 89. *Town Police Clauses Act*, 1847. Allowed the police in provincial towns and cities to direct traffic away from churches during the hours of divine service. (Remains on the statute book.)

24 and 25 Vict., c. 109. *Naval Discipline Act*, 1866. Forbade naval courts martial on Sundays. (Repealed, Naval Discipline Act, 1957.)

30 and 31 Vict., c. 103. *Factory Acts Extension Act*, 1867. Prohibited the

Sunday employment of women, young persons and children in factories. (Repealed by and incorporated in Factory and Workshop Act, 1878.)

30 and 31 Vict. c. 146. *Workshop Regulation Act*, 1867. Prohibited the Sunday employment of women, young persons and children in workshops. (Repealed by and incorporated in Factory and Workshop Act, 1878.)

34 and 35 Vict., c. 19. *Sunday Work of Jews Act*, 1871. Jewish employers and employees might work on Sundays if they did not do so on Saturdays. (Repealed by and incorporated in Factory and Workshop Act, 1878.)

34 and 35 Vict., c. 87. *Sunday Observation Prosecution Act*, 1871. Enacted that no prosecution might be brought under the 1677 Act, except with the consent of a chief police officer, two justices of the peace, or a stipendiary magistrate. (A renewable measure made permanent by Expiring Laws Act, 1922; repealed, S.L.R. Act, 1969.)

35 and 36 Vict., c. 93. *Pawnbrokers Act*, 1872. Forbade pawnbrokers to carry on their business on Sundays. (Remains on the statute book.)

38 and 39 Vict., c. 80. *Remission of Penalties Act*, 1875. Allowed the Crown to remit penalties resulting from prosecutions brought under the 1780 Act. (Repealed, S.L.R. Act, 1966.)

1 Ed. VII, c. 22. *Factory and Workshop Act*, 1901. Repealed the 1878 Factory and Workshop Act, incorporating the prohibition of the Sunday employment of women, young persons and children, but making exceptions for creameries, blast furnaces and paper mills. Made special provision for Jews. (See 1937 Factory Act.)

20 and 21 Geo. V, c. 35. *Hairdressers' and Barbers' Shops (Sunday Closing) Act*, 1930. Directed that such shops must be closed on Sundays. (Repealed and incorporated in 1950 Shops Act.)

21 and 22 Geo. V, c. 52. *Sunday Performances (Temporary Regulation) Act*, 1931. Allowed cinemas which were open on Sundays to remain open and discharged all current prosecutions under the 1780 Act. (Repealed, Sunday Entertainments Act, 1932.)

22 and 23 Geo. V, c. 51. *Sunday Entertainments Act*, 1932. Allowed cinemas to open on Sundays, subject to a form of local option, and to conditions relating to Sunday labour, donations to charity, and sums paid to the Cinematograph Fund. Allowed musical concerts, museums, galleries, zoos, gardens, lectures and debates to take place and open on Sundays, indemnified from prosecution under the 1627, 1677 and 1780 Acts. (See Sunday Cinema Act, 1972.)

23 Geo. V, c. 12. *Children and Young Persons Act*, 1933. Prohibited the Sunday employment of children under fourteen years of age for more

than two hours. (Remains on the statute book.)

24 and 25 Geo. V, c. 58. *Betting and Lotteries Act*, 1934. Declared illegal Sunday betting by means of bookmaking or totalising. (Repealed and incorporated in Betting, Gaming and Lotteries Act, 1963.)

26 Geo. V and I Ed. VIII, c. 30. *Retail Meat Dealers' Shops (Sunday Closing)* Act, 1936. Directed that butchers' shops must be closed on Sundays, with some few exceptions. (See 1950 Shops Act.)

26 Geo. V and I Ed. VIII, c. 53. *Shops (Sunday Trading Restriction) Act*, 1936. Directed that all shops must be closed on Sundays, with some few exceptions. (See 1950 Shops Act.)

1 Geo. VI, c. 67. *Factory Act*, 1937. Repealed 1901 Factory and Workshop Act and discontinued its exceptions. Prohibited the employment of women and young persons in factories on Sundays. Made exceptions for shift work and included special provision for the Jews. (See 1961 Factory Act.)

14 Geo. VI, c. 28. *Shops Act*, 1950. Repealed and incorporated the Meat Dealers and Shops Act of 1936, closing shops on Sundays. Made exceptions for certain transactions, and special provision for holiday resorts, street markets and Jews. To be enforced by the local authorities. Sunday shop workers must be given a weekday's holiday in lieu. (Remains on the statute book.)

14 and 15 Geo. VI, c. 14. *Festival of Britain (Sunday Opening) Act*, 1951. Declared that the Sunday opening of the Festival of Britain was legal.

9 and 10 Eliz. II, c. 34. *Factory Act*, 1961. Repealed and incorporated the 1937 Factory Act. (Remains on the statute book.)

1972, c. 19. *Sunday Cinema Act*, 1972. Amended the 1932 Sunday Entertainments Act, rendering it easier for cinemas to open on Sundays by abolishing local option, and wound up the Cinematograph Fund. (Remains on the statute book.)

1972, c. 26. *Sunday Theatres Act*, 1972. Allowed theatres to open on Sundays during the afternoon and night if licensed under the 1968 Theatres Act, and indemnified them from prosecution under the 1780 Act. (Remains on the statute book.)

index

Names

Places

Subjects

DATE DUE